solutions@syngress.

With over 1,000,000 copies of our MCSE, MCSD, CompTIA, and Cisco study guides in print, we have come to know many of you personally. By listening, we've learned what you like and dislike about typical computer books. The most requested item has been for a web-based service that keeps you current on the topic of the book and related technologies. In response, we have created solutions@syngress.com, a service that includes the following features:

- A one-year warranty against content obsolescence that occurs as the result of vendor product upgrades. We will provide regular web updates for affected chapters.

- Monthly mailings that respond to customer FAQs and provide detailed explanations of the most difficult topics, written by content experts exclusively for solutions@syngress.com.

- Regularly updated links to sites that our editors have determined offer valuable additional information on key topics.

- Access to "Ask the Author"™ customer query forms that allow readers to post questions to be addressed by our authors and editors.

Once you've purchased this book, browse to

www.syngress.com/solutions.

To register, you will need to have the book handy to verify your purchase.

Thank you for giving us the opportunity to serve you.

SYNGRESS®

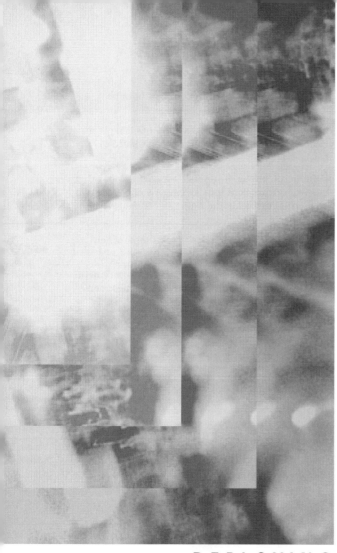

DEPLOYING
WINDOWS 2000
WITH SUPPORT TOOLS

SYNGRESS®

KEY	SERIAL NUMBER
001	ABN153WXM6
002	BRA865GHPL
003	V14587ELHN
004	TYP321KBG7
005	468ZCBMNM9
006	1LBVBC7891
007	9865ED1984
008	CCVX1534XX
009	M26719875
010	XLKMB98345

PUBLISHED BY
Syngress Media, Inc.
800 Hingham Street
Rockland, MA 02370

Deploying Windows 2000 With Support Tools

Printed in the United States of America

1 2 3 4 5 6 7 8 9 0

ISBN: 1-928994-12-1

Product Line Manager: Julie Smalley
Technical edit by: Ralph Crump
Index by: Robert Saigh
Copy Edit by: Nancy Faughnan

Proofreading by: Beth Roberts
Page Layout and Art by: Emily Eagar and
Kate Glennon
Co-Publisher: Richard Kristof

Distributed by Publishers Group West

Acknowledgments

We would like to acknowledge the following people for their kindness and support in making this book possible.

Richard Kristof, Duncan Anderson, Jennifer Gould, Robert Woodruff, Kevin Murray, Dale Leatherwood, Laurie Hedrick, Rhonda Harmon, Lisa Lavallee, and Robert Sanregret of Global Knowledge, for their generous access to the IT industry's best courses, instructors and training facilities.

Ralph Troupe and the team at Rt. 1 Solutions for their invaluable insight into the challenges of designing, deploying and supporting world-class enterprise networks.

Karen Cross, Kim Wylie, Harry Kirchner, John Hays, Bill Richter, Kevin Votel, Brittin Clark, Sarah Schaffer, Luke Kreinberg, Ellen Lafferty and Sarah MacLachlan of Publishers Group West for sharing their incredible marketing experience and expertise.

Peter Hoenigsberg, Mary Ging, Caroline Hird, Simon Beale, Julia Oldknow, Kelly Burrows, Jonathan Bunkell, Catherine Anderson, Peet Kruger, Pia Rasmussen, Denelise L'Ecluse, Rosanna Ramacciotti, Marek Lewinson, Marc Appels, Paul Chrystal, Femi Otesanya, and Tracey Alcock of Harcourt International for making certain that our vision remains worldwide in scope.

Melissa Heinlein at CoreTech Consulting Group, for all her help.

Special thanks to the professionals at Osborne with whom we are proud to publish the best-selling Global Knowledge Certification Press series.

From Global Knowledge

At Global Knowledge we strive to support the multiplicity of learning styles required by our students to achieve success as technical professionals. As the world's largest IT training company, Global Knowledge is uniquely positioned to offer these books. The expertise gained each year from providing instructor-led training to hundreds of thousands of students worldwide has been captured in book form to enhance your learning experience. We hope that the quality of these books demonstrates our commitment to your lifelong learning success. Whether you choose to learn through the written word, computer based training, Web delivery, or instructor-led training, Global Knowledge is committed to providing you with the very best in each of these categories. For those of you who know Global Knowledge, or those of you who have just found us for the first time, our goal is to be your lifelong competency partner.

Thank your for the opportunity to serve you. We look forward to serving your needs again in the future.

Warmest regards,

Duncan Anderson
President and Chief Executive Officer, Global Knowledge

Contributors

John M. Gunson II (MCSE, MCNE, CCNA) is a Consultant for CoreTech Consulting Group, Inc. CoreTech is an e-business Professional Services firm in suburban Philadelphia that excels at helping companies realize the potential of e-business through a mix of Internet technology and traditional business systems, maximizing business benefit while minimizing disruption and risk.

With over eleven years in the Information Technology field, John has a very broad background. His experience includes a number of years supporting desktop clients, as well as network administration and design in both Windows NT and Netware environments. Currently, John is working with an international corporation on its Windows 2000 migration project.

John graduated from Salisbury State University with a Bachelor of Science Degree in Geography. He holds a membership with the Network Professional Association and is also an officer in the US Army Reserve.

John lives in Phoenixville, PA with his wife, Jennifer, and two children, Molly and Brady.

Eriq Oliver Neale is a technology strategist with Nortel Networks, researching new technology solutions for inclusion in the designer workplace. He has worked in the computer support industry for eleven years and in that time has contributed to several computing technology publications. When not writing, he and his wife try to keep up with seven cats, two dogs, and a plethora of tropical fish.

Gary Rosenfeld (MCSE, MCP+I, CCNA) works as a Senior Network Systems Consultant for Lucent NetworkCare Services in Philadelphia, Pennsylvania. NetworkCare is a global provider of network consulting and software solutions for the full lifecycle of a network, including planning, design, implementation, and operations. Gary is involved in designing and implementing complex Windows NT and Windows 2000 solutions for Fortune 1000 companies. Gary lives in Pennsylvania with his beautiful wife, Jill, their wonderful son, Noah, and their lovable cat, Georgie.

Amy Thomson (A+, MOUS Master) is a software and A+ instructor for a prominent Canadian private college. She began her career in the computer industry over 10 years ago, during her military service as a communications operator. She has taught in several Canadian provinces, and has an Honours B.Sc. in Psychology. Amy currently lives in Halifax, Nova Scotia with her husband, Jeff and hedgehog, Hannah.

Robin Walshaw (MCSE, DipProjMan) was born in England, but has spent most of his life in South Africa. One of the first MCSEs in Africa, he enjoys being at the forefront of new developments in network architecture and operating systems. With a flair for developing strategic IT solutions for diverse clients, he has worked in the world of computers in eight countries, and has traveled to over thirty in the last ten years. Besides traveling, Robin is a keen sportsman and has managed to balance work with a passion for climbing the world's highest mountains, culminating in an attempt on Mount Everest.

Technical Editor

Ralph Crump (MCSE, CCNA, and a CNE 3.x, 4.x, and 5.x, with a Master CNE in Integrating Windows NT) manages a team responsible for a large scale Windows NT and Novell NetWare infrastructure for a major telecommunications company in Atlanta, Georgia. He specializes in Windows NT and BackOffice applications as well as Novell NetWare solutions. He is currently working in cooperation with Microsoft on Windows 2000 Rapid Deployment projects.

Technical Reviewer

Stace Cunningham (CCNA, MCSE, CLSE, COS/2E, CLSI, COS/2I, CLSA, MCPS, A+) is a Systems Engineer with SDC Consulting located in Biloxi, MS. SDC Consulting specializes in the design, engineering, and installation of networks. Stace has coauthored or technical edited 19 books published by Microsoft Press, Osborne/McGraw-Hill, and Syngress Media. He received a quality initiative award for his contribution to the design of a Windows NT network at Keesler Air Force Base, Mississippi. His wife Martha and daughter Marissa are very supportive of the time he spends on their home network of computers and routers. Without their love and support he would not be able to accomplish the goals he has set for himself.

Contents

Preface

The release of Windows 2000 brings an end to the largest computer software development project to date. With millions of lines of code, this is sure to be one of the largest software upgrades you have ever faced. As administrators prepare for this massive undertaking, many white papers, tools, and utilities have been and are being developed to help with deploying Windows 2000.

Despite the fact that companies use a variety of server-based technologies, such as mainframes, UNIX, and Windows NT, most organizations use a Windows-based client for some portion of their day-to-day activities. Incorporated into this new release comes Windows 2000 Professional, the client-based Windows 2000 platform. Although based upon previous operating systems such as Windows 9x and Windows NT, Windows 2000 has a number of changes and additions that will have to be addressed by all IT professionals.

Understanding how to deploy Windows 2000 Professional can be a large task in itself. It is important that as an administrator, you understand each of the methodologies that are available and the toolsets that have been provided. Not only has Microsoft prepared utilities to meet this need, but many third-party vendors are also participating in this venture. Be sure to properly investigate to ensure that the deployment process that is created meets the needs of your organization.

Organization

This book follows a pattern to not only help you understand how to deploy Windows 2000 Professional, but also to develop a deployment strategy. Each chapter provides a comprehensive view of the various components of a successful Windows 2000 Professional deployment. The chapters are broken down as follows:

- **Chapter 1:** *Tools and Techniques for Deploying Windows 2000 Professional* introduces some of the concepts and methodologies in addition to the tools provided by Microsoft for deploying Windows 2000 Professional. It provides a comprehensive introduction to the remainder of the book, including how to plan a Windows 2000 Professional deployment.

- **Chapter 2:** *Automating Windows 2000 Professional Installation* provides a detailed look at unattended installation scripts. This chapter focuses on how to use unattended installation scripts, various methods for creating and customizing them, and once completed, how to implement them.

- **Chapter 3:** *Imaging Windows 2000 Professional* discusses imaging technologies in reference to deploying this operating system. It discusses various imaging tools and techniques, how to properly prepare a computer for imaging, and also compares these methodologies to other available techniques.

- **Chapter 4:** *Remote Installation Client and Server* delves into a newer installation methodology used by Microsoft. This chapter provides a look at Remote Installation Services, how to set up and manage this service, and how to use it to deploy Windows 2000 Professional.

- **Chapter 5:** *Deploying Software with Group Policy* introduces change and configuration management and how group policy can be used to help administer a Windows 2000 Professional deployment.

- **Chapter 6:** *Managing User and Computer Settings* digs a little deeper into the details of a Windows 2000 Professional deployment. This chapter discusses some additional features, such as Folder Redirection, Roaming Profiles, and Offline Folders.

- **Chapter 7:** *Managing User Data* helps plan user data management strategies such as data storage, disk quotas, and data security.

- **Chapter 8:** *Developing a Deployment Plan for Windows 2000* discusses the finer points of pulling these methodologies together and making it happen. Primarily focusing on the project management aspect, this chapter outlines the various features and concepts that need to be addressed during a Windows 2000 Professional deployment.

- **Chapter 9:** *Windows 2000 Fast Track* provides an overview of the various Windows 2000 platforms, discusses the pros and cons of Windows 2000, including new features and the advantages of performing upgrades versus clean installations.

Audience

This book was designed and written for information technology professionals who wish to upgrade their client installation base to Windows 2000 Professional. Not only does it provide you with an overview of the various feature sets and concepts for deploying Windows 2000 Professional, it also provides step-by-step instructions on implementing these mechanisms to provide a seamless installation and migration path. The tools and methodologies provided throughout this book are especially suited for medium-to-large enterprises in which automation is a key principle in any software deployment. As organizations continue to rely more on Windows technologies such as 2000 Professional, administrators must find easier ways to deploy and implement these technologies efficiently.

Chapter 1

Tools and Techniques for Deploying Microsoft Windows 2000 Professional

Solutions in this chapter:

- Automating Windows 2000 Setup

- Deployment Tools in Windows 2000

- Deployment Techniques

Introduction

Just a few years ago no one could have foreseen the impact that the personal computer would have on the working lives of so many people. Today the modern PC is almost as ubiquitous, if not as reliable, as the pen. Idling on the desk of millions of office workers around the world is a tireless instrument that extends and facilitates our ability to deliver work. In an effort to tap the capabilities of these marvelous tools, the majority of PCs run a version of the Microsoft operating system family.

In response to the evolving world of technology, businesses have sought to adopt new operating systems in the swiftest and most economical manner possible. The Windows 2000 product group represents the largest, most technically advanced body of work undertaken by the most successful software company in the world. It is considered by many to be the single most important milestone in the evolutionary development of the Windows family. By providing a computing platform that offers stability, high productivity, and compatibility, Microsoft is hoping to extend its software presence even further. Windows 2000 includes a multitude of new features and additions, several of which address current concerns and issues with Windows NT 4.0, Windows 95, Windows 98, and Windows 98 SE (to simplify the naming scheme we will use Windows 9x when referring to Windows 95, Windows 98, and Windows 98 SE). Other features, such as Active Directory, extend the scope of computing into new and exciting territory.

As the complexity of operating systems has increased, so has the requirement to strategically deploy the operating system within the business. When Windows NT 4.0 and Windows 9x were released, they included basic tools to facilitate their deployment and adoption. These tools, while adequate, had several shortcomings that hampered effective distribution. Businesses of all sizes quickly realized the benefit of developing operating system deployment strategies, but there was still room for considerable improvement. With Windows 2000, Microsoft has provided a host of new and improved facilities for deployment.

One of the goals of the Windows 2000 design team was to ensure that it was the easiest, most efficient, and least expensive Microsoft operating system to deploy within the enterprise. The common cry of the network manager is that the expense of deploying a new operating system is exhorbitant. The requirement for skills and resources of a deployment project often outstrips supply. Even on the rare occasion when resourcing and budgetary requirements can be ignored, the complexity of deployment tools and techniques often proves problematic. Using the Windows 2000-specific deployment tools and techniques, it is possible to put an end to the network manager's lament—at least, for the time being!

An Introduction to Deployment Planning

After all the technical detail that is involved in justifying an operating system migration, the project planning stages are often overlooked. It is essential to draw up a comprehensive deployment plan to ensure the success of the project—something that we will look into in greater detail in Chapter 8, "Developing a Deployment Plan for Windows 2000."

Each business has a unique environment that influences and directs the creation and growth of a project plan. Many businesses have a well-defined project management methodology that incorporates certain variances in business processes in an attempt to leverage them as strengths. What can be established, regardless of the diversity of companies, are the common denominators to all Windows 2000 Professional deployment plans.

Assuming the common denominators listed below, what should the project be asking itself?

Project definition

- What should the scope and nature of the rollout be?
- Who should get Windows 2000 Professional?
- Why are we deploying Windows 2000 Professional?

Assessing the current network environment

- What do we have?
- What do the clients and servers look like?
- What is the logical and physical network structure?

Constructing the test lab

- How do we build a test lab?
- What do we test and who should be involved?

Training support personnel

- What is the current level of expertise?
- What level of technical excellence should be aimed for?

Conducting and evaluating the pilot rollout

- When and how do we conduct a pilot?
- What are the metrics that we use to evaluate its success?

Production rollout

- How do we incorporate the findings of the pilot rollout?
- What do we rollout? How are end users to be trained?

Change and Configuration Management—
Owning Your Network

A number of factors have contributed to the increased costs associated with managing and owning a network and its infrastructure—more demanding users, increasingly complex products, and a growing user base are just a few. Windows 2000 Professional certainly does not break the mold when it comes to developing complex products, but what it does provide is an infrastructure to reduce the cost of owning a Windows-based infrastructure.

Change and configuration management centers on the continuing requirement for administrators to manage the issues that arise while supporting their user base. Two main concepts that support the new change and configuration management techniques are IntelliMirror and remote operating system installation. IntelliMirror is a set of tools and technologies that increase availability, reduce support costs, and allow the users' software, settings, and data to follow them. Three pillars support the IntelliMirror technology:

- **User Data Management** Allows users to access their data whether they are online or offline. This includes features such as folder redirection, disk quotas, and file synchronization.

- **User Settings Management** Allows preferences to follow the user. This includes such features as roaming profiles and particular shell enhancements.

- **Software Installation and Maintenance** Ensures that users have their required software. This can include features such as self-repairing software and application deployment.

The second concept, remote operating system installation, allows administrators to build a functional, standardized workstation remotely. Providing a solid, flexible, and scalable infrastructure for operating system deployment is imperative for a successful operating system installation strategy.

Group policies can be used throughout Windows 2000 to define user and computer configuration settings such as scripts, software policies, security settings, application deployment, user settings, and document options. Using group policies allows these settings to be controlled centrally and applied across the business. Group Policy leverages the Active Directory and supports the IntelliMirror technology to control the scope and granularity of changes in configuration. By providing a well-managed desktop environment through Group Policies, Windows 2000 eases the resolution and elimination of change and configuration management issues.

The capability to control and manage the network in a scalable environment ensures that small, medium, and large businesses have the tools to reduce the cost of owning PCs and supporting users.

Windows 2000 Professional Setup Design Goals

Regardless of how advanced an operating system is, an oft-neglected feature is the capability to set up and deploy it effectively. In an effort to speed the adoption of Windows 2000 Professional, Microsoft worked with customers and IT professionals to provide a new framework for operating system deployment. With the lessons learned from the existing crop of deployment technologies and methods, Microsoft began to construct a scalable and flexible deployment framework.

The setup and installation design goals of the Windows 2000 Professional development team included:

- **Simplicity and reliability** Ensuring that the operating system is simple to install and exhibits reliability and recoverability during installation.

- **Deployment friendly** Designing the setup process in such a way that it can be deployed throughout the organization without extensive technical know-how.

- **Customization options** Providing flexibility during the installation process to satisfy the need to tailor operating systems to the needs of diverse organizations.

- **Reduction of deployment time** As operating systems have increased in size and complexity, so has their deployment time.

- **The support of disk duplication** Disk imaging has proven to be a swift and effective deployment technique that is gaining popularity.

- **Automation** Ensuring that the installation process can be fully automated.

- **Ease of deployment** Providing tools and features to make the deployment process easier.

- **Service Pack slipstreaming** Providing the facility to incorporate service pack upgrades into the deployment process with no additional impact.

Within this framework are a number of new tools and techniques targeted at easing the deployment process without sacrificing control or disrupting service. In the coming chapter we will introduce the tools and elaborate on the techniques that make Windows 2000 Professional the easiest and most versatile to deploy of the Microsoft Windows family.

Automating Windows 2000 Setup

In these days of the mega-merger it is not unusual to come across a company with more than 20,000 computer users scattered across geographically disparate areas. There are also large numbers of small-to-medium-sized corporations with a computing base ranging from a couple of hundred users to thousands of users. All these companies have one thing in common (other than a user base demanding lightning-fast service)—the requirement to deploy operating systems quickly and efficiently with maximum control.

The deployment of an operating system within a business can prove to be a complicated and repetitive task. Manual installation of even the most user-friendly operating system requires a substantial investment in time and resources. Each time an operating system is installed it requires general configuration and installation information. Such information can range from the preferred display resolution to the domain of a workstation. The process of collating the installation information and feeding it to the operating system so that it no longer requires human interaction during the installation process is called automating setup.

The information required during the setup of Windows 2000 Professional can be quite varied and includes:

- Acceptance of the end-user license agreement (EULA)
- Username and organization

- Time zone
- Computer name
- Administrator password
- Display settings
- Network settings
- Regional settings
- Browser and shell settings
- Installation folder
- Printer setup

Often the operating system settings are the same along lines of business, functional groups, or even throughout the enterprise. Installing a thousand similar configurations of Windows 2000 Professional is no one's idea of fun nor a constructive use of resources. Setup automation is undertaken by organizations that need to eliminate dead time (like repetitive operating system installation) or deploy a number of workstations within a particular time frame. The ability to rapidly deploy operating systems is considered to be of essential importance to the modern IT department. Today's operating systems are complex and sometimes difficult to understand, so it comes as no surprise to learn that the deployment process at times requires special skills and understanding. A certain level of preparation is also required before the automation of setup can take place. A knowledge of the business, project requirements and constraints, target workstations, network environment, and other technical considerations are just a few of the factors that will affect how Windows 2000 Professional is deployed.

Two deployment techniques often used in Microsoft environments to automate the setup process are automated installation scripts and disk imaging. Automated installation scripts use answer files that can be submitted to the setup program in the form of a clear text file that is relatively easy to manipulate and understand. The answer file contains information on how to automatically answer the configuration questions asked during setup. Disk imaging, on the other hand, depends on an administrator preparing a model workstation and then taking a snapshot of the model workstation. This snapshot is then distributed to other similarly configured machines.

The process of automating setup can include:

- The design of a model Windows 2000 Professional workstation.
- The creation of answer files and scripts to generate the model workstation. Alternatively, a snapshot of the model workstation could be taken using a disk imaging tool.
- Creating a centrally managed distribution point for the Windows 2000 Professional model workstation files.
- Deploying the operating system by using one of the deployment techniques mentioned later in this chapter.

Windows 2000 Setup

In order to understand how to automate the Windows 2000 Professional setup process, it is essential to understand the requirements prior to installation. A good grasp of the upgrade and installation process also helps in determining what type of installation best meets the needs of the business.

Hardware Requirements

Windows 2000 Professional provides a greater degree of stability and flexibility than its predecessors at the cost of increased hardware requirements. Microsoft has published recommended minimum hardware guidelines for running Windows 2000 Professional, but unfortunately, these recommendations provide the lowest common denominator and do not provide what everyone would agreeably call acceptable performance. Table 1.1 provides a comparison of minimum hardware requirements as issued by Microsoft and hardware recommendations based on real-world use in a corporate environment.

Table 1.1 Minimum Hardware Requirements

Microsoft Recommendations for Windows 2000 Professional	Realistic Recommendations for Windows 2000 Professional
133MHz or higher Pentium-compatible CPU	200MHz or higher Pentium-compatible CPU
64 Megabytes (MB) RAM	96 Megabytes (MB) RAM (preferably 128MB)
2GB hard disk with a minimum of 650MB free hard-disk space	2GB hard disk with a minimum of 1GB free hard-disk space

Windows 2000 Professional has a larger base operating system footprint than Windows NT 4.0 and Windows 9*x*, but, when coupled with sufficient hardware, it can outperform its older brothers. In particular, good performance gains have been associated with an increase in RAM.

Windows 2000 Professional integrates hardware and computer accessories more thoroughly than any previous Microsoft operating system, and as a result, requires hardware to undergo meticulous compatibility testing. Microsoft regularly publishes (usually quarterly) the Hardware Compatibility List (HCL), a list of Windows-compatible hardware that has passed hardware compatibility tests. Windows 2000 Professional does not yet have the same driver and manufacturer support as Windows 9*x* and Windows NT, so it is necessary to check the HCL before attempting any installations. This should be done to ensure that Windows 2000 Professional supports the hardware you are planning to use. A plain-text version of the HCL can be found on the Windows 2000 Professional CD-ROM in the \SUPPORT directory. As with Windows NT, a list of compatible hardware devices is located on the Microsoft site (www.microsoft.com/hcl). Another initiative (www.hardware-update.com) provides additional information on topics such as BIOS revisions and PC model compatibility for Windows 2000. Microsoft also provides www.microsoft.com/windows2000/upgrade/compat as a compatibility resource.

NOTE

The Hardware Compatibility List (HCL) provides a list of all hardware that is supported—meaning that Microsoft has committed to guaranteeing that specific hardware is compatible with Windows 2000. Unsupported hardware does not imply that the hardware will not work with Windows 2000, or that it is of inferior quality. What it does imply is that the Microsoft support staff cannot offer a full range of support services if problems arise with the specific unsupported hardware or driver.

Most businesses have an eclectic mix of hardware, and you will have to formulate a strategy on what action should be taken when a workstation does not meet the hardware or compatibility requirements for Windows 2000 Professional.

Actions that may be taken include:

- Replacing the hardware
- Upgrading the hardware
- Leaving non-complaint hardware in place

An excellent extension to the setup process called the pre-upgrade check can be used to check hardware and software compatibility and will be discussed in the sections on upgrades and clean installations

Application Compatibility

The function of the network and the supporting infrastructure is to service users to provide them with the tools that they need to perform their work as effectively as possible. The tools that the majority of users require are applications. Deploying Windows 2000 Professional should provide an environment that supports application requirements to an equal or greater degree than does the existing infrastructure.

The aim of application testing is to force compatibility and integration issues into the open before they become a production problem. Depending on the environment, testing can become increasingly more complex, requiring both time and skilled resources. At a minimum, there should be these two areas of exploration:

- Application compatibility
- Application integration

Testing for application compatibility is the process of ensuring that applications perform as expected. Application testing is of critical importance, even in environments that use Windows NT exclusively. Windows 2000 has undergone major architectural enhancements, several of which may change the way applications function.

Testing application integration involves determining whether applications can leverage the new and existing technology that Windows 2000 provides. A slew of exciting new technologies are available with Windows 2000, many of which are targeted at enabling applications. Some applications may need to be rewritten or may require updates to leverage the new technology.

The testing process is where a good relationship with your vendor is essential. If the application sports the *Made for Windows 2000* logo, you can be sure it is Windows 2000 compatible. Applications that comply to the Windows 2000 Application Specification (http://msdn.microsoft.com/certification) are guaranteed to be compatible and leverage the new technology afforded by Windows 2000.

Commercial applications can undergo testing by VeriTest, an independent testing company, provided they comply with the Windows 2000 Application Specification. Applications that pass the tests conducted by VeriTest can then be certified. It is important to note that applications can comply with the Windows 2000 Application Specification without being certified.

Many applications have already undergone testing, the results of which can be found on the Microsoft Web site (www.microsoft.com/windows2000/upgrade/compat/). The directory hosted by Microsoft classifies applications according to the following criteria:

- **Certified** The application completed tests run by VeriTest and takes advantage of new Windows 2000 features.
- **Ready** The application has been tested for compatibility by the vendor and supports Windows 2000.
- **Planned** The application is intended to achieve Certified or Ready status sometime in the future.

Upgrades vs. Clean Installs

Microsoft supports two methods of installing Windows 2000 Professional on target workstations: through upgrading or clean installs. Upgrading to Windows 2000 Professional implies that the target workstation already has an existing operating system that may have its own settings and configuration. If the target workstation is configured with an operating system that is supported for upgrading (see Figure 1.1 in the following section), then the setup program can be instructed to upgrade in place, migrating all user settings and applications available.

If, however, the target workstation is a new machine, requires reinstallation, or is configured with a non-supported operating system, then a clean installation must be applied to the workstation. The primary drive of the target workstation is then installed with Windows 2000 Professional without searching for existing data (though data can be preserved), applications, or configuration settings.

Administrators and support engineers should take the time to perform the upgrade and installation process numerous times to be aware of potential problems. Identifying show-stopping problems, such as that the application does not work, may be a great deal easier than handling issues (such as the profile directory has changed to the Documents and Settings folder) that manifest much more subtly.

Several factors will influence your decision whether to upgrade or to apply a clean installation of Windows 2000 Professional. These include:

- **Current workstation management levels** If modifications to the workstation's operating system and applications have followed strict change controls, then the current state of the workstation will be well known. An upgrade would best suit a well-managed environment, preserving the investment in your configuration information. If the state of the workstations is indeterminate, then a clean install of Windows 2000 Professional would allow you to revert the configuration of the workstations back to a known state.

- **User preferences and settings** If your users have a level of control over their workstations, they may have personalized certain settings and preferences. It can be difficult to determine what settings exist. To preserve these settings the best option would be to perform an upgrade.

- **Applications and data** Some users may store data on their local workstations, or install applications locally. An upgrade would be the best choice to prevent inadvertently deleting data, and would also ensure that applications would still function (if compatible with Windows 2000 Professional). Many businesses store data centrally for backup and management purposes and as a result, a clean install could be considered.

- **Existing operating systems on client workstations** The installation type you choose will also be dictated by the operating system of the client (see Figure 1.1) prior to deployment. If, for example, you are using Windows 3.1, the only option available would be to perform a clean installation. Upgrading from previous versions of Windows NT (version 3.51 and later) is inherently easier than upgrading from Windows 9*x*. This is due to the commonality between the operating system kernel architecture, device driver models, registry database, security architecture, and file systems. Upgrading from existing Windows 9x installations can present additional issues to be resolved.

■ **Operating system history** If your client workstations have been through a regular cycle of upgrades, the preferred option would be to perform a clean install, thus resolving possible legacy issues. Migrating the workstation to Windows 2000 Professional from a platform that has been repeatedly upgraded could negate some of the advantages (such as stability) of deploying Windows 2000 Professional in the first place.

There are a number of ways to start the Windows 2000 Professional setup process. The setup or upgrade process can be initiated by executing Winnt32.exe from a command line on a host operating system that is compliant with the upgrade paths in Figure 1.1 (Windows 3.51 Workstation or greater, and Windows 9*x*). The setup executable, Winnt32.exe, is found in the i386 directory on the Windows Professional CD-ROM. It is also possible to execute setup from a bootable CD-ROM containing the relevant installation files. Other solutions include using a network management application such as Microsoft's Systems Management Server (SMS), or a bootable floppy disk with network drivers and a connection to the Windows 2000 Professional installation source.

When using the setup program Winnt32.exe to install Windows 2000 Professional, the command lines used to initiate an automated installation are very similar in all methods. Winnt.exe is used when starting setup from 16-bit Microsoft operating systems such as when using a bootable floppy disk.

To summarize:

- To clean install Windows 2000 Professional on an MS-DOS, Windows 3.1, Windows 3.11, or Windows for Workgroups, run Winnt.exe from an MS-DOS prompt.

- To clean install or upgrade from Windows 9x or Windows NT, use Winnt32.exe.

TIP

Microsoft recommends a clean install of Windows 2000 Professional rather than an upgrade. The upgrade process has been extensively tested but cannot take into account every scenario. In addition, problems that existed before an upgrade may just be transferred to the new operating system.

Upgrades

Windows 2000 Professional supports the upgrade of the most recent of the Windows-based family; this includes Windows 95 (OSR 1, OSR 2, OSR 2.5), Windows 98 (and service pack), Windows 98 Second Edition, Windows NT 3.51, and Windows NT 4.0. Upgrading from Windows 3.1, Windows 3.11, Windows for Workgroups, Windows NT 3.1, or Windows NT 3.5 is not supported and will require a clean install. Additionally, those users still using Windows 2000 Professional Beta 3 and earlier must first upgrade to Windows 2000 Professional RC2 or higher before upgrading to the official release of Windows 2000 Professional.

Network installations of Windows 95 shared from a server are also not supported for upgrade to Windows 2000 Professional. To install Windows 2000 Professional on these machines, a clean installation must be completed. Other points to remember are that during the upgrade process Windows 2000 Professional searches the workstation's hard drive for other installations of Windows and will fail if there are multiple operating systems installed on the workstation. You cannot upgrade from Windows 9x to Windows

2000 Professional if *another* Microsoft Windows-based operating system is installed simultaneously. The other operating system must be removed before proceeding with the upgrade (Figure 1.1).

Figure 1.1 Upgrade paths to Windows 2000 Professional.

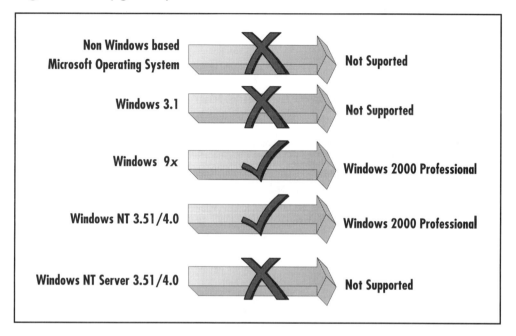

The setup program can also provide a pre-upgrade check that interrogates hardware and software for compatibility with Windows 2000 Professional before installation takes place (Figure 1.2). This check may indicate that you have to uninstall certain applications to proceed, or replace hardware or device drivers. Particular information generated may include reference to DOS configuration, Plug and Play hardware, Windows Messaging Services, and software compatibility. The check upgrade command generates a clear text report that includes all the relevant information generated and additional data, such as the amount of memory on the workstation, free disk space on the target drive, and a breakdown of the Start menu. The report can also be viewed during manual setup. The pre-upgrade check, which works for both Windows NT and Windows 9x, can be initiated from the i386 directory on the Windows 2000 Professional CD as follows:

```
Winnt32 /checkupgradeonly
```

When upgrading from Windows 9*x*, the following command line may also be used:

```
Winnt32 /unattend:\\srv1\9xupgrades\answer.txt
```

Replace \\srv1 and the path as necessary for your environment.

Figure 1.2 The pre-upgrade check has found an incompatibility on the target workstation.

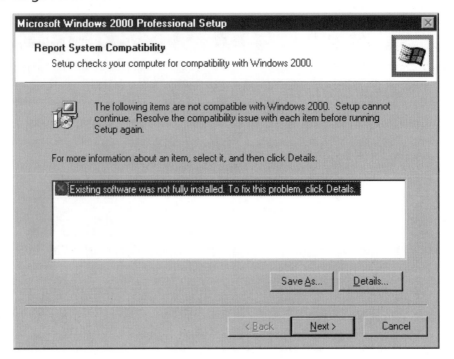

The file answer.txt referred to in the Windows 9*x* example above is a clear text file that may resemble the code:

```
[unattended]
win9xupgrade=yes
[win9xupg]
ReportOnly=yes
SaveReportTo=\\srv1\9xupgrades\%computername%.txt
```

The option to use an answer file (a file that contains details on how setup should run) to specify that a pre-upgrade check must be executed allows the administrator greater flexibility in collating the information gathered from the workstations. An answer file to store the results of the pre-upgrade check centrally will only work for Windows 9*x*. Answer files are extremely useful in automating setup, and their format will be explained in greater detail in later chapters.

TIP

It is possible to check the hardware and software compatibility of workstations without using the Winnt32.exe pre-upgrade check. A compatibility tool, chkupgrd.exe, is available from the Microsoft Web site. This tool provides the same functionality as the pre-upgrade check included in the Windows 2000 setup program, but can be run as a standalone application without requiring Windows 2000 source files.

The Windows NT pre-upgrade check stores its report in the winnt32.log file in the %windir% directory and could be used in a batch file similar to:

```
winnt32.exe /CheckUpgradeOnlyQ

copy %windir%\winnt32.log \\srv1\ntupgrades\%computername%.txt
```

To automate the pre-upgrade check of Windows NT workstations, use winnt32.exe /CheckUpgradeOnlyQ instead of winnt32.exe /CheckUpgradeOnly. Appending the Q to CheckUpgradeOnly forces setup to create the winnt32.log file without requiring user input.

To minimize issues during the upgrade process it is always recommended that you visit your vendors' Web sites for compatibility information, updated drivers, and other information. During the setup of a test lab you will be able to run the upgrade process on production-type machines to gain an understanding of what issues may need to be resolved. As a general rule, custom power-management tools and custom Plug and Play solutions should be removed before upgrading Windows NT and Windows 9x.

TIP

The pre-upgrade check can be run manually at any time, the results of which will be saved to %windir%\upgrade.txt for Windows 9x and %windir%\winnt32.log for Windows NT. This will detail the applications that may not work, what device drivers may require upgrading, and which hardware is incompatible. This report can also be run from the automated setup process, login script, or other management utilities and may be saved to a network share for later perusal. Each report can be uniquely saved in the central location as the computer name of the machine where the pre-upgrade check ran.

Upgrading from Windows 9x

A great deal of effort has been invested to ensure that the upgrade from Windows 9x to Windows 2000 Professional is as smooth as possible. This said, upgrading from Windows 9x is the least optimal of the upgrade paths available. Most administrators will be familiar with the fact that there are distinct differences between Windows NT and Windows 9x, notably with the registry, the accounts database, and operating system structures. This implies that some applications designed specifically for Windows 9x will not work under Windows 2000 Professional, and that some hardware that functions under Windows 9x will not function with Windows 2000.

During compatibility testing, Windows 2000 Professional developers found that applications would not function as expected after the upgrade process from Windows 9x for several reasons:

- The application setup routine detected that it had been installed on Windows 9x and had installed Windows 9x-specific files.

- Some applications made calls to Windows 9*x* application programming interfaces (APIs) not found in Windows 2000 Professional.

- During application setup certain registry data would be stored under Windows 9*x* in a different place than where it is installed in Windows NT or Windows 2000 Professional.

- Changes to the operating system. As part of the design criteria, Windows 2000 developers always chose stability or robustness of the operating system over application compatibility.

To allow companies to resolve application compatibility issues, Microsoft provides an extension mechanism called migration DLLs that plug into setup. These migration DLLs attempt to resolve application compatibility issues during setup through a software-based solution, and can be used to replace Windows 9*x* specific binaries and registry settings with Windows 2000-compatible binaries and registry settings. These DLLs are quite easy to integrate into the upgrade process as they are based on the standard Win32 API and comprise a single DLL and any files that must be copied to the target workstation to resolve the particular application issue. A possible issue to beware of is the uninstallation of applications changed by the migration DLLs. Unless the uninstall log for the specific application is modified by the migration DLL, notifying it of file and registry changes, the uninstallation process may be unsuccessful. A toolkit is available to aid in the DLL development and can be downloaded from www.microsoft.com/msdn.

Several system utilities are not migrated during the upgrade process, such as Scandisk, Defragger, and DriveSpace, since they are replaced with equivalent functionality within Windows 2000 Professional. Compressed drives will also not be upgraded and must be decompressed before upgrading. Certain Windows 9*x* specific binaries, called VxDs, will not migrate during the upgrade to Windows 2000 Professional along with .386 drivers. The [386Enh] section of the system.ini file on Windows 9*x* workstations details the VxDs that are loaded.

As stated earlier, all released versions of Windows 9*x* are supported for upgrade. The upgrade process will preserve the system and user state; that is, the file system, drive letters, and user accounts. Windows 2000 Professional supports a wide range of file systems, including FAT32 introduced with Windows 9*x*. The upgrade process supports FAT32, though no changes are made to the file system during the migration. The setup process can be instructed to convert partitions to NTFS v5, or to leave the file system alone. Networking components may also not upgrade, though Windows 2000 does ship with some clients in the /i386/win9xupg folder on the Windows 2000 Professional CD-ROM.

TIP

NTFS v5 provides a number of advantages over FAT32, including encrypted file system, volume mount points, increased security, and NTFS directory junctions. Windows 2000 Professional workstations should be converted to NTFS to leverage these advantages.

The method with which the setup program detects incompatibilities in Windows 9*x* is more complex than that used for Windows NT. The Plug and Play IDs of the hardware devices are compared against those listed as compatible in the Windows 2000 Professional source files. If entries for 16-bit drivers are found in the config.sys, they are flagged in the pre-upgrade check.

Additional considerations when upgrading include:

- **Specifying the installation directory** This cannot be changed from the current Windows directory.
- **Machine accounts** Windows 9*x* machines do not require machine accounts in the domain, but Windows 2000 Professional workstations do.
- **User accounts and profiles** During the migration process the setup program will attempt to migrate profiles and user accounts.

Software incompatibilities are found by examining installed applications for API calls that will not work with Windows 2000. The setup process also compares executable files on the target workstation with a database of known issues in the Windows 2000 source. Setup writes incompatibilities to the pre-upgrade check under the following categories:

- **Programs that do not work under Windows 2000** A flag is raised for all those applications that must be upgraded, or an alternate compatible application installed.

- **Programs that work but with minor issues**

- **Programs that must be removed before upgrading** Some applications have been found to adversely affect the installation process and must be removed before proceeding with setup.

- **Programs that are removed by Setup** Some programs become redundant, with similar or identical functionality built into the operating system.

- **Programs that should be reinstalled** Programs that are identified to install differently when installed on different operating systems should be reinstalled.

To summarize, resolving compatibility issues when upgrading from Windows 9*x* to Windows 2000 Professional could entail:

- **Obtaining updated device drivers** Drivers based on the Windows Driver Model (WDM) will work on Windows 2000, but manufacturers may have to release updated drivers to replace VxDs and other non-compatible drivers.

- **Securing a migration DLL** Application-specific migration DLLs are coded to resolve compatibility issues encountered after the migration process.

- **Re-installing the application after upgrade** This may resolve issues caused by the initial installation program detecting that it was installed on Windows 9*x* and installing Windows 9*x* specific binaries, modifying registry keys specifically for a Windows 9*x* installation, or installing files in the wrong directory.

- Sourcing third-party network drivers not distributed with the Windows 2000 Professional source.

- Removing custom Plug and Play and custom power management solutions.

- Acquiring software or hardware to replace components that are not compatible.

Upgrading from Windows NT

Windows NT 4.0 and Windows 2000 share a common architecture in many key areas, such as the registry, file system, security, and operating system kernel structures. This eases the upgrade path. Applications also have common compatibility requirements for Windows NT and Windows 2000. Testing has revealed that there is a significantly higher success rate in upgrading from Windows NT than from Windows 9*x*. So much so, in fact, that Microsoft recommends that part of the preparation process for Windows 2000 Professional deployment is to migrate as many workstations to Windows NT as possible.

When upgrading, Windows 2000 Professional supports a great deal of the Windows NT 4 legacy hardware, though this does not necessarily imply that the same hardware is supported for clean installs.

The main software incompatibility culprits include anti-virus programs, file system filters (as used by backup programs and even storage devices such as CD-ROMs), and disk quota software. Third-party networking components may also need close examination, though Windows 2000 does ship with some clients in the /i386/winntupg folder on the Windows 2000 Professional CD-ROM. It is always a good idea to ensure that the machines' BIOS revisions are up to date. Migration DLLs cannot be used for Windows NT, but an alternate process can be used to help resolve upgrade issues.

If a particular component is known to be problematic during the upgrade process, then you can alert Setup to the problem and configure what action should be taken. Dosnet.inf is processed during the first phases of setup and can instruct Setup to disable services or even to halt the installation process, if necessary. This is done by copying the Dosnet.inf from the i386 directory on the Windows 2000 Professional CD and modifying the [ServicesToDisable] section to include items that you wish to disable during the upgrade. Editing the [ServicesToStopInstallation] will determine what services will prevent setup from continuing.

When examining Dosnet.inf, the following key determines function type:

- **(d)** DLL
- **(f)** File
- **(s)** Service
- **(r)** Registry

To allow Setup to halt installation or disable a service, the correct entries need to be detailed in the Dosnet.inf in a format similar to that detailed below:

```
r, key_name, value_name, expected_value, html_file, text_file,
%description%

f, file_name, version, html_file, text_file, %description%

s, service_name, html_file, text_file, %description%
```

- *key_name* is the registry key to search for. Correct format should be HKEY_LOCAL_MACHINE.
- *value_name* is the value name to search for under the key specified in *key_name*.
- *expected_value* is the registry value to search for. If it is found, then the appropriate action is taken according to which section the entry appears in.
- *html_file* is the name of a .htm file that will be displayed when the entry is found.
- *text_file* is the name of a .txt file that will be displayed when the entry is found.

- *%description%* is the name of the incompatibility displayed to the user. The friendly name is expanded with a corresponding entry in the [Strings] section of Dosnet.inf.
  [Strings]
  Description = "A description of the incompatibility."

- *file_name* is a fully qualified file name of a file to detect.

- *version* is the file version of *file_name* to detect. If this version is not detected, no action is taken. Multiple file entries can be used to detect multiple versions.

- *service_name* is the name of the service as it appears in the Windows NT registry. This name is the same as that shown in Control Panel. It is important to know that the majority of device drivers run as services.

Associated HTML and text files are provided to supply more information on what corrective action to take when an incompatibility is encountered. The HTML file can even be used to point the user to the location of a replacement file as required. These parameters (even if they point to empty files) must be included or the entry in the Dosnet.inf file will not be executed. The HTML and text files should all be contained in the Compdata directory, a child of the i386 directory.

TIP

The pre-upgrade check can be modified to contain additional incompatibilities as you deem appropriate, such as inhouse, custom-written applications. By modifying the Dosnet.inf file, which is parsed when the pre-upgrade check is initiated, you can provide your own incompatibility entries.

The setup program can then be run with the /m switch to copy replacement files from an alternate location. In the following example, a replacement Dosnet.inf has been copied to the \\srv1\ntup-grades share to prevent the running of a particular service.

```
\\srv1\distribution\winnt32.exe /unattend /m:\\srv1\ntupgrades
```

Clean Install

The process of installing Windows 2000 on a workstation whose hard drive can be formatted (thus erasing all data), or on a workstation that will be booting between operating systems, is known as a clean install. In order to proceed with a clean installation, the only requirements are that the workstation should meet the minimum hardware specifications for Windows 2000 Professional and that the hardware be present on the HCL. A clean install will not have any settings other than those entered during setup and may require individual customization.

To speed up the installation process, winnt32 can be run with the Syspart switch. The Syspart switch causes all of the installation files to be copied to the target disk drive. When the drive is then removed and placed in another workstation, it will continue with the next stage of setup. This option is particularly useful for reducing deployment time in environments with dissimilar hardware, or for use with disk imaging software. Syspart can only be used on workstations that already have Windows NT 3.51, Windows NT 4.0, or Windows 2000 installed—it is not supported on the Windows 9x platform. Another consideration is that Syspart must be used with the Tempdir switch.

You must perform a clean install when:

- Target workstations are configured to use a shared copy of Windows 95 running from a server
- Target workstations are running Windows 3.1, Windows 3.11, and Windows for Workgroups

- Target workstations are running a non-Microsoft operating system

- Target workstations do not have an operating system installed

- Target workstation must be built from CD-ROM

TIP

For a workstation to use a CD-ROM for automated setup, it must have El-Torito No Emulation support for bootable CD-ROMs. Boot the workstation from the Windows 2000 CD-ROM and insert a floppy disk containing an answer file named winnt.sif. After the computer has finished reading the contents of the floppy disk, remove it and allow the installation to continue.

Microsoft has ensured that Windows 2000 Professional supports a good number of file systems. During the installation process the following changes are affected:

- **When not multi-booting** All local NTFS volumes are converted to NTFS v5 (this is the default behavior, and occurs whenever an NTFS volume is mounted locally on a Windows 2000 workstation). Boot/system volumes formatted with FAT16 can be converted to NTFS v5. Volumes that are not boot/system volumes are not converted.

- **When multi-booting** If you are multi-booting with Windows NT Service Pack 3, then a new NTFS driver is installed in the Windows NT Service Pack 3 directory to enable you to read NTFS v5 volumes. If you are multi-booting with Windows NT Service Pack 4, you will be able to access any basic volumes formatted by Windows 2000. If you are multi-booting with a version of Windows NT earlier than Service Pack 3, then you will not be able to access NTFS volumes.

For IT Professionals

Deploying Windows 2000 Professional in an International Environment

Globalization is a fact of life and a growing part of the modern work ethic. To serve the diverse groups of people wishing to collaborate as painlessly as possible, Microsoft has provided multilanguage capabilities for Windows 2000 Professional. By facilitating work in a mixed language environment and reducing the cost of owning a MultiLanguage operating system, Windows 2000 Professional makes working in a multilingual business a manageable reality.

Three language versions of Windows 2000 Professional are available:

- Windows 2000 Professional English Version allows you to input, view, and print in 60 languages.
- Localized language editions of Windows 2000 Professional provide a fully localized user interface and all the benefits of the English version.
- Windows 2000 Professional MultiLanguage Version allows users to switch the user interface to the language they prefer and still provide all the benefits of the English version.

Multilingual editing and viewing (which is part of Windows 2000 Professional English version) allows users to work with documents written in a different language without the need to reboot. The MultiLanguage version of Windows 2000 Professional allows for the adoption of a single worldwide deployment strategy, as users would be able to change their user-interface language as required.

Continued

> In a more controlled environment, the user-interface language could be controlled centrally by administrators, using group policies. MultiLanguage Windows 2000 Professional also reduces some support and administration overheads due to the elimination of localized versions of operating systems.

Common to both the upgrade and clean install process is the issuing of the setup program Winnt32.exe (unless a clean installation from a 16-bit platform is required. In that case, winnt.exe is used). Some of the more common winnt32 switches are detailed in Table 1.2.

Table 1.2 Winnt32.exe Switches

Winnt32.exe switch	Meaning
/?	Launches comprehensive Help screen.
/s:sourcepath	Specifies the location of the Windows 2000 installation files.
/tempdrive:drive_letter	Setup places temporary files on the specified partition and installs Windows 2000 on that partition.
/unattend[seconds]:[answer_file]	Upgrades/installs Windows 2000 in unattended Setup mode. All user settings are taken from the previous installation, requiring no user intervention.
/copydir:folder_name	Instructs Setup to copy a specified folder and all of its contents from the source folder to the folder where the Windows 2000 files are installed on the target workstation, and create a folder within the folder where Windows 2000 is installed.
/copysource:folder_name	Creates a temporary additional folder to be used during the setup process. This folder is deleted after setup is complete.
/cmd:command_line	Forces Setup to execute a specified command before its final phase.

Continued

Winnt32.exe switch	Meaning
/udf:id[,UDF_file]	Indicates an identifier (ID) that Setup uses to specify how a Uniqueness Database (UDB) file modifies an answer file.
/Syspart:drive_letter	Setup copies just the startup files to a disk and marks them as active. This allows the disk to be inserted into another workstation.
/checkupgradeonly	Performs the pre-upgrade check.
/checkupgradeonlyq	Checkupgradeonlyq can be used as the silent alternative for Windows NT.
/cmdcons	Installs the Recovery Console for repairing Windows 2000. It can only be used after setup.
/m:folder_name	Setup copies replacement files, such as the Dosnet.inf, from an alternate location.
/makelocalsource	Setup copies installation files to the local hard disk.
/noreboot	Setup does not restart after the file-copy phase of winnt32 is complete. This is often used so another command can be issued.

Setup Issues

In a perfect world the upgrade and installation process would be a seamless activity that worked right every time. The fact that support engineers have such productive careers is evidence enough that information technology is all but perfect. What can be done, however, is to provide proactive troubleshooting and fault resolution. Obviously the pre-upgrade check should be conducted on the target workstation or on a workstation of similar configuration before attempting to install Windows 2000 Professional. It is not possible to discuss all of the problems that can arise during the setup process, or even be too specific, but a brief summary of some of the major generic issues may provide insight on where to begin.

- **Insufficient hard disk space** The obvious solution to this is to free up additional disk space.

- **Windows 2000 Professional does not install or start** An initial step would be to determine if the target workstation's hardware is represented on the HCL. Establish whether the workstation can boot off the particular installation device.

- **Dependency service does not start** Verify that settings and drivers used during the setup process are correct.

- **Stop messages** One of the first actions after receiving the "Blue Screen of Death" should be to consult the HCL. Document the error carefully and search the TechNet and Microsoft Web site for information on the error code. Try removing exotic hardware from the workstation configuration.

- **Network connectivity problems** Verify that network settings and drivers are correct. Confirm that registering with network entities can take place. For example, establish that the workstation can be or has already been added to the domain.

- **Setup stops in text mode** Verify that the BIOS is up to date and compatible with Windows 2000 Professional. In particular, check Advanced Configuration and Power Interface (ACPI) compliance and settings and any IRQ assignments. ACPI is responsible for the interface between the operating system and the workstation's power management and Plug and Play features.

- **Setup stops in GUI mode** During the GUI portion of Setup, device detection takes place. With some hardware this can prove problematic. Check the vendors for information and the HCL.

TIP

After Setup has completed, a number of log files are available for troubleshooting and general support information. %Windir%\Setupact.log contains a description of the actions performed during setup in chronological order. %Windir%\Setuperr.log contains a detail of errors that occurred during setup. %Windir%\Setupapi.log contains information on the use of INF files.

Deployment Tools in Windows 2000

Every deployment strategy has a foundation that is built on a set of reliable deployment tools. A deployment tool is the mechanism or utility with which the initial automated operating system build is created and deployed. These tools can either provide an automated interface into the setup program or provide a means of taking an exact copy of a model workstation so that it can be replicated to other workstations. Without a sufficiently diverse set of deployment tools, an operating system would not be able to fulfill the number of different deployment requirements that are a function of the complexity of the modern computing environment. As a result, Windows 2000 has a variety of deployment tools that provide a great deal of flexibility.

Careful consideration needs to be taken regarding installation type, as it directly impacts on the choice of deployment tool—some deployment tools do not provide the capability to upgrade to Windows 2000 Professional.

Windows 2000 Support and Deployment Tools

A number of deployment and support tools are available with Windows 2000 Professional, and most can be found on the Windows 2000 Professional CD-ROM. In particular, the Windows 2000 Support Tools provide administrators with a rich array of tools, not only for deployment, but also for general administration and trouble shooting. The distribution set is located in the SUPPORT\TOOLS directory on the Windows 2000 Professional CD. If necessary, several of the utilities can be individually extracted from cabinet files. Cabinet files (.CAB) are used to minimize the size of software distributions and are based on a non-proprietary compression format.

The Windows 2000 Support Tools consist of:

- **SETUP.EXE** The Windows 2000 Support Tools installation program
- **2000RKST.MSI** Windows 2000 Support Tools Microsoft Installer file

- **SREADME.DOC** Contains late-breaking information not included in the help files
- **SUPPORT.CAB** Cabinet file containing all the individual support tools

An additional cabinet file, DEPLOY.CAB, contains general deployment tools:

- **DEPTOOL.CHM** A compiled HTML Help file containing help on Setup Manager, Sysprep, and unattend.doc
- **README.TXT** A text file containing complementary or late-breaking information that supplements the Microsoft Windows 2000 Guide to unattended Setup
- **SETUPCL.EXE** A complementary utility to Sysprep
- **SETUPMG.EXE** A wizard-based tool for automating setup
- **SETUPMGX.DLL** Associated binary for Setup Manager
- **SYSPREP.EXE** A disk duplication utility
- **UNATTEND.DOC** Document detailing answer file parameters

The deployment tools do not have an installation routine and have to be extracted from the cabinet file manually. To decompress the deploy.cab file on Windows 95, use the EXTRACT command. Users of Windows 2000 and Windows 98 have a much easier time and can extract the files directly by right-clicking on the files and choosing EXTRACT.

Before using any of the tools and techniques in this book, take the time to read through the Readme.txt for late-breaking information regarding automated installs. Browsing through the compiled HTML Help file, Deptool.chm, will provide you with additional information on the deployment tools.

Running Setup.exe or, if you have Microsoft Installer installed, 2000RKST.MSI, will install the Windows 2000 Support Tools. Read the initial welcome screen (Figure 1.3) and follow the very simple installation wizard to install the tools and utilities.

Figure 1.3 Windows 2000 Support Tools Setup Wizard.

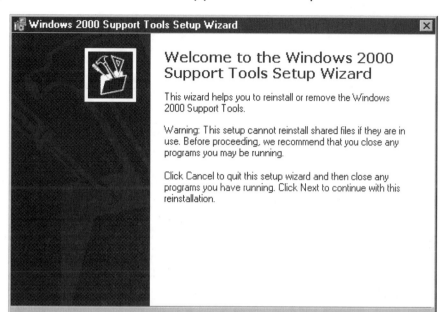

After the initial welcome screen, the Windows 2000 support tools wizard will guide you through the remainder of the installation steps. Selecting a typical installation, as in Figure 1.4, will install all of the tools and will also create the Start menu item titled, "Windows 2000 Support Tools."

When browsing the default directory for the Windows Support Tools installation files, C:\Program Files\Resource Kit, you will notice that there are a large number of utilities. The tools, a subset of the Windows 2000 Resource Kit, provide a surprising amount of functionality. Description and usage notes for these utilities can be found in the Tools help file in the Windows 2000 Support Tools folder in the Start menu. Launching the Deployment Planning Guide from the Support Tools folder in the Start menu will also provide a great deal of information on automating and deploying Windows 2000 Professional.

Figure 1.4 Selecting the installation type for Windows 2000 support tools.

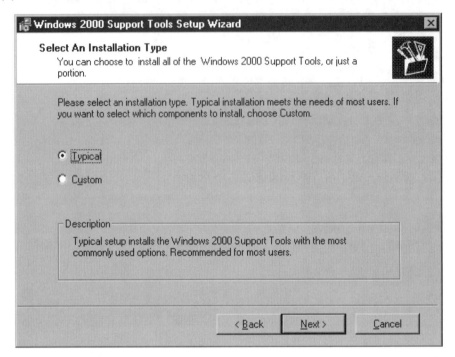

Automated Installation File

The automated installation file is a plain-text file that can be fed to the operating system during setup to automate the installation process. An automated installation file can be used during an upgrade or a clean install. During manual setup the operating system asks the user a number of questions relating to the configuration of the computer and its environment. When the Windows 2000 Professional setup program is launched in a specific manner, the setup program can interrogate an automated installation file for answers to the setup questions. This answer file can also provide configuration information beyond the scope of the normal installation program, including details on how to interact with the distribution folder. The automated installation file is a plain-text file (usually called unattend.txt) and is often referred to as the answer file. When an answer file is being used to automate the installation completely, setup is said to be running in unattended mode. A simple way to launch setup with an automated installation file may look similar to:

```
Winnt32 /unattend:\\srv1\9xupgrades\unattend.txt
```

The setup process progresses through the same steps as when run manually. For example, Plug and Play device detection is still carried out, enumerating all hardware devices.

An answer file is divided into sections, each with a section header. Within each section are key/value pairs. The keys are allocated values by using the = sign. There is an extensive set of pre-defined section headers (detailed in the Microsoft Windows 2000 Guide to Unattended Setup document on the Windows 2000 Professional CD-ROM), though some section headers can be user defined. Answer files can vary considerably in size since not all key/value pairs need to be present. The terms *answer file, automated installation file,* and *unattend.txt* (the usual answer file name) are often used interchangeably.

Error handling is rather basic and usually results in the setup process behaving incorrectly or displaying an error during setup. The code extract below details some of the key/value pairs that can be used for an automated installation file to set up a workstation WKS001 in the xyzcompany.com domain.

```
[Data]

    AutoPartition=1

    MsDosInitiated="0"

    UnattendedInstall="Yes"


[Unattended]

    UnattendMode=FullUnattended

    OemSkipEula=Yes

    OemPreinstall=No

    TargetPath=\WINNT
```

```
[GuiUnattended]

     AdminPassword=password

     OEMSkipRegional=1

     TimeZone=33

     OemSkipWelcome=1


[UserData]

     FullName="Bilbo Baggins"

     OrgName=XYZCompany

     ComputerName=WKS001


[Identification]

     JoinDomain=xyzcompany.com
```

Answer files are the most flexible deployment tool as they allow you to fully tailor the setup process and at the same time allow for variants in hardware. Configuration changes are easy to apply since it usually only requires changes to the automated installation file. By renaming unattend.txt to a different file name, you can maintain a number of different answer files for different machine configurations or lines of business.

The answer file can be created in a number of ways, such as by using a text editor like Notepad, or by using the easy to follow Setup Manager.

Other examples of the use of automated installation files include:

- **Winnt.sif**, used for CD-ROM-based automated installs
- **SysPerp.inf**, used for automating the final stages of disk imaging

Setup Manager

One of the most obvious improvements in Windows 2000 Professional is the number of wizards used to ease operating system configuration and tool usage. Microsoft has extended the use of wizards to some of the deployment tools. Setup Manager is a wizard-based deployment tool that assists administrators in automating the clean installation or upgrade process of Windows 2000. One of the first iterations of Setup Manager was to automate the setup of Windows NT. Feedback from users and the IT community have helped Microsoft improve substantially on the earlier version, providing a much more complete and functional tool. The end product of using the Setup Manager is an answer file and possibly a distribution share. An answer file, as mentioned earlier, is a plain-text file that contains information that the setup process can use to reduce or eliminate any user interaction. In short, an answer file can be used to facilitate the automation of the setup process.

The Windows 2000 Professional operating system files used for the setup process are obtained either from a CD-ROM (in the i386 directory) or over the network from what is called a distribution share. This distribution share acts as a central repository, not only for the operating system files, but also for installation information such as updated drivers and automation information (such as the answer file).

To run Setup Manager, extract Setupmgr.exe and Setupmgx.dll from Deploy.cab, and place the files into a directory on your hard drive. The obligatory Windows Welcome message, as shown in Figure 1.5, introduces the Setup Manager after double-clicking Setupmgr.exe.

Along with creating new answer files, it provides the ability to duplicate the current computer's configuration and edit existing answer files. Five user interaction levels provide different levels of automation as shown in Figure 1.6. Setup Manager also creates answer files for:

- Windows 2000 unattended installations
- Sysprep
- Remote installation services

Figure 1.5 Welcome screen for the Setup Manager Wizard.

Figure 1.6 Setup Manager product-install screen.

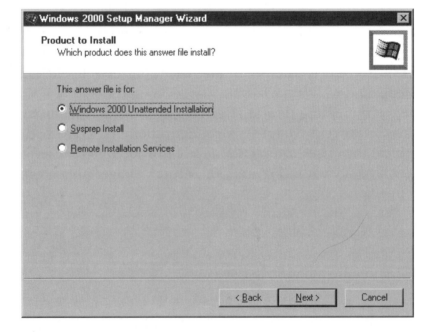

Setup Manager also provides five different levels of automation:

- **Provide defaults** The answer file you create will provide default answers that the installer can then review.

- **Fully automated** The answer file fully automates the setup process with no user interaction.

- **Hide Pages** If all the answers for a particular wizard have been supplied in the answer file, that particular wizard will be hidden from the installer.

- **Read Only** If a wizard is not hidden from the installer, the values are Read Only.

- **GUI unattended** This automates only the text-mode portion of setup.

It is no coincidence that Setup Manager reflects the real setup process very closely, allowing administrators to use a tool that is as intuitive as the setup process itself, as shown in Figure 1.7.

Figure 1.7 Sample Setup Manager configuration window.

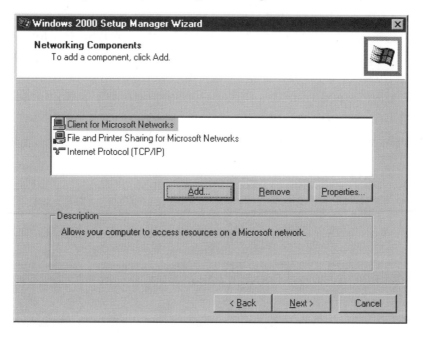

Sysprep

A tool used frequently in Windows NT and Windows 9*x* environments is disk-imaging software. It allows the administrator to take a snapshot of a workstation and copy it to another identical workstation. This is a particularly fast way of deploying a fully configured (including software and operating system settings) workstation to multiple target workstations. Initially, Microsoft did not support disk imaging, but its growing popularity and public pressure forced them to reconsider. With Windows 2000 Professional, a model workstation, including applications and configuration settings, can be prepared for disk imaging by using the Sysprep utility.

Disk cloning is often confused with disk imaging. Disk cloning is a hardware process that involves making an exact copy of an original drive and inserting it into a new workstation. Disks can be prepared for cloning using Winnt32 and the Syspart switch.

When Sysprep is executed it changes several registry settings during the preparation process. After the workstation has shut down (see Figure 1.8), the third-party disk-imaging software can then be used. When the image is applied to another workstation, a new Security Identifier (SID) is applied on the next boot. A mini-wizard also runs on the next boot and requests basic information for configuration purposes. A script file called Sysprep.inf, which is syntactically identical to an answer file, can be used to answer the configuration questions and make the setup totally automated.

Certain restrictions apply to using Sysprep, including that the model and target workstations are identical in the following aspects:

Figure 1.8 Sysprep confirmation dialog box.

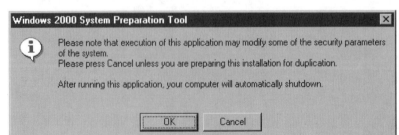

- Advanced Configuration and Power Interface (ACPI) support
- Hardware Abstraction Layers (HALs)
- Mass-storage device controllers

Plug and Play devices need not be the same since Sysprep redetects these devices on first reboot.

WARNING

Sysprep distributed with Windows 2000 does not support Windows NT. If you wish to use Sysprep for an operating system other than Windows 2000, be sure to obtain a version that works with the specific operating system.

Additional Tools to Help Deployment

Several new developments have heralded an increased ability to manage and support Windows-based infrastructure. Increased manageability translates into a more effective and customizeable means of upgrading and installing operating systems and applications.

The following technologies and tools are an essential part of Microsoft's Windows 2000 strategy. An important point to note is that the advantages of these tools can be realized prior to Windows 2000 deployment and can pave the way to a well-controlled deployment process. Some of the new tools and technologies include:

- **Active Directory Services Interface** (ADSI) In businesses today there are usually a number of disparate directories—repositories of information—such as network operating systems and e-mail systems, each with its own method of accessing the information it contains. ADSI provides a well-defined, open set of interfaces for managing these directories. ADSI can be used with equal ease to add a user to the Active Directory, to the Windows NT Directory Service, to the Novell Directory Service. ADSI can be considered to be the ODBC (Open Database Connectivity) of directory services.

- **Windows Management Instrumentation (WMI)** To provide a comprehensive management platform, Microsoft has developed a means of engineering software and hardware components. WMI's kernel-level technology allows it to monitor, view, and manipulate components. WMI publishes information, configures device settings, and supplies event notification from device drivers.

- **Windows Scripting Host (WSH)** The limitations of batch files are well documented, and the need for a replacement mechanism to automate tasks has been long overdue. WSH is a language-independent scripting host that natively supports VBScript and JScript (and the capability to leverage Internet Explorer). Scripting is a powerful way to efficiently automate tasks, both for the administrator and the power user.

- **Microsoft Installer (MSI)** In order to address the shortcomings of the installation processes during deployment in Microsoft-based environments, MSI was developed to provide a more robust installation method. It manages shared resources effectively, enforces installation rules, reduces DLL conflicts, simplifies rollback installations, eases customization, and offers a self-repair facility.

You might wonder how these tools help to deploy Windows 2000 Professional. Consider the following example: A technology company requires the deployment of Windows 2000 Professional and Office 2000 to all users who would like to be early adopters. Since all technologies discussed above are part of the drive to make Windows more manageable, they are freely available from the Microsoft Web site. What's more, they work equally as well on Windows NT and Windows 9*x* as on Windows 2000. Our resourceful support engineer has written a script using VBScript (which runs very nicely on each workstation thanks to Windows Scripting Host) to ask the user whether he or she would like to be an early adopter. The script writes the usernames and machine names of all those requesting to be early adopters to a centrally located file.

The second part of the script only executes if the user indicated that he wanted to be an early adopter of Windows 2000

Professional. The administrator knows that the workstations are well specified, but could be short on disk space. Using Windows Management Instrumentation, he interrogates the amount of free space left on the users' primary drive and notifies the user of how much disk space he or she would have to free up to allow the upgrade to commence over the weekend. The script then exits.

The weekend of the migration, the support engineer runs another VBScript which, using ADSI, adds the early adopters to the Active Directory and, according to a pre-defined matrix, adds them to the relevant Active Directory groups according to the groups they had belonged to in the Windows NT domain. The workstations are then migrated over the weekend, with the last part of the migration being the installation of Office 2000 (which comes prepackaged in MSI format) using Microsoft Installer.

This hypothetical scenario illustrates a very basic use of the tools previously mentioned. Each of these technologies contains more than enough functionality to warrant the publication of a set of books on their use. The possible uses for these tools are endless and are only limited by the imagination of the user.

Deployment Techniques

The methods available for deploying Windows 2000 Professional are fortunately varied and flexible. These methods, called deployment techniques, provide an outline for the basic processes that an installation or upgrade will follow. These techniques may overlap with different deployment tools, using the specific tool that will get the job done as required.

Remote Installation Services

Total Cost of Ownership (TCO) is an idea that has gained considerable momentum in recent years. Microsoft has introduced a strengthened change and configuration management infrastructure aimed at reducing TCO and improving management of its Windows 2000 products. Remote Installation Services (RIS), a key component of the new change and configuration management infrastructure, provides administrators with an enterprise class deployment technique to deliver Windows 2000 Professional remotely to clients in a well-managed fashion.

What can RIS do for you? It provides a mechanism for delivering Windows 2000 Professional to target clients in the following three ways:

- Normal Windows 2000 Professional manual installation with all of the usual setup questions
- **Automated Windows 2000 Professional installation** An answer file is used to automate the setup process. To make the process even easier, you could use Setup Manager as it provides an option to generate RIS answer files.
- **Cloned image of a model workstation** A model workstation will typically contain Windows 2000 Professional, applications and customized settings—these can all be delivered through RIS to a new target workstation.

RIS is easy to install and configure, but relies heavily on the Windows 2000 infrastructure. During the RIS installation process, you are guided through the relevant steps by the RIS setup wizard (Figure 1.9).

During the installation process the wizard requests the Windows 2000 Professional source files and copies them to a directory created for the Remote Installation Service (Figure 1.10).

WARNING

Remote Installation Services is tightly coupled with the Windows 2000 network infrastructure, and its benefits cannot be realized without the following required services:

- **Dynamic Host Configuration Protocol (DHCP)** This service allows
  remote boot-enabled clients to retrieve an IP address and other network configuration information.
- **Domain Name Service (DNS)** Acts as a locator service.
- **Active Directory (AD)** Enables deployment servers and the client computer accounts.

Figure 1.9 Remote Installation Wizard.

Figure 1.10 Copying the Windows 2000 Professional source files.

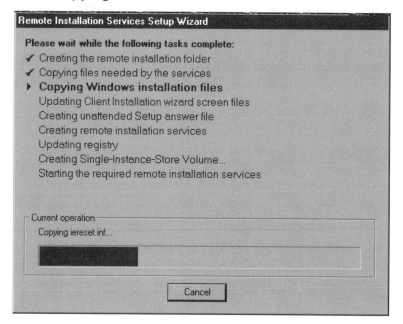

RIS provides a great deal of functionality, but not only must you meet Windows 2000 infrastructure requirements with Active Directory, DHCP, and DNS, but target workstations must still meet the Windows 2000 compatibility requirements and satisfy one of the following boot requirements:

- Network PC (NetPC) compliant, which includes the capability to boot from the network
- A pre-boot execution-(PXE) compatible network card (found on PC98 compliant workstations)
- An RIS supported PCI-based network card

RIPrep.exe, an RIS utility, allows an image of a model workstation to be taken and dumped to disk. This image can then be delivered to target workstations that meet the RIS boot requirements. A frequently encountered problem is that model workstation images often take up a great deal of disk space. RIS intelligently manages disk space by using the single-instance store that trawls through the disk images and removes duplicate files, replacing them with a pointer to the original copy of the file.

RIS is managed through the Active Directory Users and Computers MMC snap-in. The Properties window shown in Figure 1.11 provides the basic interface into managing images, clients, tools, and security.

Disk Imaging

Installing, configuring, and deploying operating systems can be a tremendously time-consuming and onerous task. A common question from the non-technical user is, "Can't we just copy it, like a floppy disk, from one to another?" The response, more often than not, is, "No you can't ... uhhh, well, you can—but it's not quite that simple you know...." Such ingenuous questioning paved the way for a deployment technique called disk imaging.

Disk imaging allows an administrator to configure a model workstation, with operating system and applications installed, and use it as a template for other workstations with similar hardware specifi-

Figure 1.11 Remote Installation Properties window.

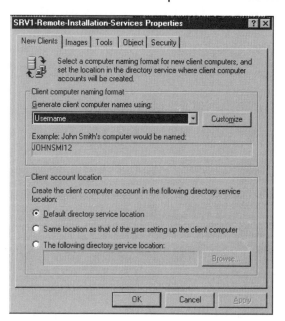

cations. The usual method employed by disk imaging software is to copy the hard drive of the model workstation sector by sector. An important point is that, prior to imaging the disk, the Sysprep utility must be used to prepare the drive for imaging. Obviously, a sector-by-sector copy means that all files—data files, application binaries, hidden files, super-hidden files (as found in Windows 2000 Professional), operating system files, configuration settings—are copied faithfully. The disk image is then stored, often in a compressed form, in a central location for easy access and deployment. When a new workstation is designated for operating system installation it can be booted from a specially configured floppy disk that downloads the image onto the target workstation. In a very short space of time the target workstation has been identically configured to the tested model workstation. As a result, disk imaging can significantly reduce the management and support costs of deployment.

Disk imaging software also has other attractions. It can be used to deploy multiple operating systems, such as Windows 9x, and back up critical systems. Consider the following scenario: The CEO's workstation "meets its maker" (that is, has to be returned to the manufacturer for repairs). Needless to say, he wants a resolution to his problem yesterday. Fortunately our battle-hardened support engineer backed up the CEO's workstation with disk imaging software. In no time at all, the backup image was applied to another functioning workstation and the CEO hardly knew the difference.

This idea can obviously be extended further to help facilitate support. Every support engineer will tell you that he has at some stage been driven to distraction, and lost an untold amount of hair, because a workstation that appears to be identical to all others, but refuses to function as expected. Hours (sometimes even days) of costly troubleshooting could be avoided in this scenario by simply redeploying the model image to the sickly workstation.

Third-party vendors of disk imaging software include Symantec, Powerquest and Altiris. Disk imaging may seem like a deployment nirvana, but, as with most strategies, it has its pitfalls. The number of PC models that are cycled through a production environment seems to grow every year. Each one of these models has a different hardware specification and as a result, a specific image may be required to service that model. Over time this adds up to a significant disk space requirement to store the model workstation images. Managing the images can also be problematic. The image itself is not something that can be actively manipulated since it is a sector by sector copy, with little cognizance of the contents. Even the slightest changes or variations require that a new image must be generated and stored.

Disk imaging software companies have stepped up their efforts to make their software more enterprise friendly by increasing scalability, flexibility, manageability, and security. Images can be of considerable size and deployment could incur a sizeable network bandwidth cost. With multicasting, disk-imaging companies provide a means of reducing bandwidth requirements by transmitting a single image to multiple target workstations. Using this IP broadcast technique allows the image to be broadcast once, but received by many machines simultaneously.

Automated Installation Scripts

We have discussed two methods of deploying Windows 2000 Professional using disk imaging and Remote Installation Services.

Automated installation scripts provide the third means of delivering Windows 2000 Professional to workstations. Automated installation scripts are scripts that collate all the necessary information needed to deploy the operating system without the need for human intervention. Some examples of automated installation scripts we have already encountered include:

- **Answer files**, such as the unattend.txt used in conjunction with the setup program winnt32.exe and winnt.exe
- **Sysprep.inf**, which is used to complete the automated setup of Windows 2000 Professional after a disk image has been applied to a target workstation
- **Winnt.sif**, which automates CD-ROM based setup

An automated installation script could be placed on a bootable floppy and issued to engineers who are responsible for upgrading workstations, or it could be located centrally to automate setup after a disk image has been applied to a workstation. The script contains the necessary code to initiate the automated setup process. The setup process could then be launched and guided to completion by an answer file.

A number of tools, such as Windows Scripting Host, Windows Management Instrumentation, Active Directory Services Interface, and Microsoft Installer can be used to provide additional functionality to the automated installation scripts.

A Comparative View of Deployment Techniques

Comparing deployment techniques is a difficult and sometimes fruitless task. For a particular business, one advantage may outweigh all of a specific deployment technique's pitfalls, no matter how numerous. The decision to choose a deployment technique must be based on many factors; use the technique (or techniques—a combination may be suitable) that best fits the requirements at hand.

Table 1.3 contains a few of the more obvious advantages and disadvantages of the deployment techniques.

Table 1.3 A Comparison of Deployment Methodologies

	Advantages	Disadvantages
Remote Installation Services	■ Single Instance Store greatly reduces image sizes ■ Target workstations can utilize different storage mass controllers ■ Can be used with automated installation scripts ■ Can be used with images to deploy more than just the operating system. Applications can be contained within images. ■ Integrated with Active Directory ■ Managed from a Microsoft Management Console	■ Requires a Windows 2000 Server to act as an RIS Server ■ Requires DHCP, DNS, and Active Directory ■ Only works for Windows 2000 Professional ■ Target clients must either be NetPC, PXE enabled, or have a compatible PCI-based network card ■ Limited number of available network drivers for boot floppy—cannot be modified by administrator ■ Laptops without docking stations with PCI-based network cards are not supported ■ RIS can only provide images for the C:\drive
Disk Imaging	■ Fast deployment method ■ Multicasting decreases bandwidth requirements during large rollouts ■ Can be used for multiple operating systems ■ Can be used for alternative purposes, such as disaster recovery and support ■ Software is written by a company that specializes in disk imaging ■ Easy to use—can lower management and support costs	■ Target workstations must be similar and have identical mass-storage controllers ■ Changes to model workstation requires re-imaging ■ Can be difficult to manage multiple images ■ Disc space requirements can be extensive even with compression

Continued

	Advantages	**Disadvantages**
Automated Installation Files	■ Most flexible option ■ Changes can be made easily ■ Takes up least amount of disk space ■ Can be used to upgrade target workstations	■ Requires technical knowledge of the setup process ■ Minimal infrastructure, or third-party, requirements

Summary

Operating systems have progressed remarkably in terms of capability and complexity in recent years. Unfortunately, productivity gained by using technologically advanced operating systems has been offset by the high cost of owning and deploying them. Effective operating system deployment within an organization has become a focus of intense interest, manifesting in the development of a host of tools and technologies for Windows 2000 deployment.

Automating setup eliminates the need for human intervention during the installation process. Depending on the requirements of the business, the appropriate deployment technique needs to be leveraged to create and deliver the Windows 2000 Professional configuration. The steps for automating the setup of Windows 2000 Professional include the design of a model Windows 2000 Professional workstation that reflects the organization's preferred configuration. Next, a tool needs to be used to aid the creation of the model workstation (this could be done with automated installation files, Sysprep, or Setup Manager). Following this, a distribution point should be created to store the automated install centrally.

Before deploying, it is essential to check that the target workstations' hardware is represented on the Hardware Compatibility List, and that it meets the minimum hardware requirements for Windows 2000 Professional. An excellent tool to determine hardware and software readiness is the pre-upgrade check run by winnt32.

The first goal in attempting to automate setup is determining what type of installation should be carried out—is it an upgrade or a clean install? Several criteria affect what installation type to choose, including workstation management levels, user preferences and settings, applications and data, and operating-system history. Upgrading any operating system is a complex process that places a great demand on resources and time. Only Windows NT 3.51 and higher and Windows 9*x* family workstations can be considered for upgrading to Windows 2000 Professional. All other workstations require a clean install.

Even though a great deal of research has been invested in smoothing the upgrade process from Windows 9*x* to Windows 2000, some applications and hardware will not work after upgrading. Migration DLLs can be used by developers to help bridge the gap between applications being exclusively Windows 9*x* compatible to being Windows 2000 compatible.

Windows NT and Windows 2000 Professional share a common architecture in many key areas, which eases the upgrade path tremendously. Problematic services identified prior to upgrade can be halted during the setup process as required using the Dosnet.inf file.

A clean installation is the preferred installation type, ensuring that legacy issues are not propagated to the new platform.

A deployment tool is the mechanism or utility with which the initial automated operating system build is created and deployed. The Windows 2000 Support and Deployment tools provide valuable utilities to aid in the deployment process. Automated installation files are plain-text files that can be fed into the setup process to eliminate the need for any human intervention. They also allow interaction in certain ways with the distribution source providing additional functionality. Setup Manager is a wizard-based deployment tool that generates answer files for Remote Installation Services, unattended installations, and Sysprep installations. Sysprep is a tool used for preparing a disk for disk imaging. After Sysprep is executed on a target workstation, the drive can be imaged. When the image is transferred to a target workstation, a mini-Setup Wizard is launched, requesting answers to a series of configuration questions. These questions can be eliminated by using the Sysprep.inf answer file, which is syntactically identical to an answer file.

Deployment tools can be used with different deployment techniques. Automated installation scripts require a certain amount of technical know-how, but are the most flexible of the deployment techniques. RIS provide the facility to use both automated installation files and disk imaging, but place a heavy burden on infrastructure. Disk imaging can be a very fast and efficient method of deploying Windows 2000 Professional, but can prove to be difficult to manage and maintain. No single deployment technique can be considered preeminent—a business needs to understand its requirements and capabilities and choose the deployment technique and tools appropriately.

FAQs

Q: When undecided whether to upgrade or clean install, which should I choose?

A: If the advantages and disadvantages are of equal weight, then go for a clean install. It allows you to know exactly what is present on target workstations while ensuring that you do not inherit legacy issues.

Q: What are the differences between the way Remote Installation Services uses the Riprep tool and the way disk imaging software works?

A: The end result of using each is exactly the same. You are able to distribute an image that has both the operating system and applications included. Disk imaging software is of benefit since it is multifunctional, and usually works across a larger range of network cards than RIS does. RIS is free, but carries with it considerable infrastructure requirements.

Q: I have a disk with the Setup Manager executables. Why is it not wizard based?

A: The version you are using is the one that ships with
Windows NT 4. Setup Manager has been considerably upgraded
for Windows 2000.

Q: Are there options other than upgrading or clean installing all of
our workstations to gain the benefits of Windows 2000
Professional?

A: Windows 2000 Server ships with an excellent service that allows
a diverse range of client workstations to experience Windows
2000 Professional. Terminal Services allows existing Windows
client machines to connect to the Windows 2000 Server via a
Terminal Services Client and run a session on the server that
emulates a fully functional Windows 2000 Professional
workstation. The obvious advantage of the thin client concept is
that workstations do not need extensive hardware upgrades and
can continue to run operating systems such as Windows 3.11.

Chapter 2

Automating Windows 2000 Professional Installation

Solutions in this chapter:

- **Preparing for Setup**

- **Customizing Windows 2000 Professional Setup**

- **Preparing the Destination Computer**

Introduction

One of the techniques available for automating the installation of Windows 2000 is using unattended installation scripts. Think of an installation script just as you would a script for a play. Each actor has lines to say, and those lines are spoken at certain points during the play. An installation script provides answers (the lines of the play) to the questions asked by the setup process when they are needed, without the need for someone to sit at the console and provide the answers.

There are a number of benefits to unattended installation scripts, including:

- Most flexible option for large-scale deployments of Windows 2000
- Creates consistent installs
- Reduces overall deployment time
- Reduces user interaction

In opposition to the benefits listed above, one of the shortcomings of this automated installation method is that the per-computer install time is longer than other automated installation methods, such as disk imaging. The average install time using unattended installation scripts is about 45 minutes to one hour, depending upon system resources.

Several steps must be taken to use unattended installation scripts (the terms *installation script* and *answer file* are used interchangeably throughout this chapter). First, the source files for completing the installation must be made available. This can be done via a network share or by using the source CD-ROM. Next, the target computer must be prepared properly, including backing up any required existing data. Last, the install process is initiated manually or by using a batch file or systems management software.

This chapter covers all aspects of performing a fully automated installation using unattended installation scripts, with detailed coverage of how to use Setup Manager to prepare the distribution folder and installation scripts.

Preparing for Setup

As with most projects in life, one of your first steps is preparation. With respect to automated installations, preparation involves making sure that the setup process has all the files and settings it needs to complete the installation of Windows 2000.

All of us who have been in this industry for more than a few weeks realize that most software, including operating systems, require a setup or installation procedure. Windows 2000 installation is initiated much as it was with previous versions of Windows NT—you launch the installation by typing winnt32.exe or winnt.exe from a command line (winnt.exe is only used when installing from 16-bit operating systems, such as Windows 3.*x* and MS-DOS. winnt.exe is not discussed in detail in this chapter). There are a number of options when running winnt32.exe, and most are discussed throughout this chapter. For a thorough listing of all options, you can type Winnt32 /? at a command prompt.

Inside WINNT32.EXE

The command-line options we concentrate on pertain to the topic at hand—automated installs. Before we talk further about preparation, it is a good idea to have a firm understanding of the command-line options required to execute Windows 2000 Setup in unattended mode.

```
Winnt32 [/makelocalsource] [/s:sourcepath] [/tempdrive:drive_letter]
[/unattend[seconds]] [:answer_file]] [/udf:id[,udf_file]]
```

/makelocalsource

This option instructs Setup to copy all source files to the local hard disk. This is usually used when performing a CD-ROM installation if the CD-ROM drive becomes unavailable during the installation process.

/s:sourcepath

This option points Setup to the location of the Windows 2000 files. You have the option of specifying additional /s:sourcepath (up to eight) as part of winnt32.exe to indicate multiple source locations. Setup can then copy files from multiple locations, thereby speeding the installation process and taking the load off a single server. If you are using multiple source paths, make sure that the first source path listed is available when the installation starts, or Setup will fail.

/tempdrive:*drive_letter*

This option instructs Setup to copy setup files to the specified drive letter and to install Windows 2000 to that drive.

/unattend[:*answer_file*]

This option runs Setup in unattended mode. Without the *answer_file* specified, the existing operating system is upgraded and all users' settings are preserved. If an answer file is specified, you can customize information during the setup process.

/unattend [*seconds*] [:*answer_file*]

This option is similar to the previous one with the exception of the *seconds* setting. *Seconds* specifies the number of seconds Setup should pause after copying files to the destination computer and rebooting the computer. This option is only available on machines you are upgrading from Windows NT 4.0.

/udf:[*id*,[*udf_file*]]

UDF stands for "uniqueness database file." Its role is to provide additional customization to the unattended answer file for each computer being upgraded. By indicating an id and a .udf file, Setup will override information provided in the answer file with the specific info provided in the .udf file for the id specified. For instance, you can provide unique computer names for each computer by using a .udf file.

Here is an example of a complete winnt32.exe command for an unattended installation (this example assumes that drive h: is mapped to the share for the distribution files):

```
h:\winnt32.exe /s:h:\ /unattend:h:\unattend.txt /udf:comp1,unattend.udf
```

Included with Windows 2000 is an End-User License Agreement (EULA). This statement pertains to Windows 2000 and the rules that bind it. By using these options to create an unattended installation, you must agree to bind by this agreement for all computers with which this install process is used. One important tip: OEM versions of Windows 2000 will not be able to use these options because of the EULA.

Network Distribution Point

Now that we are comfortable with the winnt32.exe command, let's see what is required to be in place prior to typing in that command.

At the most basic level, a distribution point is a network share that includes the contents of the \i386 folder from the distribution CD-ROM for Windows 2000 Professional. Instead of placing the CD-ROM into the CD-ROM drive and starting the installation, you point winnt32.exe to the network share and launch Setup from there. The distribution folder also includes the unattended answer file, named "unattend.txt," by default. If you are using a .udf file, that, too, will reside in the distribution folder.

Distribution Point Directory Structure

Taking a deeper look, we see that the network distribution point is made up of a number of subdirectories, each of which plays an important role during an unattended installation.

Figure 2.1 is a screen shot of a distribution folder. From this screenshot we see that our distribution point is a folder named win2000dist. You can name this folder with any name you wish. This folder is shared, and the share is the focus of the \s command option for winnt32.exe discussed previously. You place the contents of the \i386 directory in the root of this folder. In addition to the folders of the \i386 directory, we see a OEM folder and a number of subfolders. This section concentrates on the OEM folder and its subfolders.

Figure 2.1 Screenshot of network distribution point.

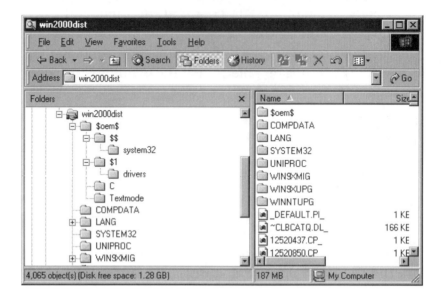

\$OEM\$

As part of an unattended installation, you may need to provide additional files required by Setup that are not included with the Windows 2000 distribution. These files include computer HALs, mass-storage device drivers, and Plug and Play drivers. OEM acts as the root for files and folders that are required during the setup process.

\$OEM\$\\$$

This folder includes system files that are copied to the Windows 2000 installation folder on the computer being upgraded. The $$ is equivalent to \%windir%. So, if your install directory is \winnt, $$ is equal to \winnt. \$OEM$\$$ can include subfolders that represent the subfolders in the system folder, such as \system32.

\$OEM\$\\$1

This folder contains files that are copied to the system drive. $1 is equivalent to the %systemdrive% environment variable. For instance, if you are installing Windows 2000 to the C: drive, then $1 is equal to C.

OEM*drive_letter*

As we saw in Figure 2.1, this equals OEM\C. This folder contains additional files and folders that should be copied to the corresponding drive on the computer. This differs from the $1 folder in that the drive letter is hard-coded for this folder. This allows you to copy files and folders to additional drives if they exist on the computer.

OEM\Textmode

This folder is very important when dealing with installations on computers with dissimilar hardware. In it you can place files that support different HALs and mass storage device drivers that are not included with the distribution files.

All this information is good to know, but it can seem very complicated. Luckily, Windows 2000 provides a tool called Setup Manager to help automate the creation of a distribution folder. The next section covers this tool in detail.

Customizing Windows 2000 Professional Setup

If you decide to launch a Windows 2000 installation from an existing Windows NT or Windows 9*x* install using the /unattend command option without specifying an answer file, the system will be upgraded using all the existing user settings. If you want to customize the upgrade, you will need to use an answer file and the OEM directory structure discussed earlier. The answer file provides answers to the questions asked by the setup process and instructs Setup on what to do with the distribution folders and files contained under OEM. This section provides some insight into the answer file and then walks you through using Setup Manager to create an answer file and the OEM structure.

Answer Files

An unattended answer file is simply a text file that is formatted similar to an .ini file. Its role is to provide the setup process with the data it needs to complete the installation of Windows 2000 without having a user type in the information.

For IT Professionals

Automated Installs from a Bootable CD-ROM

This chapter focuses primarily on performing an automated install from a network share. Windows 2000 also can be installed in an automated fashion locally on a workstation using a bootable CD-ROM.

Prior to initiating a CD-ROM-based install, you must make sure these preliminary requirements are met:

- Place the answer file onto a floppy disk and name it winnt.sif.
- Ensure that the destination computer supports booting from a CD-ROM and supports the El-Torito non-emulation specification.
- The answer file needs to contain a valid [Data] section. The [Data] section needs to include the following parameters:

UnattendedInstall=Yes

MSDosInitiated=No

AutoPartition=1; if this value is set to 0, the end user is prompted to select the installation partition during setup.

Create the answer file using Setup Manager as discussed in detail in this chapter. Modify the answer file with the [Data] information provided above. Boot the destination computer using the Windows 2000 CD-ROM and place the floppy disk containing the winnt.sif file into the floppy drive.

Here's the kicker: Windows 2000 does not support upgrading Windows 9x or Windows NT 4.0 systems when booting from CD-ROM. Booting from CD-ROM only supports a fresh installation of Windows 2000. If that didn't hurt enough, installing from a CD-ROM doesn't support the OEM directory structure discussed in the Network Distribution Point section of this chapter. Needless to say, much of the flexibility of automated installations is stripped away when using a bootable CD-ROM.

An answer file is made up of a number of headings, and under each heading are pairs of parameters and their assigned values. The format looks like this:

[Heading1]

Parameter1=value1

Parameter2=value2

[Heading 2]

Parameter3=value3

You are welcome to create the answer file manually using a text editor like Notepad, but I would recommend that you allow Setup Manager to automate this process. After the answer file has been created, you can then go back and add additional values or edit the answer file to further customize the installation.

Setup Manager

Setup Manager has been mentioned a number of times so far, but what is it and what does it do? Setup Manager is a wizard-driven program that queries the user on a number of topics in order to prepare an unattended answer file and construct the distribution folder. You can run through the wizard any number of times to prepare additional answer files to address all of your installation needs. In this section we will walk through the Setup Manager wizard, providing thorough descriptions of each screen and suggestions as to what information to provide.

First we need to start Setup Manager. The files needed to run Setup Manager are available on the Windows 2000 distribution CD-ROM in the deploy.cab file under \support\tools. You need to extract the Setupmgr.exe and Setupmgx.dll files to your local hard drive and run the Setupmgr.exe. Once you launch Setup Manager, the wizard walks you through a number of dialogs extracting the information it needs to prepare the answer file and OEM directory.

1. The first screen you see is the Welcome screen, which doesn't need to be shown here. Click NEXT to continue.

2. The next window asks whether you wish to create a new answer file or to modify an existing one (see Figure 2.2). The first time through Setup Manager you will select to create a new answer file. If you are creating an additional answer file for a unique unattended installation, you can choose to modify an existing answer file. This choice takes an existing answer file you specify and places the data from that file as defaults throughout the Setup Manager Wizard, allowing you to make changes along the way. The second selection is fairly self-explanatory in that each wizard screen defaults to the current settings of the computer on which Setup Manager is being run. For our example, we are creating a new answer file. Make your selection, and click NEXT.

Figure 2.2 Create a new answer file or modify an existing one.

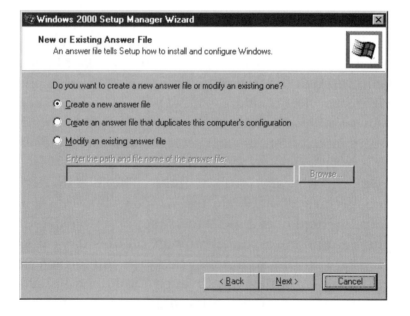

3. The dialog shown in Figure 2.3 asks you which type of answer file to create: Unattended installation, Sysprep, or Remote Installation Service. Setup Manager will display select screens based on your choice. Sysprep is discussed in Chapter 3, and Remote Installation Services is discussed in Chapter 4. We make the appropriate choice for an unattended installation. Click NEXT to continue.

Figure 2.3 Indicate which type of answer file to create.

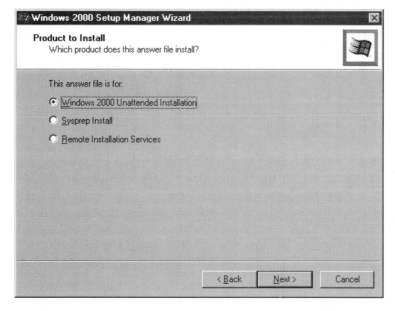

4. Next, we must indicate which platform is to be installed,Windows 2000 Professional or Server (shown in Figure 2.4). We select Professional, and click NEXT.

5. In Figure 2.5, we must decide what level of user interaction we wish to take place during the installation. The choices and descriptions are as follows:

Provide defaults

The answers you select during Setup Manager are displayed as the defaults during Windows 2000 installation. The user has the opportunity to change any setting. This does not result in a fully automated installation.

Figure 2.4 Select the appropriate Windows 2000 product.

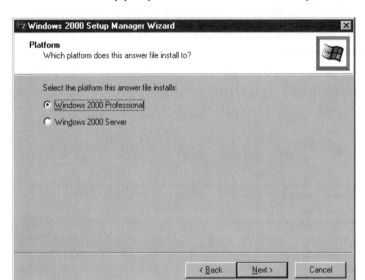

Fully automated

As its name implies, by selecting this option, the installation will proceed without any user interaction—the answer file must supply all answers.

Hide pages

Selecting this option results in a partially automated installation. If the answer file supplies answers, then the relevant installation pages are not displayed to the user performing the installation. If no answer is available, the page is displayed and the user must provide an answer manually.

Read only

This setting includes the settings for "Hide pages" and "Provide defaults" with an additional twist. If the page is not hidden, it is displayed to the user in read-only mode, restricting the user from making any changes.

GUI attended

By making this selection, you automate the text mode portion of Setup, but leave the GUI portion requiring user input.

For our example, we want a fully automated installation, so that is the choice we'll make.

Figure 2.5 Select the level of user interaction.

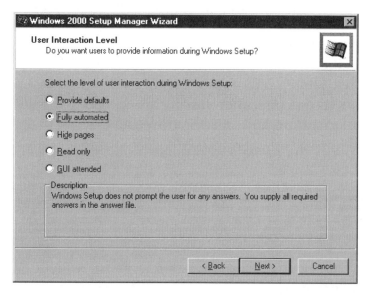

6. The next window (Figure 2.6) requires that you accept the
   EULA on behalf of the end user. To comply with Microsoft
   licensing, ensure that the end users have the opportunity to
   review the license and understand it. Click NEXT to continue.

Figure 2.6 Respond with your acknowledgment that you accept the
terms of the EULA.

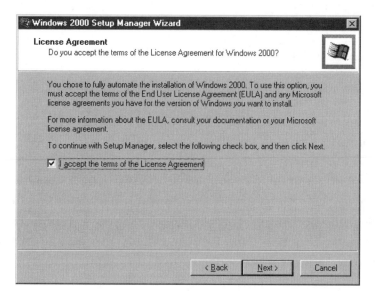

7. The next dialog (Figure 2.7) asks you to enter a Name and Organization. Keep in mind that this information is applied to all computers that use this answer file. You can create additional answer files if different settings need to be applied, or use a .udf file, which is discussed later in this chapter. Simply put, a .udf file provides additional, per-computer, customization during an unattended install. Enter the information, and click NEXT to continue.

Figure 2.7 Specify the name and organization to be applied to the installation.

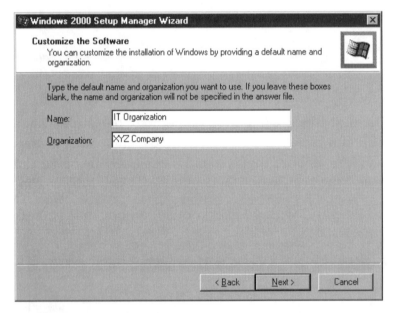

8. Figure 2.8 displays the next wizard screen, which asks you to specify how you want to create computer names. You have a few options: You can manually enter the list of computer names for the machines that are being installed; you can import a text file that includes a list of computer names, one per line with carriage returns; or you can have the answer file generate random names based on the organization name you provided in Step 7. If you already have your Active Directory installed, you can add the computers into Active Directory and export the listing using

the tools available in Active Directory Users and Computers. The file can then be imported into this dialog. In this example, a list of names was imported from a text file. Click NEXT to continue.

WARNING

There is no support for names with all numbers. All-numeric computer names are not supported in Windows 2000; however, Windows NT supported this feature. For instance, in Windows NT you could name a computer "100". This name is invalid in Windows 2000 due to the fact that all-numeric names can be interpreted incorrectly during name resolution. Instead of a computer name, the number is treated as an IP address.

   If you are upgrading a Windows NT system that has an all-numeric name, Windows 2000 will perform the upgrade and retain the name. Any changes to that name are then restricted by the naming conventions of Windows 2000.

Figure 2.8 Enter the names of destination computers, or allow the answer file to generate them automatically.

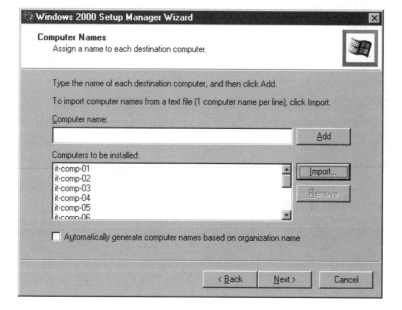

9. Next, you are asked to enter the administrative password for the destination computer as shown in Figure 2.9. You can also specify whether the Administrator account should be automatically logged on after the computer reboots and, if so, how many times. This feature is useful if you are going to perform automated application installations after Setup completes and the installations require an admin account (see Step 21).

Figure 2.9 Supply Administrator account information.

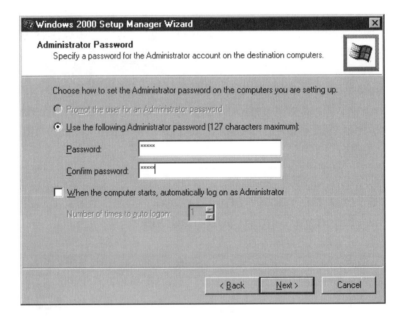

WARNING

The administrator password is Clear-text. When you supply the Administrator password during this step, the password is placed as clear-text in the answer file. Whoever has access to this file has the ability to view the Administrator password you have assigned, so limit access to this file. This password is for the local Administrator account.

A copy of the answer file is left on the destination computer after the automated installation process, but the password entries are deleted from this copy. The original file still contains the clear-text passwords.

10. Figure 2.10 shows the wizard screen prompting you to customize the display settings. As the window shows, you have the ability to select values for colors, screen area, and refresh frequency. If you decide to change these settings, and the settings you wish to use are not available in the pull-down menus, you can customize your settings by clicking CUSTOM.... Figure 2.11 is displayed, allowing you to enter specific data.

Figure 2.10 Select display settings.

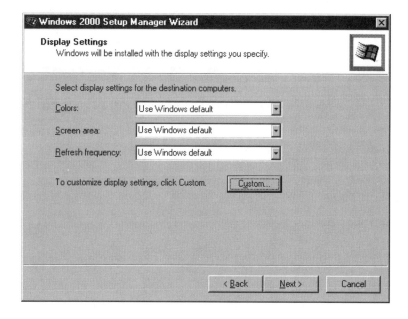

11. The next window, shown in Figure 2.12, prompts you to choose the typical settings for the network configuration or to customize these settings. For most, the default settings are adequate, providing TCP/IP and DHCP with the Client for Microsoft Networks. By selecting "Custom settings," you can include additional network interface cards and additional network components. In our example, the typical settings are fine. Click NEXT to continue.

12. Figure 2.13 displays the window asking whether the destination computer will be part of a workgroup or part of a domain. When joining the destination computer to a

Figure 2.11 Result of clicking CUSTOM… in the Display Settings
window.

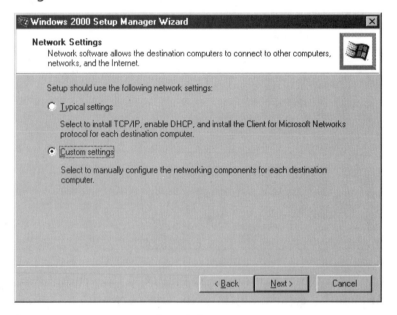

Figure 2.12 Accept typical network settings or choose to customize
these settings.

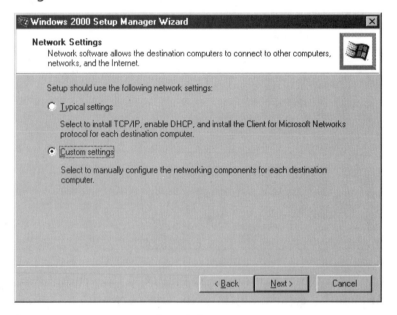

domain, you must select "Create a computer account in the
domain" and specify the appropriate credentials *even* if the
computer account has already been created. The reason for
this is that Windows 2000 uses Kerberos authentication,
which requires that you provide a valid domain account.
When you specify this information, the following lines are
added to the answer file:

[Identification]

    JoinDomain=<domain name>

```
DomainAdmin=<domain account>
DomainAdminPassword=<account password>
```

13. Next, you can select the time zone setting for the destination computers. Since I set up house in the Keystone state (Pennsylvania, that is), I've selected Eastern Time. This is shown in Figure 2.14. Click NEXT to continue.

Figure 2.13 Specify whether the destination computer will join a workgroup or domain.

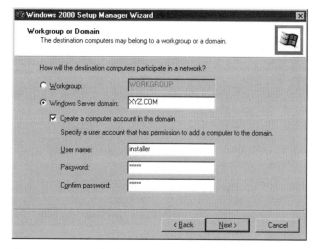

14. At this point, you have the option to further customize the unattended installation or accept the defaults for these settings (Figure 2.15.) The additional settings include telephony, language, browser, printer installation, and Windows 2000 installation folder configurations. If you decide not to customize these settings, you can skip to Step 22. Each of these additional settings is prefaced by the word "optional" in the following steps.

15. (Optional) Figure 2.16 displays the Telephony settings window. The settings you specify here will only apply to destination computers that have modems installed.

16. (Optional) Next, you can specify any additional regional settings that may be required on the end-user systems (Figure 2.17). If you don't require any additional regional settings aside from those on the Windows version currently installed, select to use the default. By specifying additional

regional settings, you give end users the ability to use regionally specific currency, keyboard layout, and measurement settings. For each additional regional selection you make, the necessary files are copied to a \lang folder under \OEM. Make your selection, and click NEXT to continue.

Figure 2.14 Make the appropriate time zone selection.

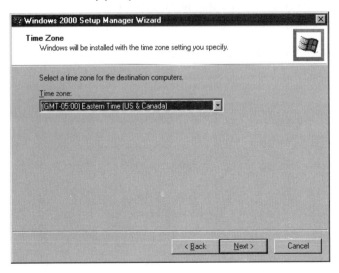

Figure 2.15 Select whether or not you wish to edit additional settings.

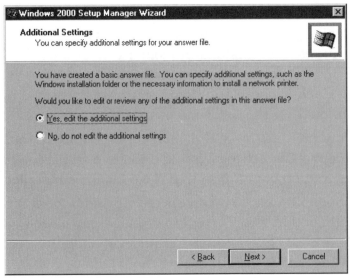

Figure 2.16 Select telephony settings for the destination computers.

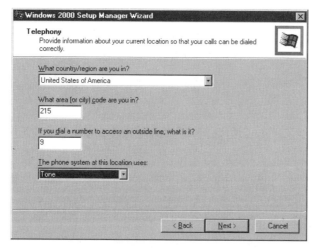

17. (Optional) Figure 2.18 shows the Languages settings screen. By specifying additional languages, you allow the end users to create and read documents in the languages that are made available on the system. Click NEXT to continue.

Figure 2.17 If necessary, specify any additional regional settings.

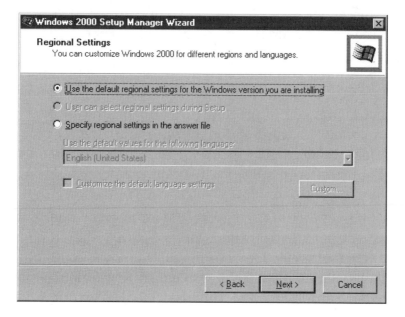

Figure 2.18 Include support for additional languages.

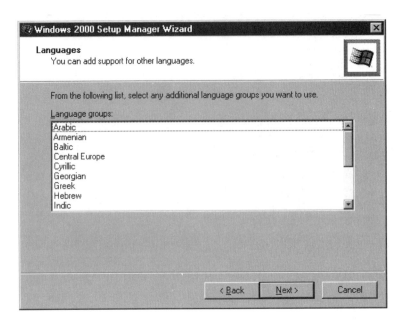

18. (Optional) In the window shown in Figure 2.19, you have the option of customizing the behavior of Internet Explorer. Your options include the self-explanatory "Use default Internet Explorer settings." In addition, you can select "Use an auto-configuration script created by the Internet Explorer Administration Kit" to configure your browser. If you select this setting, you must specify an .ins file, which is copied to the \OEM folder. An .ins file is an Internet settings file that allows you to preconfigure and lock down Internet Explorer. The third option allows you to specify proxy and default home page settings for IE. Since this isn't a book about customizing IE, we'll accept the default settings. Click NEXT to continue.

19. (Optional) Figure 2.20 prompts you to enter information about the folder to which Windows 2000 should be installed. The default selection is to install Windows 2000 into a folder named winnt. By choosing to generate a uniquely named folder, Setup will name the install folder \winnt.*x* (*x* being

Figure 2.19 Specify browser and shell settings.

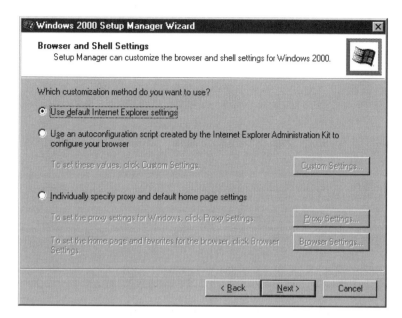

0,1...999) if a folder named winnt already exists on the disk. You also have the option of specifying the name of the folder to which Windows 2000 should be installed. The format for this entry is the path name without a drive letter (i.e., windows2000.) If you want to specify the drive letter, use the */tempdrive* parameter with winnt32.exe. For our example, we are going to leave any existing winnt folders and allow setup to create a new folder.

20. (Optional) If you need to preconfigure printers on your destination computers, you can do this using the dialog shown in Figure 2.21. Enter the UNC name of the printer share when specifying a printer to be installed the first time a user logs on after Setup completes. Note that the user logging on must have the appropriate permissions to add the printer in order for this feature to work. Click NEXT to continue.

Figure 2.20 Select the folder in which Windows 2000 should be installed.

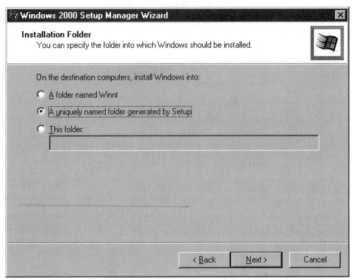

21. (Optional) If you want to run any programs automatically after the first user has logged on, you can set this up using the dialog shown in Figure 2.22. This can be combined with automatically logging on the Administrator account *x* number of times after Setup completes, as is discussed in

Figure 2.21 Configure network printers to be installed on destination computers.

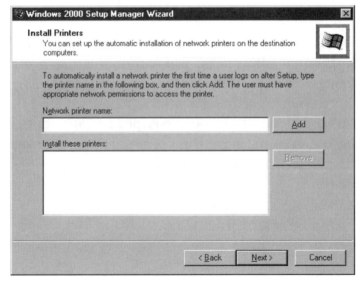

Step 9. In Figure 2.22, I've entered a command to run notepad.exe with the readme.txt file. This would launch the readme.txt file, which includes some introductory material for the end user. This program would only run once. In this case, we would not want the Administrator account logged on automatically. Click NEXT to continue.

Figure 2.22 Enter commands to run after the first user logs on to the system after Setup completes.

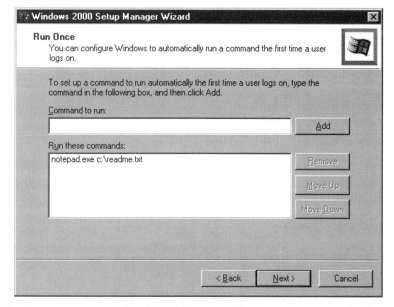

22. Next, you can instruct Setup Manager to create the distribution folder or modify an existing distribution folder, as shown in Figure 2.23. By selecting "Yes," Setup Manager will next prompt you for a folder name and share name for the distribution folder (Figure 2.24). Setup Manager also creates the OEM file structure under the distribution folder. Also, if you selected "Yes," Setup Manager will copy the Windows 2000 source files to the root of the distribution folder to be used during the unattended installation. If you are installing from the CD-ROM, select "No" and see "For IT Professionals: Unattended Installations from a Bootable CD-ROM" in this chapter for more guidance.

Figure 2.23 Instruct Setup Manager to create or modify a distribution folder.

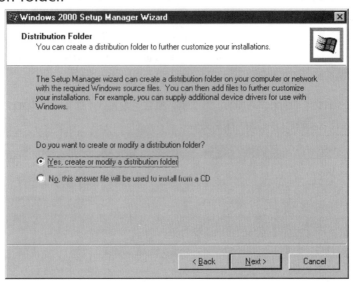

23. If the SCSI devices on your destination computers do not have drivers available with the Windows 2000 source files, you can add them to the unattended installation by including them in the window shown in Figure 2.25. The

Figure 2.24 Provide a name and location for the distribution folder and a name for the share.

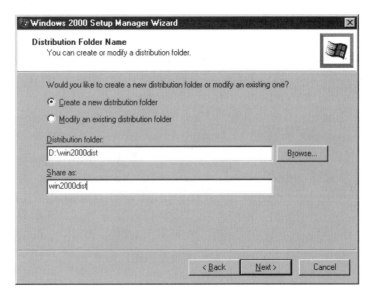

Windows 2000 drivers for your mass storage device should be available from the vendor. For most hardware devices, Plug and Play will detect and install the appropriate drives. But, in order for Plug and Play to work, mass storage devices must be properly installed prior to initiating.

Figure 2.25 Specify new or additional drivers for your mass storage devices.

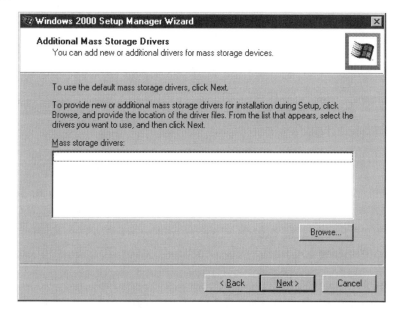

24. If the vendor of your computer systems provides a custom Hardware Abstraction Layer (HAL), you need to provide this file during the unattended installation. This is accomplished by providing the file in the dialog shown in Figure 2.26.

25. Previously, you were given the opportunity to enter commands to be run once after the first user logged on to the system after Setup completed (see Step 21). Figure 2.27 displays a dialog that prepares commands to be run immediately after Setup, but prior to the system restarting. Each command you enter here is included in a cmdlines.txt file placed in the OEM folder. For more information about cmdlines.txt, refer to Chapter 3.

Figure 2.26 If necessary, change the default HAL to the custom HAL provided by your computer vendor.

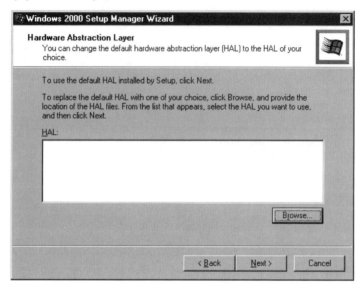

26. Many companies, especially VARs, want to include some type of name branding on the machines they deploy. The OEM Branding dialog shown in Figure 2.28 provides inputs to include logo and custom background bitmaps that are displayed during the GUI mode portion of Setup.

Figure 2.27 Enter commands to be run immediately after Setup.

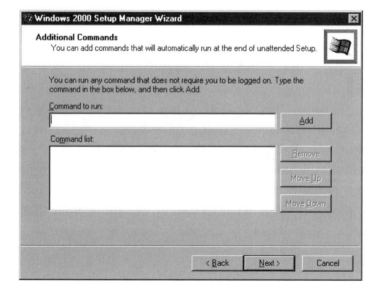

Figure 2.28 Enter bitmap files to be displayed during the GUI portion of Setup and as a custom background.

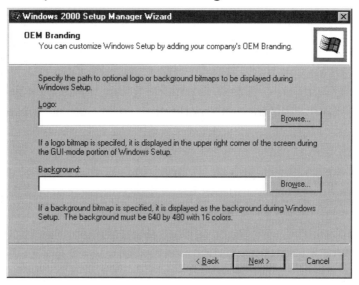

27. Back in Step 21, we added a command to run notepad.exe to launch a readme.txt file from the c: drive. Prior to launching this command, we need to place the readme.txt file onto the c: drive. In Figure 2.29, Setup Manager provides the opportunity

Figure 2.29 Add additional files or folders to the destination computer.

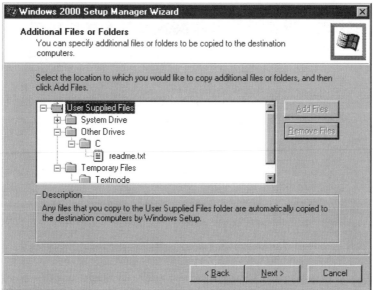

to add additional files and folders to the destination computer drives. You can see in the figure that I've already added the readme.txt file to the C: folder, which represents a c: drive on the destination computer. Referring to Figure 2.29, you cannot add files directly under the root of User Supplied Files. Nor can you add files directly under the Other Drives folder. The Temporary Files\Textmode folder holds files needed by Setup during the text-mode portion of Setup. These include mass storage device drivers and HALs. If you selected additional mass storage device drivers and HALs in the previous steps, you don't need to add them again here. The System Drive\Windows folder holds files that are placed in the Windows system directory, such as \winnt. Under the Other Drives folder is a list of drive letters that represent the drives on the destination computer. Figure 2.29 shows only one drive, C, but you can add additional drive letters.

28. The last steps finalize the Setup Manager process, asking you to name the answer file and specify the location of the setup files. The screens are shown in Figures 2.30 and 2.31. You can name the answer file anything you wish; you do not need to accept the default, unattend.txt. Setup Manager also creates a

Figure 2.30 Specify the location and name for the answer file.

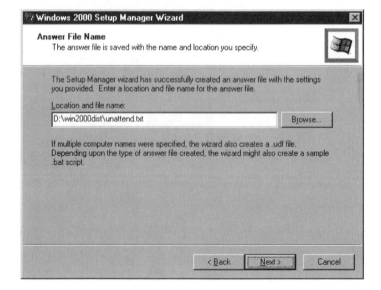

uniqueness database file (.udf file) if multiple computer names are provided. In addition, a .bat file is created, which is listed below. This is a sample file that is executed by entering UNATTEND at the command line, followed by a computer name or ID that matches a computer name in the .udf file. More information on .udf files is provided in the next section.

NOTE

When you name your answer file, that same name is applied to the .udf and .bat files. For example, if you name your answer file myanswerfile.txt, you also end up with myanswerfile.udf and myanswerfile.bat.

```
@rem SetupMgrTag
@echo off

rem
rem This is a SAMPLE batch script generated by the Setup Manager Wizard.
rem If this script is moved from the location where it was generated, it
rem may have to be modified.
rem

set AnswerFile=.\unattend.txt
set UdfFile=.\unattend.udf
set ComputerName=%1
set SetupFiles=\\WIN2K-SERVER\win2000dist

if "%ComputerName%" == "" goto USAGE

\\WIN2K-SERVER\win2000dist\winnt32 /s:%SetupFiles% /unattend:%AnswerFile%
/udf:%ComputerName%,%UdfFile% /makelocalsource
goto DONE

:USAGE
echo.
echo Usage: unattend ^<computername^>
echo.

:DONE
```

Figure 2.31 Point Setup Manager to the location of the Windows setup files.

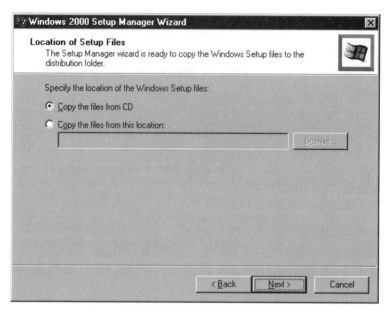

29. The last window in the Setup Manager wizard requires you to click FINISH so that Setup Manager can complete its work.

In addition to copying the Windows source files to the distribution folder and any other files you indicated, Setup Manager generates an answer file and places it at the root of the distribution folder. A sample of an answer file that was generated by the responses provided during the Setup Manager walkthrough is provided here.

```
;SetupMgrTag
[Data]
    AutoPartition=1
    MsDosInitiated="0"
    UnattendedInstall="Yes"

[Unattended]
    UnattendMode=FullUnattended
    OemSkipEula=Yes
```

```
    OemPreinstall=Yes
    TargetPath=*


[GuiUnattended]
    AdminPassword=admin
    OEMSkipRegional=1
    TimeZone=35
    OemSkipWelcome=1


[UserData]
    FullName="IT Organization"
    OrgName="XYZ Company"
    ComputerName=*


[TapiLocation]
    CountryCode=1
    Dialing=Tone
    AreaCode=215
    LongDistanceAccess="9"


[SetupMgr]
    ComputerName0=it-comp-01
    ComputerName1=it-comp-02
    ComputerName2=it-comp-03
    ComputerName3=it-comp-04
    ComputerName4=it-comp-05
    ComputerName5=it-comp-06
    ComputerName6=it-comp-07
    ComputerName7=it-comp-08
    ComputerName8=it-comp-09
    ComputerName9=it-comp-10
    ComputerName10=it-comp-11
    ComputerName11=it-comp-12
    ComputerName12=it-comp-13
    DistFolder=D:\win2000dist
```

```
    DistShare=win2000dist


[GuiRunOnce]
    Command0="notepad.exe c:\readme.txt"


[Identification]
    JoinDomain=xyz.com
    DomainAdmin=installer
    DomainAdminPassword=mypassword


[Networking]
    InstallDefaultComponents=Yes
```

You should be able to disseminate what each heading means and where the data comes from by going back through the Setup Manager steps. For a thorough discussion of all the available parameters for an answer file, refer to the unattend.doc file included in the \support\tools\deploy.cab folder on the Windows 2000 distribution CD-ROM.

Further Customization with UDF

One answer file usually does not cut it for most deployments since it only provides a single source of answers for the setup process. You could create multiple answer files for each destination computer, but that can become quite tedious. A better approach is to utilize a uniqueness database file (.udf). This was introduced at the beginning of this chapter, and more detail is provided in this section. One way to think about the purpose of a .udf file is that the answer file specifies the defaults, and the .udf file specifies the exceptions. Any settings included in the .udf file for a computer override the settings provided in the answer file.

The .udf file generated by Setup Manager only provides unique computer names for the destination computer. You need to add additional information if necessary to further customize setup on individual systems. Here is a sample of the unattend.udf file created by Setup Manager (some of the repetitive data has been omitted).

```
;SetupMgrTag

[UniqueIds]

    it-comp-01=UserData

    it-comp-02=UserData

.

.

    it-comp-13=UserData


[it-comp-01:UserData]

    ComputerName=it-comp-01


[it-comp-02:UserData]

    ComputerName=it-comp-02

.

.

[it-comp-13:UserData]

    ComputerName=it-comp-13
```

As you can see, the first heading, [UniqueIds], correlates with subsequent headings, which include the ComputerName parameter. These subsequent headings are prefaced with the UniqueId (i.e., it-comp-01) followed by an equals sign and UserData. UserData is an answer file heading that is included in the unattend.txt file listed earlier in the chapter. You can provide additional parameters under this heading, or add additional headings for each computer as long as the UniqueId of the computer prefaces them. Let's take a look at some samples.

Suppose you want to include unique user and organization names to each computer. In order to do this, you need to add additional parameters to the UserData portion of the .udf file for each machine. Here's an example:

```
[it-comp-02:UserData]

        ComputerName=it-comp-02

        FullName=John Doe

        OrgName=XYZ Affiliates
```

If you want to add additional headings you can do that as well. Below is an example that illustrates how to join computers to different domains using parameters under the Identification heading.

```
[it-comp-03:Identification]
        JoinDomain=sub01.xyz.com
        DomainAdmin=installer
        DomainAdminPassword=mypassword


[it-comp-04:Identification]
        JoinDomain=sub02.xyz.com
        DomainAdmin=installer
        DomainAdminPassword=mypassword
```

TIP

In Windows NT, all you needed to worry about was which domain to join when adding a new workstation. In Windows 2000, you need to consider which Organizational Unit (OU) you want to join as well. Luckily, unattended installations provide a way to specify the OU that the destination computer should join. This is accomplished using the MachineObjectOU parameter under the Identification heading. Here is an example:

```
[Identification]
        JoinDomain=xyz.com
        DomainAdmin=installer
        DomainAdminPassword=mypassword
        MachineObjectOU= "OU = legal, DC = xyz, DC = com"
```

The syntax for MachineObjectOU is the full LDAP path name of the OU. In the example above, the OU name is legal and the domain is xyz.com.

The command line to launch Setup with a .udf file is:

```
Winnt32.exe /s:<location of setup files> /unattend:< unattend file>
/udf:<UniqueID>, <udf file>
```

There are a number of ways to launch this command. You can use the batch file that was created by Setup Manager and provide the computer name. You can include similar batch file commands in a logon script that is launched when the user logs on to the system. A word of caution about this method: It could overwhelm your distribution servers if a large number of users log on at the same time and receive the same logon script. A third install option is to use a system's management application, such as Microsoft Systems Management Server, to deploy Windows 2000.

Preparing the Destination Computer

You have an answer file and a .udf file and are ready to start your automated installations. The final step is to prepare the destination computers for upgrade. This involves ensuring that existing applications and utilities are supported under Windows 2000, data on the disk is backed up, and that the drives to which Windows 2000 is to be installed are healthy and have adequate space for the larger footprint of Windows 2000.

Looking Out for Incompatibilities

When upgrading a computer to Windows 2000, there are some issues to watch out for. What those issues are depends on whether you are upgrading from Windows NT or from Windows 9x. When upgrading from Windows NT, look out for the following incompatibility issues:

- **Anti-virus applications and disk management applications that rely on system filters to operate** Due to changes in how Windows 2000 handles these processes, legacy applications should be uninstalled prior to the upgrade.
- **Custom Plug and Play utilities** Since Windows NT did not natively support Plug and Play, some third parties developed

tools to emulate this functionality that was so convenient for laptop users. Windows 2000 fully supports Plug and Play, so these custom utilities should be removed.

- **Custom power management utilities (usually for laptop systems.)** Windows 2000 uses Advanced Configuration and Power Interface (ACPI) and Advanced Power Management (APM) to address power management. Any existing power management utilities on the Windows NT system must be removed prior to the upgrade.

- **Protocols and clients.** Networking protocols and clients that are not automatically updated during the Windows 2000 installation

When upgrading from Windows 9x systems, watch out for these incompatibilities in addition to the ones mentioned under Window NT:

- Any applications or utilities that make use of virtual device drivers and .386 drivers.

- Any Control Panel applications installed by third parties. These often include network interface card utilities or display adapter utilities.

You also want to check the Hardware Compatibility List (HCL) maintained by Microsoft on their Web site at www.microsoft .com/windows2000/upgrade/compat/. Microsoft also offers a great utility for checking the hardware and software on your current system for compatibility with Windows 2000. This utility is called the Readiness Analyzer and is available at the same URL as the HCL.

Please, Back Up Your Data

Once you are sure that your system and software are free of any known incompatibilities and you have tested your automated installation in a lab and in pilots (see Chapter 8, "Developing a Deployment Plan for Windows 2000," for more information about planning), you need to back up the data on the destination computer in case the automated installation fails. This is definitely one of the most often "shoulda dones" spoken by IT professionals–"I shoulda backed up the data!" Don't make the same mistake so many of your contemporaries have made. Although it extends the deployment time frame and can be an unglamorous job, backups are essential to prevent disasters.

When backing up Windows NT systems, also be sure to back up the Registry. If your backup software doesn't support this function, you can use the Regback.exe utility available in the Windows NT Resource Kit.

Do a Disk Checkup

If you perform an upgrade on a sick disk drive or one with inadequate space, your installation will fail. Take some steps to repair any disk problems and provide adequate disk space prior to the upgrade to Windows 2000.

Use disk utilities that are available on the current operating system, like ScanDisk and Defrag (Windows 9*x* systems), to check your disks and repair any problems. Next, make sure that there is enough room for Windows 2000 to be installed. Windows 2000 is a much larger product than either Windows NT or Windows 9*x*. The minimum available free space needed for a Windows 2000 Professional installation that takes place over a network is over 650MB. This increases to over 1G when installing the Server product.

By taking these simple precautionary steps, you afford yourself a greater chance of experiencing a problem-free automated installation.

Summary

This chapter covered the steps to prepare and execute a fully automated installation of Windows 2000 using unattended installation scripts.

Preparing for setup involves understanding the various command-line options available with winnt32.exe and how to use them. You also should understand what the network distribution point is and the files and folders that compose it.

In order to customize the automated installation, it is necessary to use an answer file. Although it is possible to manually create the answer file, it is much easier to use the wizard-driven dialogs provided by Setup Manager.

Since a single answer file might not be flexible enough for a diverse user population, uniqueness database files (.udf) give you the means to further customize settings applied to individual systems—the answer files is the default, the .udf is the exception.

In order for your automated installation to run as smoothly as possible, take the time to prepare the destination computers. Check for hardware and software incompatibilities, and back up the drives prior to upgrading to Windows 2000.

To further wear out a well-worn cliché: There are no free lunches. It takes a great deal of testing and trial and error to get an unattended installation to run correctly. Once you've nailed down and mastered the process, the time and money saved are very gratifying.

FAQs

Q: Our company wants to have our computers join a domain during an unattended installation, but we don't want to place an account password into the answer file in clear text. What are the alternatives?

A: This is a legitimate concern. One alternative is to first join the computer to a workgroup during the automated installation process. After your systems have been installed, you can use the NETDOM.EXE tool available in the support.cab file in \support\tools on the Windows 2000 distribution to join the computers to a domain. The syntax for this command is

```
NETDOM JOIN /Domain:domain [/OU:ou path] [/UserD:user]
```

```
[/PasswordD:[password | *]] [/UserO:user] [/PasswordO:[password | *]]
/REBoot
```

/Domain= Name of the domain to which the workstation is to be joined. If an account does not already exist for the workstation, one will be created.

/OU= The full distinguished name of the OU under which the computer account will reside.

/UserD and **/PasswordD=** User account and password used to connect to the domain specified with /Domain. If the * is used, the user will be prompted for a password.

/UserO and **/PasswordO=** User account and password to connect to the computer to be joined.

/REBoot= Instructs the computer to be rebooted after the NETDOM command completes.

Q: The computers on which we are installing Windows 2000 have a couple of Plug and Play devices for which Windows 2000 does not ship drivers. Where can we put the drivers so that they are available during setup?

A: You will want to copy your Plug and Play drivers to the OEM\$1\PnPDrivers folder in your network distribution point and make some modifications to your answer file. Name the PnPDrivers folder anything you wish, up to eight-characters long. This folder is copied to the %systemdrive% folder on the destination computer during setup. Next, you need to tell Setup where to look for these files by modifying the answer file. Add the OemPnPDriversPath parameter under the [Unattended] heading of the answer file specifying the folder in which you placed the drivers. For example, if you named your PnPDrivers folder PNPSource, you would edit your answer file to include the following:

```
[Unattended]
OEMPnPDriversPath="PNPSource"
```

Q. I am trying to install Windows 2000 from a bootable CD-ROM. I know my machine supports this, but the computer is not booting from CD-ROM. What can I do?

A: If you are sure that your machine's CD-ROM drive and BIOS support this feature, you need to check your system's BIOS setup. Follow your machine's manual to enter your system's BIOS setup (this usually involves pressing a key or key sequence during system startup to enter this configuration mode). Once there, make sure that the CD-ROM is available as a boot drive.

Q. We currently have Systems Management Server (SMS) deployed in our organization. Is this an option for performing our automated installation?

A: Yes, SMS is an excellent tool for upgrading to Windows 2000. Keep in mind that you can only perform an upgrade or clean installation with SMS. You cannot perform a new installation on a system with no current operating system installed.

Chapter 3

Imaging Windows 2000 Professional

Solutions in this chapter:

- Selecting an Imaging Tool

- Preparing Windows 2000 for Imaging Using Sysprep

- Automating Setup of a Target Computer

- Imaging vs. Automated Installation Scripts

Introduction

As organizations have grown larger, relying more heavily upon desktop systems, the need to quickly deploy new workstations has risen. A technology known as disk imaging has surfaced as a popular method of meeting this demand. Imaging tools are used to take a snapshot of a standard workstation and use this image to recreate an exact copy on one or more additional computers.

In the past, Microsoft has taken a "don't do it" stance on using imaging tools to distribute Windows NT. Microsoft's primary argument against imaging Windows NT was that all target machines to which a single image was installed would have identical security identifiers (SIDs). The effects of duplicate SIDs on a network are not immediately evident, but could cause problems down the line. Microsoft changed their position with the release of the System Preparation (Sysprep) tool, which prepares disks prior to the imaging process. Unfortunately, Sysprep's availability was limited to companies that participated in Microsoft's Select Open or Enterprise licensing programs. Third-party vendors addressed the unique SID issue by releasing tools that would generate unique SIDs on the imaged computers. Microsoft's Sysprep performs the same function.

With the release of Windows 2000, Microsoft has acknowledged that imaging tools are a sound and effective way of deploying their operating system, so they decided to ship Sysprep with Windows 2000 and provide support to systems that were created from images that used the tool. This does not have an impact on third-party imaging tool vendors, since Sysprep doesn't actually create an image file from a disk. It only prepares the operating system to be imaged and distributed.

Selecting an Imaging Tool

Disk imaging has been around for a while, ever since PCs became popular in corporate environments. Imaging was developed when PC technicians were tasked with setting up and configuring large numbers of desktop systems. If you only have to install five systems, manually installing the operating system and applications and then configuring the whole thing is not too daunting. When you are faced with deploying 500 systems, however, and all with a standard setup, the manual process quickly fades into the ether. In this case, you need a tool that will take a snapshot of a standard desktop. This snapshot can then be used to quickly build the 500 systems.

For the most part, each imaging product operates in a similar fashion. The process is to configure a source machine to your specifications. You then shut this machine down and boot it using a DOS boot floppy running the imaging software's disk imaging tool. The software reads a partition or the entire drive, sector by sector, compressing it and storing the final image to some storage media. You then boot a target machine using a special boot floppy, identify the image file, and write it to the hard drive.

Microsoft's Sysprep tool is used to *prepare* a system to be imaged; it does not have the functionality to actually generate the image file. This requires a third-party tool. There are a number of third-party tools available. Each provides a base set of imaging features with additional functionality added to differentiate one product from another in the marketplace. This section discusses what to look for when shopping for an imaging tool, and takes a brief look a some of the more popular imaging tools on the market today.

NOTE

RIPrep provides limited imaging functionality. To state that Windows 2000 does not ship with an imaging tool is not completely accurate. As you will learn in Chapter 4, "Remote Installation Client and Server," RIS uses file images created by the RIPrep tool. RIS is limited to deploying Windows 2000 Professional, and the remote-boot functionality will only operate on computers with PCI-based network interface cards that are included on the remote-boot disk. This list is currently limited to about 25 cards.

Determine Requirements

Determining what requirements you have for an imaging tool may seem like a silly task. Of course, you want a tool that can create an image and transfer that image from a *source* to a *target*. Fortunately, today's disk imaging tools offer a much wider range of features that help create and manage disk images.

Here are some questions you need to ask yourself to prepare a set of requirements to be used while evaluating products:

- *How will I distribute the images to target disks? Will I use my network, CD-ROM, or some other means?* To make an imaging tool useful you need some way of taking the image you created from the source disk and distributing it to a target machine. When evaluating imaging products, you need to look at the different ways they enable this. Almost every "corporate" version of the imaging tools available provides some means to distribute the image over a network. Most support TCP/IP as the network protocol for the transfer. Some support multiple protocols, including IPX and NetBEUI. If your needs require you to visit the target systems, you can transfer the image onto CD-ROM or other external media, such as Iomega Zip or Jaz cartridges or tape, or you can hook the source and target up using a parallel port or USB port and transfer the image that way (one-to-one connections like this are limited to smaller deployments).

- *Do I want to image disk partitions as well as whole disks?* In addition to creating an image of an entire disk, you may wish to only create an image of one partition on the disk. This is valuable if the source machine's hard drives were divided into multiple partitions and you installed the operating system and applications onto only one of the partitions. It would be more efficient to only image that partition and not the entire disk.

- *What level of compression do I require?* This is something to consider when you are concerned about the space needed to store images and how fast the image can be applied to the target machine. For the most part, the higher the compression ratio, the longer it takes to actually create the image. With a higher compression ratio, the image itself is smaller and can be transported across a network more quickly.

- *Do I need to multicast an image to a number of workstations at the same time?* To multicast an image to more than one workstation at a time is a recent development for imaging tools. This function allows an image to be sent as a single communication stream to multiple target systems at one time. This minimizes the traffic created by pulling images since the same amount of bandwidth is used if one client or one hundred clients are receiving the image.

- *How much money do I want to spend on licensing an imaging tool?* This is a straightforward, budgetary question. Each vendor licenses its products differently. Some require you to pay a license fee for each imaged disk created from an original. Others allow you to pay a flat rate for unlimited use of the product. Examine each product's licensing scheme closely and ask the sales representatives what types of discounted rates are available.

- *Do I need to perform post-cloning activities?* Along with multicasting, this is a fairly new function that is shipping with some imaging applications. This feature allows you to apply machine-specific information to a system after the image has been applied. The type of information that can be manipulated includes computer name and IP address.

- *What types of file systems do I need to support?* Windows 2000 introduces NTFSv5. If you wish to use this file system on your workstations, you need to ensure that your imaging software supports this new file system. Most products provide support for FAT16, FAT32, and NTFSv4.

Once you have put down on paper what features you require from an imaging tool, you can start evaluating the imaging products available on the market today.

Third-Party Tools

There are a number of third-party imaging tools available. We will briefly look at three of these products and give a summary of their functionality. Each vendor offers a trial version of their product, which is downloadable from the vendor Web site.

Symantec Norton Ghost

"Ghosting" disks has become synonymous with the imaging process. Ghost was released a number of years ago by Binary Research and became widely popular as a shareware product. The product was then bought by Symantec.

Norton Ghost is a mature product with a rich feature set. At this time, Norton Ghost 6.0 is available from Symantec. Norton Ghost's advantage over its competitors has been its speed and compression ratios. It also has the ability to create and resize partitions automatically.

With version 6, Symantec has also improved the management of the imaging process and the administration of creating and editing images. For more information, you can visit Symantec's Web site at www.symantec.com.

Innovative Software ImageCast IC3

ImageCast IC3, available from Innovative Software, is another strong imaging tool competitor with an equally impressive feature set as that provided by Norton Ghost. One strong feature of ImageCast is its built-in boot disk creator. The boot disks are used to boot the target systems and receive images from a master control center. The current release of ImageCast, version 4.0, is claiming that it is the only imaging tool that supports Sysprep. For more information, you can visit Innovative Software at www.innovativesoftware.com.

Altiris RapidDeploy

Altiris' RapidDeploy offers many of the features available from ImageCast and Norton Ghost. One nice feature of the RapidDeploy product that is also available with ImageCast is the capability to modify the image files to change configuration settings. This feature allows you to change the computer name and IP address on the target from a central management console and send it out to the client. RapidDeploy also has a solid boot-disk creation utility, something that Norton Ghost lacks. For more information, you can visit Altiris at www.altiris.com.

Preparing Windows 2000 for Imaging Using Sysprep

You've purchased your imaging tool of choice and you are ready to start imaging your computer. Before you jump right into creating images, it is best to understand what features the Sysprep tool includes and the correct sequence of steps to take when preparing a system to be imaged.

Overview of Sysprep

Simply stated, the Sysprep tool prepares a computer disk to be imaged and copied to another disk. First, the Sysprep tool generates a unique SID for the target machine when the target system first reboots. Second, it runs a modified version of the GUI setup that takes only five to ten minutes and can be fully automated. Third, Sysprep will run Plug and Play detection to detect any hardware devices that exist on the target, but may not have existed on the source machine.

Sysprep Requirements

One limitation of using imaging to deploy Windows 2000 is that there is a requirement that some of the system hardware of the source be identical to that of the target. This requirement is much stricter with NT 4.0, since that operating system does not support Plug and Play. Since Windows 2000 supports Plug and Play, certain hardware components can be different on the target than those that existed on the source install.

For IT Professionals

HAL and ACPI Explained

In order to use the Sysprep for imaging disks, it is necessary that the source and target have identical Hardware Abstraction Layer (HAL) and Advanced Configuration and Power Interface (ACPI) support. The question is, "What the heck are these things?"

The HAL is just what its name implies: it is software that *abstracts* the hardware from the operating system so that all hardware looks the same to the operating system itself. One example is that the HAL enables Windows 2000 to run on both single-processor and multi-processor systems without having to change the operating system. Some companies, such as Compaq and Dell, have developed their own HALs that can be installed so the operating system makes use of the hardware architectures used on some of their systems.

The ACPI specification provides additional enhancements to the Plug and Play specification. It includes system board and BIOS interfaces that extend Plug and Play to include power management. Windows 2000's Plug and Play support is optimized for systems that include ACPI system boards. Developers utilize the ACPI specification to integrate power management features throughout the system. By utilizing the ACPI specification, Windows 2000 is better able to manage which applications are active when evaluating the system for power management. More information about ACPI can be found at www.teleport.com/~acpi/.

In order to take advantage of Sysprep disk duplication using imaging, the following components must be the same on both the source and target:

- Hardware Abstraction Layer (HAL)
- Advanced Configuration and Power Interface (ACPI) support
- Size of the target disk must be equal to or larger than the source

Any Plug and Play devices, such as sound cards, network interface cards, and modems, do not have to be identical on the source and target. If different Plug and Play devices exist on the target machines, you must make sure that drivers are available from the Windows 2000 distribution or added to the distribution location in order for these devices to be installed correctly during Plug and Play detection. How to do this is discussed in more detail later in this chapter.

NOTE

At about the same time Windows 2000 was released, Microsoft posted a new version of the Sysprep tool, Sysprep 1.1, to their Web site (www.microsoft.com/windows2000/downloads). When using Sysprep 1.0, there was a requirement that the mass storage device controller on the source computer be the same on the destination computer. The reason for this was that Plug and Play detection required a properly installed mass storage device (i.e., hard drive). Sysprep 1.1 eliminates this requirement so long as the device controllers are Plug and Play or use Plug and Play mini-ports. If your destination computers host different mass storage device controllers, using Sysprep 1.1 can greatly reduce the number of images you need to create. It is strongly recommended that you download the updated tool from Microsoft's Web site and read the included documentation. If your destination computers host similar mass storage device controllers,there is no additional benefit to using the 1.1 version of Sysprep.

Sysprep Step by Step

The Sysprep installation process usually involves three or more devices. The first machine is your source machine. The source machine is the computer on which you install the operating system and applications and customize the configuration. Sysprep is run on this machine to prepare for disk imaging. The disk image is created using a third-party application and is stored on a network share or on external media, such as CD-ROM, tape, or Jaz. The image is then loaded onto one or more target devices.

Following are the steps necessary to create and load a disk image using Sysprep and a third-party imaging tool. The tasks that require more discussion are explained in detail later in this section.

1. Install Windows 2000 Professional on the source machine. When Setup prompts you as to whether you wish to join a workgroup or domain, select workgroup. Do not choose to join a domain. Additionally, leave the administrator account password blank. If you do not leave the password field blank, you will not be able to change it during the setup process on the target.

2. Once the computer has rebooted, log on as Administrator and install and configure additional applications and services. Be aware that some applications, like Microsoft Office, will create user-specific settings for the currently logged-on user. These settings might not be available to users logging on to the target system after imaging takes place.

3. Test the operating system and applications to ensure that they are functioning correctly.

4. Create a folder in the system root called "Sysprep" (i.e., c:\Sysprep).

5. Open deploy.cab from the \support\tools folder of the Windows 2000 distribution CD and extract Sysprep.exe and setupcl.exe to the \Sysprep folder on the system drive.

6. If full or partial automation is desired, run Setup Manager to prepare the Sysprep.inf answer file. The Sysprep.inf file can be saved in the \Sysprep folder or on a floppy disk.

7. Run Sysprep with any optional parameters and shut down the system. DO NOT REBOOT THE SYSTEM. If you reboot the system, Sysprep will launch the mini-Setup Wizard on the source computer.

8. Create an image of the disk according to the imaging product's instructions.

9. Transfer the image to the target machine according to the imaging products instructions.

10. Reboot the target machine, which initiates Plug and Play detection and runs the mini-Setup wizard. If you are using a Sysprep.inf file that is stored on a floppy disk, insert it during the Windows startup process.

11. The Sysprep folder is deleted automatically and the system reboots, prompting for the first logon.

Steps 1–5 are fairly straightforward and don't require much additional explanation. An important point is that the \Sysprep folder must exist on the system drive, and Setupcl.exe must be present in that folder to run Sysprep. Setupcl.exe is responsible for generating a unique SID and for running the mini-Setup wizard on the target machine.

Step 6 is optional, but if you wish to use Setup Manager to create a Sysprep.inf file, you can find more information in the section "Automating Setup of a Target Computer" later in this chapter.

Step 7 instructs you to run Sysprep.exe with any optional switches. To do this, open up a command prompt and change the directory to point to the \Sysprep folder you created in Step 4 by typing **cd Sysprep**. At this point, you type **Sysprep.exe** and one or more optional switches. The options available with the Sysprep command include:

- **/QUIET** This switch runs Sysprep without displaying onscreen messages.

- **/NOSIDGEN** This switch runs Sysprep without creating a unique SID for the computer.

- **/PNP** This switch forces Plug and Play to initiate after the target system reboots.

- **/REBOOT** This switch will automatically restart the computer after Sysprep has done its work. Do not use this switch if you will be creating an image from this disk because mini-Setup wizard will launch after reboot.

Once you run Sysprep, the message window shown in Figure 3.1 pops up, warning you that some security parameters will be changed on the system. Select OK to continue.

Figure 3.1 Sysprep warning message.

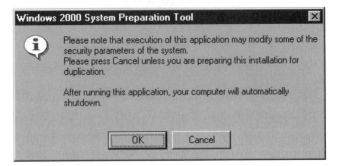

Sysprep then configures the system to prepare it for imaging and shuts down. You then need to use the tools available from your imaging software vendor to create an image of the disk and store it to the proper media as indicated in Step 8.

TIP

Most imaging tools allow you to view and modify the contents of an image file. In order to further reduce the size of an image file prepared using Sysprep, you can delete the hyberfil.sys (hibernation file, if it exists), pagefile.sys, and setupapi.log files from the image. Each of these files is recreated during the mini-Setup wizard.

Step 9 involves transferring the disk image to the target machine. There are a number of ways to do this and you need to refer to your imaging software vendor's documentation to see what methods are supported by their product.

Step 10 indicates that after the image is transferred to the target machine, the machine needs to be rebooted. The machine starts up and displays the normal Windows 2000 boot information and proceeds through the boot process. The GUI phase of the boot process initiates Plug and Play detection. Then the mini-Setup Wizard starts by displaying its Welcome screen. After clicking NEXT at the Welcome screen you are presented with a series of dialog boxes prompting you for configuration information specific to this computer. The type of information you are required to enter includes:

- End-user License Agreement
- Product ID Key
- Regional Settings
- Name and Company
- Network Configuration
- Workgroup or Domain Selection
- Time zone

Once you have completed the mini-Setup, the wizard displays a summary screen and requires you to select Finish. The system will then restart and the first user is prompted to log on.

Running Sysprep During Automated Installation

You may want to run Sysprep as part of an automated installation on a computer. In order to do this, you need to create a special Sysprep folder as part of the distribution folder hierarchy. This folder is located at \I386\$OEM$\$1\SYSPREP. The $1 is equivalent to the system drive letter. Type in $1, not the actual drive letter. You then need to place the Sysprep.exe and Setupcl.exe files in this folder along with the optional Sysprep.inf answer file.

To run Sysprep automatically after the automated installation completes, you need to modify the automated installation answer file that is usually named unattend.txt. Open this file in a text editor, such as Notepad, and locate the [GUIRUNONCE] section. Add the Sysprep command by typing **%SYSTEMDRIVE%\SYSPREP\ SYSPREP.EXE –QUIET**. This runs Sysprep in quiet mode and will not display message windows.

Automating Setup of a Target Computer

You eliminate a great deal of the time required to deploy Windows 2000 by running Sysprep and creating an image of the disk. What if you could even automate the mini-Setup wizard discussed earlier? This would eliminate the need for someone to be sitting at the console when the target is rebooted the first time and the mini-Setup wizard runs. You can use a Sysprep answer file, called Sysprep.inf, to provide—you guessed it—answers to the questions posed by mini-Setup. This section covers the elements that make up Sysprep.inf and how to create this file using Setup Manager.

Creating an Answer File Using Setup Manager

Creating a Sysprep.inf answer file using Setup Manager is an optional step when preparing a system using Sysprep. When a target system first boots with an image prepared by Sysprep, a mini-Setup wizard runs and asks the user for user- and machine-specific information. The information required by the mini-Setup wizard includes:

- End-user license agreement
- Name and organization
- Whether the computer should join a domain or workgroup
- Regional settings
- TAPI info (if the computer has a modem)
- Network protocol and services configuration

In order to fully or partially automate this wizard, you can use a Sysprep.inf answer file. The Sysprep.inf file can be created manually (it is in a text-file format) or by using the Setup Manager tool, which was also discussed in Chapter 2. The Sysprep.inf file is very similar to the answer file created for unattended installs that was discussed in Chapter 2, but only contains a subset of the values. The following sections and keys are supported in the Sysprep.inf answer file:

[Unattended]
OemSkipEula
OemPnPDriversPath
InstallFilesPath
ExtendOEMPartition

[GuiUnattended]
AdminPassword
AutoLogon
TimeZone
OEMDuplicatorString
OEMSkipWelcome

[UserData]
ComputerName
FullName
OrgName
ProductID

[LicenseFilePrintData]
AutoMode
AutoUsers

[GuiRunOnce]

[Display]
BitsPerPel
Vrefresh
Xresolution
Yresolution

[Regional Settings] *Note: These files must exist on the disk prior to setup.*

InputLocale

Language

LanguageGroup

SystemLocale

UserLocale

[Networking]

InstallDefaultComponents

[Identification]

DomainAdmin

DomainAdminPassword

JoinDomain

JoinWorkgroup

MachineObjectOU

[NetClients]

[<MS_MSClient parameters>]

BrowseDomains

NameServiceNetworkAddress

NameServiceProtocol

[<MS_NWClient parameters>]

DefaultTree

DefaultContext

LogonScript

PreferredServer

[TapiLocation] *Note: These keys only apply when the target system has a modem installed.*

AreaCode

CountryCode

Dialing

LongDistanceAccess

TIP

If your deployment requires different information to be entered during the mini-Setup wizard for different machines, you can create multiple Sysprep.inf files. Each Sysprep.inf file contains machine-specific information. In order to accomplish this, you will need to remove any copies of Sysprep.inf from the \Sysprep folder on the system drive and supply a floppy with the appropriate Sysprep.inf file during the Windows 2000 startup.

To use Setup Manager to create the Sysprep.inf:

1. Open deploy.cab from the \support\tools folder of the Windows 2000 distribution CD and extract Setupmgr.exe and Setupmgx.dll to a folder on your local hard drive.

2. From the local folder, double-click on setupmgr.exe to launch the program.

3 The first window you see is the Welcome screen as shown in Figure 3.2. Click NEXT.

4. You are then asked whether you want to create a new answer file or modify an existing one as illustrated in Figure 3.3. You create a new answer file since this is the first time through Setup Manager. Click NEXT.

Figure 3.2 Setup Manager Wizard Welcome screen.

Figure 3.3 Select whether to create a new answer file or modify an existing one.

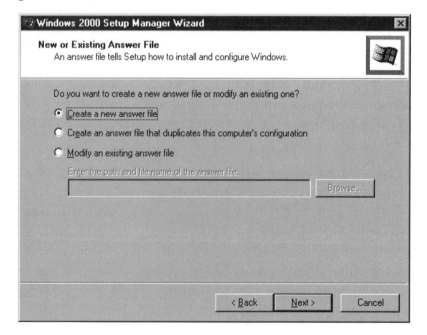

5. The window shown in Figure 3.4 appears and asks what the answer file will be used for. All the choices are self-explanatory. For our example, we select Sysprep Install and click NEXT.

Figure 3.4 Select the installation method for which the answer file will be used.

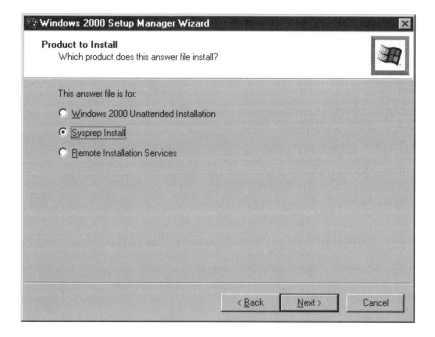

6. The window shown in Figure 3.5 then asks you to specify whether you are installing the Professional or Server version of Windows 2000. We have selected Windows 2000 Professional for our example. Click Next.

7. The End-User License Agreement (EULA) window is shown in Figure 3.6. In order to prepare a fully automated installation using Sysprep, the acceptance of the EULA needs to be bypassed by selecting "Yes, fully automate the installation." Microsoft instructs OEMs using disk imaging to not automatically accept the EULA, requiring the system recipient to manually accept the licensing agreement. Click Next.

Figure 3.5 Select the platform for which the answer file will be used.

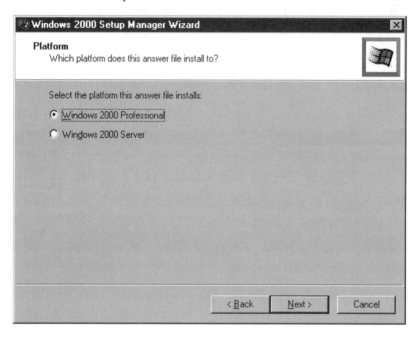

Figure 3.6 Automate the acceptance of the EULA.

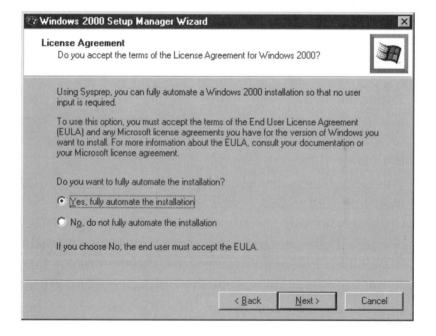

8. In the next dialog window, shown in Figure 3.7, you enter the default name and organization. Remember, this information is applied to all systems that use this Sysprep.inf file during mini-Setup. Click NEXT.

Figure 3.7 Enter name and organization.

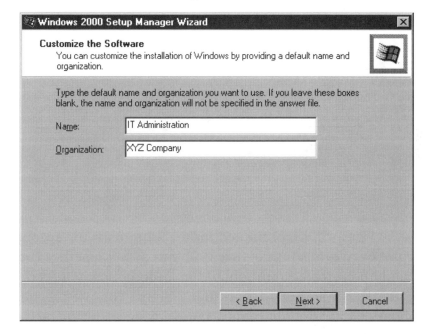

9. Next, you are prompted to enter a computer name for the destination system, as shown in Figure 3.8. If you are using this answer file to create more than one target (which I'm sure you are), you will want to create unique names for each machine. When using Sysprep for duplication, you can modify the Sysprep.inf answer file after Setup Manager creates it by changing the ComputerName key under [UserData]. You then save each unique answer file to floppy to be used when the mini-Setup wizard runs on the target computer. A second option is available if the imaging tool you purchase allows for post-imaging modifications of this type of configuration. Altiris RapidDeploy is one product that provides this function.

Figure 3.8 Enter the computer name for the target system.

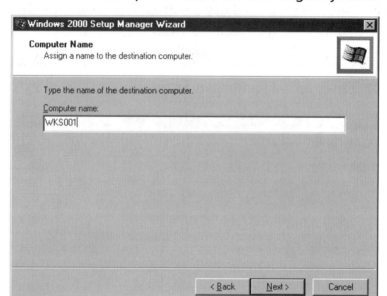

10. Next, you will be prompted for an Administrator account password (shown in Figure 3.9) and asked whether the administrator account should be automatically logged on after setup and, if so, how many times. You are only able to change the administrator account password if the account of the source computer is null. If it is not null, then the target computer will receive the password of the source computer. Having the administrator user log on after the system first reboots is useful when you need to install applications that require administrative permissions on the local machine. These applications can be initiated from the answer file by entering the proper commands under [GUIRUNONCE].

11. The next window allows you to enter display settings for the target systems (see Figure 3.10). If you require unique display settings, you can use the pull-down selection boxes to make your choices, or customize the settings by selecting "Custom." We are sticking with Windows defaults. Click NEXT to continue.

Figure 3.9 Enter the administrator password and indicate whether the administrator account should be automatically logged on when the target computer restarts.

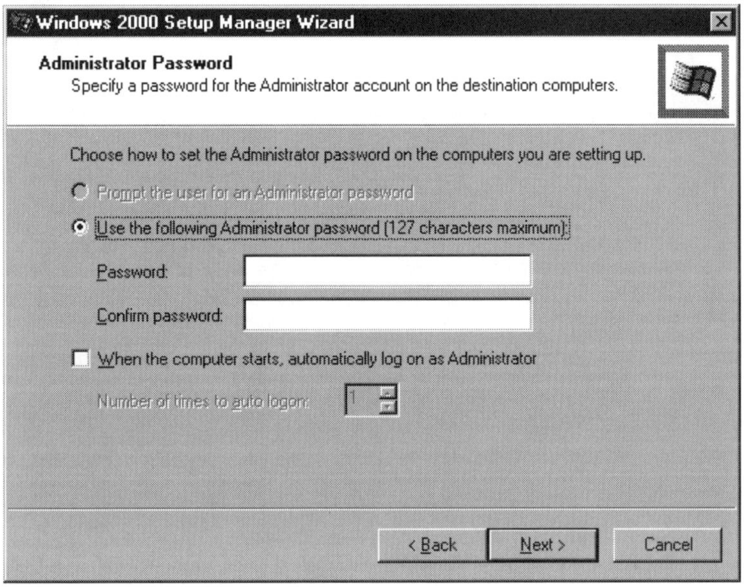

WARNING

Consider carefully whether you wish to supply the administrative password in the Sysprep.inf file. This information is not encrypted and is easily accessible to any user who has access to the Sysprep.inf file in the\Sysprep folder or the floppy, if the Sysprep.inf file was copied there.

12. Setup Manager then asks you to configure network settings (see Figure 3.11). If you select Typical settings, the target systems will run TCP/IP and obtain their IP address and other settings from a DHCP server. The Client for Microsoft Networks is also installed, allowing the user to connect to Windows 2000 or Windows NT systems. If you wish to customize these settings or add additional protocols and clients, select Custom settings. For our purposes, the Typical settings are what we need. Click NEXT to continue.

Figure 3.10 Enter display settings.

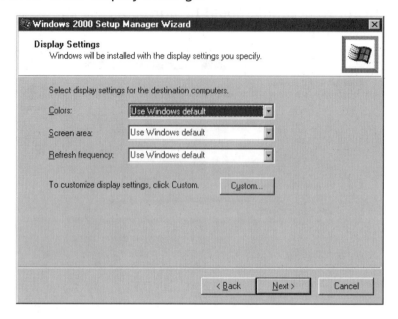

Figure 3.11 Select to use default network settings or to customize the network settings.

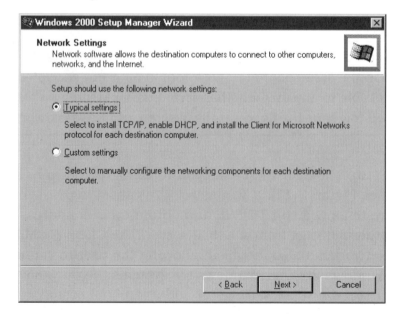

13. You are then prompted to specify whether the computer should join a Workgroup or Domain, as shown in Figure 3.12. If you are joining computers to a Windows 2000 domain, you have the choice of specifying a username and password with permissions to add computer accounts. You must ensure that you are using a method for applying unique computer names as discussed in Step 9. For our purposes, we will join our computers to a workgroup named Workgroup (no points for creativity here). Click NEXT to continue.

Figure 3.12 Select whether the target systems will join a workgroup or domain.

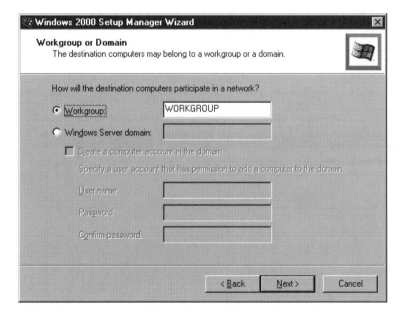

14. The next dialog prompts you to enter data about the time zone in which the target machines are situated (see Figure 3.13). Make the appropriate choice, and click NEXT.

15. The next window, shown in Figure 3.14, asks if you wish to enter additional settings, such as add network printers,

Figure 3.13 Select time zone information for target computers.

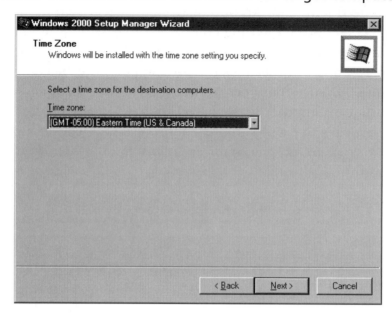

Figure 3.14 Select whether you want to specify additional settings for the answer file.

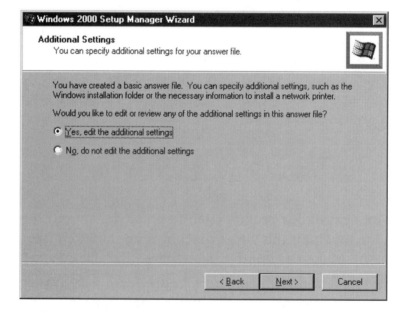

additional language groups, run once commands). If you wish to fully automate your installation, it is recommended that you proceed through the additional dialog boxes to minimize user interaction during the mini-Setup wizard. If you decide not to specify additional settings, you can continue to the OEM Duplicator String dialog in Step 25. Steps 16–24 walk through the dialog boxes that pop up when you do select to specify additional settings. They are marked Optional to show that they only appear when additional settings are selected.

16. (Optional) If you specified that you wish to enter additional settings in Step 15, the next dialog window (Figure 3.15) queries you for telephony settings. These settings only apply if the target computer has been configured with a modem. Click NEXT to continue.

Figure 3.15 Specify telephony settings for systems with modems.

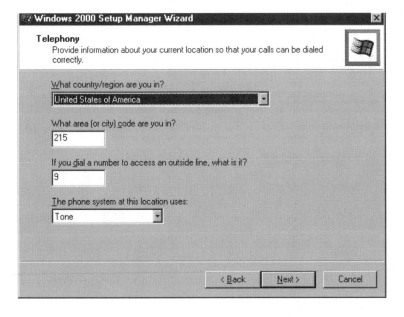

17. (Optional) Figure 3.16 prompts you to enter information about regions and languages that may be different from the Windows version you are installing. Therefore, if you are

installing the English version of Windows 2000 and you are deploying this image in Greece, you must make the appropriate selection here in order to support the unique regional requirements of Greece, such as currency, measurements, and keyboard layouts. The files needed for supporting additional regional settings are loaded into the Sysprep folder under OEM\LANG. The option to allow users to select their regional settings during Setup is only available if you did not choose to automatically accept the EULA as described in Step 7. If you want to allow your users to specify regional settings *and* accept the EULA, forgo fully automating the setup. For our deployment we will stick with the default configuration of the English version of Windows 2000 Professional. Click NEXT to continue.

18. (Optional) The next window, shown in Figure 3.17, actually gives you the opportunity to install support for additional languages. With this support installed on the system, users are able to create and read documents in different languages. Click NEXT to continue.

Figure 3.16 Specify any additional regional and language settings to be included in the image distribution.

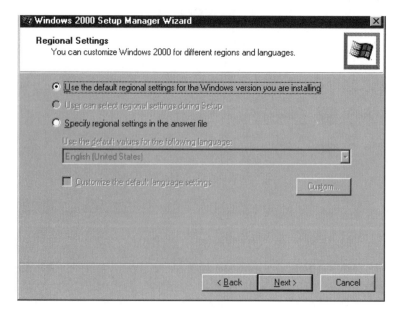

Figure 3.17 Select any additional language groups that you need to support.

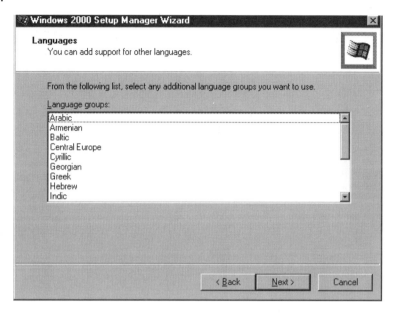

19. (Optional) Next, you have the opportunity to specify printers you want to preconfigure on the target systems. Figure 3.18 shows the dialog for adding printers to the target computer. As illustrated in the screenshot, you use the UNC name of the printer share when specifying a printer to be installed the first time a user logs on after the mini-Setup wizard completes. Note that the user logging on must have the appropriate permissions to add the printer in order for this feature to work. Click NEXT to continue.

20. (Optional) The next window, shown in Figure 3.19, gives you an opportunity to enter commands that will run the first time a user logs on to the imaged system. As you can see, the network printer we want installed has been entered automatically as a RUN ONCE command. Commands execute in the order listed. You can reorder the commands by selecting the command and using Move Up and Move Down.

Figure 3.18 Specify network printers to be installed when the first user logs on to the system.

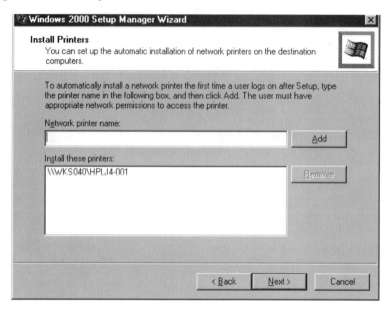

Figure 3.19 Indicate commands that should be run the first time a user logs on to the system.

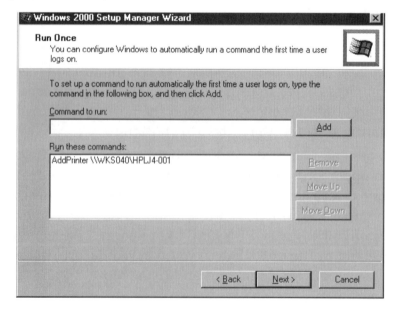

21. (Optional) Setup Manager then asks you whether you want it to create a new Sysprep folder or modify an existing Sysprep folder, as illustrated in Figure 3.20. Select Yes, especially if you have indicated additional language support or additional device drivers. This allows Setup Manager to load the correct files and copy them to the \Sysprep folder for use during mini-Setup.

22. (Optional) The Additional Commands window shown in Figure 3.21 at first appears to serve the same purpose as the RUN ONCE commands entered in Step 20. The difference is that the commands you enter in this window run right after the mini-Setup wizard completes; therefore, running without any user logged on. The commands you enter here are put into a cmdlines.txt file, which is discussed in more detail later in this chapter. Click NEXT to continue.

Figure 3.20 Select whether you want Setup Manager to create the Sysprep folder, or whether you will create it manually.

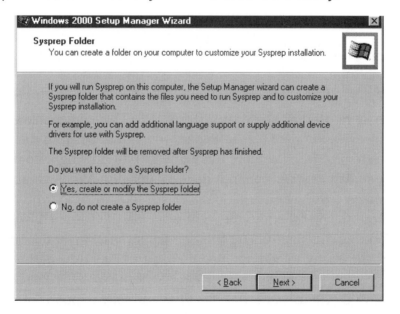

Figure 3.21 Enter commands to be run when the mini-setup completes.

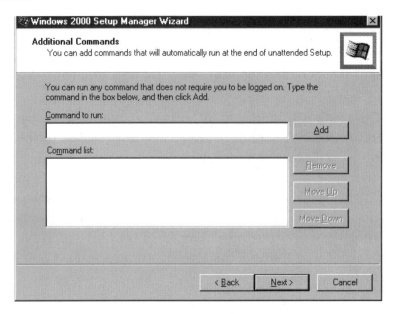

23. (Optional) The OEM Branding window shown in Figure 3.22 allows you to enter bitmap files that you want to appear during the mini-setup process. For instance, you can enter your company logo and a custom background image. Click NEXT to continue.

24. (Optional) The next dialog to appear is the Additional Files or Folders window shown in Figure 3.23. This screen allows you to specify additional files or folders you want copied to the target systems. This has more functionality when using automated installation scripts than it does for imaging. When creating an image, if you want additional files or folders added you only need to copy them to the right place on the source hard drive prior to imaging. Where this screen is valuable for disk imaging is the ability to add additional Plug and Play drivers that are not included on the Windows 2000 distribution CD-ROM. So, if you have new hardware that has Plug and Play support, but its drivers didn't make it to the Windows 2000 CD-ROM, you can add them here. Click NEXT to continue.

Figure 3.22 Include file locations for graphics that you want displayed during the setup process.

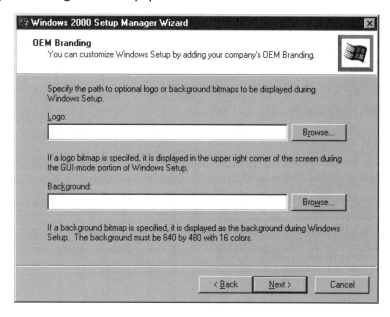

Figure 3.23 Add additional files or folders to be available during setup.

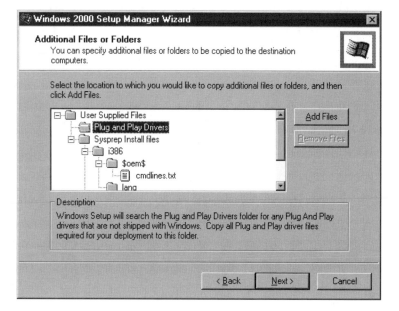

25. You are then prompted to enter an OEM Duplicator String in the dialog shown in Figure 3.24. This information is important when evaluating systems to determine which image was used to clone the machine. The OEM Duplicator String appears in the Registry under HKEY_LOCAL_MACHINE\System\Setup. You are able to enter a maximum of 255 characters for the string text. Sysprep also adds a CloneTag value noting the date and time the image was created. Enter your information, and click NEXT.

26. The next screen (Figure 3.25) prompts you to enter the file name and location for the Sysprep.inf file. The default is to place this file in the Sysprep folder you created earlier. Even if you plan on transferring the Sysprep.inf file to floppy for your deployment, it is suggested that you allow Setup Manager to save it to the \Sysprep folder. You can perform modifications to the file after Setup Manager has finished. Click NEXT.

Figure 3.24 Enter OEM Duplicator String.

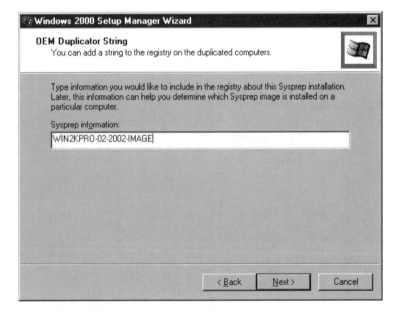

Figure 3.25 Enter location and file name for Sysprep answer file.

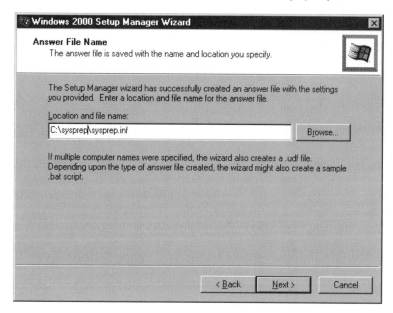

27. The last window to appear is a summary window indicating that Setup Manager will create the Sysprep.inf file and a Sysprep.bat file and place them in the folder specified in the previous screen. This window is shown in Figure 3.26. Sysprep.bat is a simple batch file that launches Sysprep.exe. Click FINISH to allow Setup Manager to create these files.

The end result is that Setup Manager creates an answer file, Sysprep.inf, which will look something like this:

```
;SetupMgrTag
[Unattended]
    OemSkipEula=Yes


[GuiUnattended]
    AdminPassword=admin
    OEMSkipRegional=1
    OEMDuplicatorstring=WIN2KPRO-02-2000-IMAGE
    TimeZone=35
    OemSkipWelcome=1
```

```
[UserData]
     FullName="IT Department"
     OrgName="XYZ Company"
     ComputerName=WKS001

[TapiLocation]
     CountryCode=1
     Dialing=Tone
     AreaCode=610

[SetupMgr]
     DistFolder=C:\sysprep\i386
     DistShare=win2000dist

[Identification]
     JoinWorkgroup=WORKGROUP

[Networking]
     InstallDefaultComponents=Yes
```

As it is shown above, this Sysprep.inf answer file will automate all aspects of mini-Setup wizard except one: the need to enter a Product Key. The person performing the image transfer and running through mini-setup will be prompted to enter a valid Product Key from the back of the CD-ROM case. In order to automate this step, you need to add a ProductID parameter under [UserData] and give it a value equal to a valid Product Key. You can edit Sysprep.inf manually by double-clicking on it in the \Sysprep folder. The modified [UserData] section would look like this (the Product Key shown is made up, and Windows 2000 will not accept it):

```
[UserData]
     FullName="IT Department"
     OrgName="XYZ Company"
     ComputerName=WKS001
     ProductID=11111-AAAAA-11111-AAAAA-11111
```

Figure 3.26 Summary of Setup Manager wizard tasks.

> **NOTE**
>
> Using the ProductID value creates identical product IDs. If you enter the Product Key information into the ProductID parameter in your Sysprep.inf file, you may run into some difficulty when trying to support these systems down the road. The reason is that each system will have an identical Product Key that can make it difficult to differentiate machines for support purposes when calling Microsoft.

Running Additional Programs After Mini Setup

You can use the cmdlines.txt file to run additional programs after the mini-setup process is complete. If you used Setup Manager to create an answer file, you were able to enter the commands for cmd-lines.txt (see Step 22). To manually configure this functionality, you must create a \i386\$OEM$ folder in the \Sysprep folder created for Sysprep.exe and Setupcl.exe. All files that are needed to run the application launched by cmdlines.txt must be placed in the \$OEM$ subfolder. The syntax for the cmdlines.txt file is as follows:

```
[Commands]
"<command1>"
"<command2>"
```

Note that these are required quotation marks surrounding the command lines that launch the applications.

After editing cmdlines.txt in a text editor, place the file in the \OEM folder and add the following line to the Sysprep.inf file:

[Unattended]
InstallFilesPath = %systemdrive%\Sysprep\i386

The commands listed in the cmdlines.txt file are executed under the system account and do not support multiple-user configurations. Any application-specific user settings are applied to the default user registry area and will be used by all future users created on the computer.

Imaging vs. Automated Installation Scripts

You learned about automated installations in Chapter 2. After reading this chapter, you now have an understanding as to what is involved in deploying Windows 2000 using imaging. Let's compare the two methods. Table 3.1 describes a number of deployment scenarios and specifies whether you can use imaging or automated installs, or both.

Table 3.1 Determining When You Should Use Imaging versus Automated Installs

Scenario	Imaging	Automated Install
You deploy Windows 2000 to multiple systems with different mass storage devices.	Yes	Yes
You deploy Windows 2000 to multiple systems with different HALs.	No	Yes
You upgrade an existing installation to Windows 2000.	No	Yes
You need to quickly deploy a standard Windows 2000 build to a large number of desktops with identical hardware.	Yes	Yes, but imaging is quicker in this scenario
You need to run a number of commands when the first user logs on to the system.	Yes	Yes

Summary

Late in the life cycle of Windows NT 4.0, Microsoft admitted that imaging disk drives in order to deploy their operating systems is a valuable tool for system administrators. To address the issues surrounding identical security identifiers (SIDs) caused by duplicating a single build, Microsoft released the System Preparation Tool, Sysprep, to their enterprise-licensing clients. With Windows 2000, Microsoft is shipping Sysprep on the distribution CD-ROMs.

Sysprep's value is as a preparation tool and requires you to purchase a third-party imaging application. There are a number of such applications available on the market today, including Symantec Norton Ghost, Innovative Software ImageCast IC3, and Altiris RapidDeploy. Aside from basic imaging functionality, these tools provide features for managing and customizing the disk-imaging process. Take the time to figure out what your requirements are for a disk-imaging tool, and then download the trial versions of two or three products to see if they meet these requirements.

The Sysprep tool is used to prepare a system for imaging. To take advantage of Sysprep, the source and target machine(s) must both have the following components in common:

- Hardware Abstraction Layer (HAL)
- Advanced Configuration and Power Interface Support
- Size of the target disk must be equal to or larger than the source

After installing and configuring Windows 2000 and the applications you require on the source disk, run Sysprep and shut down the computer. Use your imaging software to create a disk or partition image and save that image to a network share or external media. The image is then transferred to the target disk using tools available with your imaging software. The target system is rebooted and a mini-Setup wizard runs. The mini-Setup wizard can be automated using an answer file called Sysprep.inf. This answer file can be manually created or created using Setup Manager.

There are differences between using disk imaging and automated installation scripts. The most important is that Sysprep has limitations requiring certain hardware components to do the same on the source and target systems.

FAQs

Q: I don't want to purchase another product to create my disk images. What are the alternatives?

A: Windows 2000 Server does ship with the Remote Installation Service, which provides functionality similar to the disk-imaging products. It does have two major limitations: First, it only works for Windows 2000 Professional, and second, its remote boot capabilities for the target workstation are limited to a defined set of PCI-based network interface cards. If you decide that your Windows 2000 deployment can fully or partially take advantage of disk images, I suggest that the cost savings from not having to babysit an entire install on numerous machines will more than pay for the cost of a disk-imaging product.

Q: Is there a way to automate the product licensing key portion of mini-Setup wizard without having every target system end up with the same license key?

A: As with a few of the parameters set in the Sysprep.inf answer file, entering a value for the licensing key results in every system having the same key. In order to assign unique product-licensing keys to target systems, you will need to create unique Sysprep.inf files for each install. This is not as daunting a task as you may think. All it entails is modifying the [UserData]|ProductID key in the Sysprep.inf file and saving the file to a floppy. This floppy-based Sysprep.inf file is then used during the mini-Setup wizard on the target computer.

Q: I want certain applications to be installed after the first user logs on to the target system so that the configuration information is stored in that user's profile. How do I do this?

A: To set up a program to run after the first user logs on, you need to provide that information in the RUN ONCE dialog of Setup Manager or manually modify the Sysprep.inf file. In either case, the information needs to be present under the [GUIRUNONCE] section of the answer file. For example, if you want to install Application X and Application Y after the first user logs on, the Sysprep.inf file needs to include the following lines:

```
[GuiRunOnce]
"appx.exe"
"appy.exe"
```

These programs are then installed in the context of the first user who logs on to the system.

Chapter 4

Remote Installation Client and Server

Solutions in this chapter:

- Installing a Remote Installation Server
- Remote Install Services Configuration and Administration
- Remote Client Installation

Introduction

With Windows 2000, there are many new techniques and tools to enhance the deployment process. Remote Installation Services is one of those new tools.

Remote Installation Services (RIS) allows an administrator to install Windows 2000 Professional on a client PC without having to visit each workstation. It uses a technology called Preboot Execution Environment (PXE) to enable the network card to download a boot-strap program and boot without having an operating system installed. With the Client Installation Wizard, one can install Windows 2000 with a username, password, and domain name provided by the administrator. In most cases, the administrator will not have to be present for this operation.

While this functionality is exciting, it does require some up-front planning. First, you cannot even begin to take advantage of RIS without having an Active Directory infrastructure and PCs that have a PXE-compliant network card.

Several steps are required to set up and configure RIS. First, the server components must be installed and the server must be authorized in Active Directory. Understanding how to create new OS images and administer RIS is also very important. Lastly, the client must be set up and configured properly to allow remote services to function. This chapter will walk you through these steps and introduce the technologies that are running in the background.

Once all of these pieces are in place, you will have a robust environment from which to install Windows 2000 Professional. Let's start by looking at the planning process for implementing RIS.

Planning for Remote Installation Services

Arguably, the most important step in implementing RIS in your organization is the initial planning process. There are a number of factors that you must consider before adding the first RIS server to your infrastructure. Here are a few of the important questions that you must answer:

- Will your server hardware handle the additional load of RIS?
- Will your network infrastructure handle the additional load of operating system installation over the wire?
- Do your PCs meet the specifications for Windows 2000 Professional?
- Do you have a well-planned Active Directory infrastructure?

Hardware Requirements

Let's start with the hardware requirements for RIS. You need to ensure that your server and PC hardware will support the additional load of the RIS components. Following are Microsoft's minimum specifications for servers and client PCs.

Server Requirements

- Pentium 200MHZ or greater
- 128MB of RAM (256MB if other services have been installed, such as DNS or DHCP)
- 2GB NT File System (NTFS–formatted partition dedicated to the RIS images)
- Network interface card (NIC)
- CD-ROM drive

Client Net PC Requirements

- Pentium 166MHZ-or-greater Net PC client computer
- 32MB of RAM at minimum

- 800MB-or-greater hard disk
- PXE DHCP-based boot ROM version, .99c or greater

Client Non-Net PC Requirements

- Pentium 166MHZ or greater
- 32MB of RAM at minimum
- 800MB-or-greater hard disk
- Supported PCI Plug-and-Play network card
- PXE DHCP-based boot ROM version, .99c or greater

When choosing the hardware for your RIS server, you should avoid going with the minimum specifications if possible. I would recommend using a Pentium II 400MHZ-or-faster processor and installing 256MB of RAM. You will need at least 2GB dedicated to the RIS, in addition to the basic requirements for running Windows 2000. The RIS partition needs to be formatted as NTFS v5. You will want to install SCSI hard disks on a fast controller. The RIS service is very I/O dependent, so eliminating a bottleneck here will pay off in the end. If you intend on creating multiple images, you will probably want to increase the dedicated disk space. RIS helps to limit the amount of disk space used by implementing a technology called Single Instance Store (SIS) to help reduce the number of redundant files being stored on the server. This is discussed in the next section.

The requirements for the client PCs are also on the low side. It is highly recommended that you install no less than 64MB of RAM on your client PCs, and128MB if your users work with Office suites or e-mail/groupware applications.

Active Directory Planning

Once you understand the hardware requirements for implementing RIS, you need to look at your Active Directory structure. You should have a good idea of how your Directory is going to look. When you designed your Directory, you made planning decisions based on geographic, organizational, and political criteria. For example, you may have decided to create a site for every physical location. You may also have decided to subdivide your Directory with Organization Units, rather than subdomains, such as business.domain.com. This information will be very important when you begin to plan for the deployment of RIS servers in your enterprise.

When you start to place your RIS servers, you will want to follow a basic rule, which is to keep the servers close to your users. For a small organization, this will be easy to follow, as you may only have one or two physical locations. For larger locations it becomes harder to follow, since you may have tens or hundreds of locations, connected by slow links, such as ISDN, up to faster T-1s and T-3s. While it seems obvious that you don't want your clients to try to install the operating system over an ISDN connection, you may not want your clients attempting that installation in a campus environment either.

For IT Professionals

What Is a Net PC?

Every year, Microsoft teams with Intel to devise a standard machine build that will accommodate the operating systems and software applications that are currently in vogue. This standard is called the PCxx standard; for instance, the current standard is named PL99. This specifies a minimum list of components that must be present. A Net PC is a machine built to the PL99 standard and would include support for Wake-on-LAN, PXE, Web-based Enterprise Management (WBEM), and Windows Management Initiative (WMI). You can add certain components from the Net PC standard, such as a network card with the PXE Remote Boot ROM, to gain some of the Net PC's functionality.

At this point, you should have a better idea of the planning required to implement Remote Installation Services. Now, let's look at the components that make up RIS.

Examining the Technology Behind RIS—PXE, BINL, TFTP, and SIS

These acronyms sound like a stand-up comedy routine. In actuality, they are the major components underneath the hood of Remote Installation Services. PXE, or PreBoot Execution Environment, works on the client side of RIS. PXE is a remote-boot technology whose functionality is added to a network card by way of a Remote Boot ROM. BINL, or Boot Information Negotiation Layer, is the service running on the RIS Server that listens for requests from PXE network cards and supplies the name of the boot image to the client PC. The third component is TFTP, or Trivial File Transfer Protocol. This service is responsible for downloading the boot image to the client. The last component is SIS, or Single Instance Store. This engine also runs on the server and works to reduce the number of redundant files stored on the server (hence the name *single instance*).

Pre-boot Execution Environment (PXE)

There are normally three devices by which you can boot your PC: the floppy drive, the CD-ROM, and the primary hard disk. When you add a network card to your PC with a PXE Remote Boot ROM, you boot your PC from a fourth device, the network adapter.

When you boot from the NIC, the network card is responsible for obtaining a boot image from a server on the network. However, before it can do this, it must request an IP address from a DHCP server, and request the address of a server that holds the boot image. Figure 4.1 shows the communication between the PXE client and the DHCP server.

Figure 4.1 Communication between a PXE client and the DHCP server.

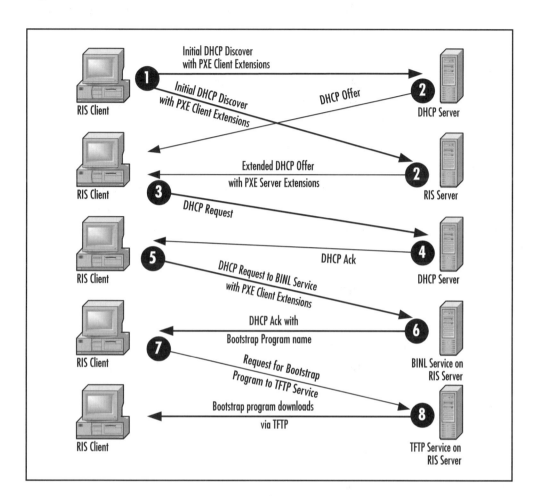

As you can see in Figure 4.1, there are a number of broadcasts and replies between the PC and the DHCP server.

1. The Client PC sends out a DHCP Discover broadcast for a DHCP server and the name of a Boot Server (this is done by adding extensions to the DHCP packet that identify the client PC as a PXE client).

2. This request is answered by both the DHCP server and the RIS server. The DHCP server replies with a lease offer. The

RIS server replies with a DHCP packet that contains information about the BINL service on the RIS server.

3. The Client PC sends a DHCP Request to the DHCP server.

4. The DHCP server sends an Acknowledgment back to the client. The Client PC now has a valid IP address.

5. The Client PC sends a request to the BINL service requesting the name of the Bootstrap program.

6. The BINL service (explained in the next section) responds by sending the Bootstrap program name.

7. The Client PC sends a TFTP request to the RIS server requesting the Bootstrap program.

8. The TFTP service running on the RIS server sends the Bootstrap program to the Client PC via TFTP. This allows the PC to begin the boot process.

There is no need for a vendor-specific driver since NICs that are PXE capable use the Universal NIC Driver Interface (UNDI). Additional programs are sent to the client PC following the bootstrap program. These are usually custom programs, such as RIS's Client Installation Wizard, which provides a menu program for the user to navigate.

Boot Image Negotiation Layer (BINL)

The Boot Image Negotiation Layer (BINL) is a service that runs on the RIS server. As you can see in Figure 4.1, the BINL service listens for the DHCP request from the PXE client. Once it receives a valid request with the PXE Client Extensions, the BINL service performs two major tasks. First, it validates the PXE client against the Active Directory. Later in the chapter we'll discuss configuring the RIS server to ignore requests from unknown client PCs. The second major function the BINL service provides is to send a DHCP acknowledgment back to the PXE client that includes the name of the boot image in the DHCP extensions. Once the PXE client receives the name of the boot image, it sends a download request to the TFTP service running on the RIS server. This leads us to the discussion of the next technology used by RIS—TFTP.

Trivial File Transfer Protocol (TFTP)

The Trivial File Transfer Protocol (TFTP) is an application that is used to exchange files. It does not use authentication (as FTP does), and depends on User Datagram Protocol (UDP) rather than Transmission Control Protocol (TCP) for file transfer. The TFTP service running on the RIS server is responsible for hosting the bootstrap program, as well as the Client Installation Wizard files (which will be discussed later in the chapter). Once the TFTP service receives the download request, it sends the requested files back to the PXE client. In the case of RIS, these files include the boot image and the Client Installation Wizard files.

Single Instance Store (SIS)

SIS is another service that runs on the RIS server. When you begin to add images to the RIS server, the SIS service attempts to limit the number of redundant files stored. For instance, if you have five different Windows 2000 Professional images, you could have five copies of every system file in the operating system. SIS scavenges the images and makes a copy of each unique file. It stores the copy, and places a pointer to the file in each image's directory.

Now that we have a better idea of what is running behind the RIS service, we are going to look at the installation and configuration of Remote Installation Services.

Installing and Configuring Remote Installation Services

The first step in the preparation of Remote Installation Services is to install the components on the server. RIS is not installed by default when you install Windows 2000. There are two ways to install the components: You can add them during the installation of Windows 2000, or you can install them from Add/Remove Programs after the server has been built.

Installing RIS during Server Setup

It is very easy to add the RIS components during the installation of the server. On the Windows Components screen, merely choose the Remote Installation Services box when you are selecting other components to install, such as Internet Information Server. When the server installation is complete, you can run the setup program to finish the RIS installation.

Installing RIS from Add/Remove Programs

If you choose to add the Remote Installation Server components after your server has been built, you can do so with the Add/Remove Programs utility.

Choose Start and then choose Settings. Open the Control Panel and choose the Add/Remove Programs utility. Now, choose the Add/Remove Components button on the left side of the screen. This will launch the list of optional components for Windows 2000 Server. Place a check mark in the box next to Remote Installation Services as shown in Figure 4.2. Now, click NEXT to finish the setup.

NOTE

You cannot install the RIS components on Windows 2000 Professional. They are only available on the Windows 2000 server products.

Once you have added the RIS components to your server, you can begin the process of configuring the service.

Figure 4.2 Adding RIS to your server.

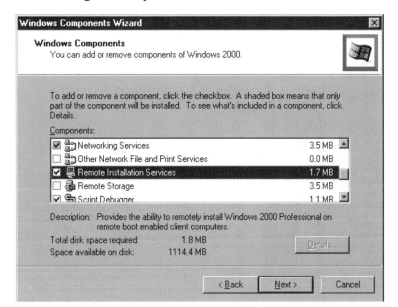

RIS Setup

The majority of the setup for RIS is performed in this section. You will specify where the service will be installed, make choices regarding how the server will respond when the setup is completed, and you will create the first image.

To begin the customization process, you will run the RIS Setup Wizard. To run the Wizard, choose Start, then Run, and type:

```
risetup.exe
```

Click OK to start the wizard. Figure 4.3 shows the welcome screen for the Remote Installation Services Setup wizard.

The first step is to specify the location of the Remote Installation directory. This directory must be located on a separate partition than the system partition. The partition must also be formatted as NTFS. The default name for the folder is RemoteInstall. Figure 4.4 shows the dialog box for choosing the directory location.

Figure 4.3 Welcome screen for the Remote Installation Services Setup wizard.

Figure 4.4 Specifying the RIS folder location.

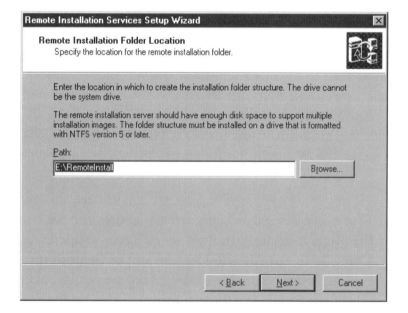

After you have chosen a location, click NEXT. Your next option is to allow the server to begin accepting client requests at the completion of the configuration. If you are installing a simple configuration of one CD-based image, you can probably select this option. Otherwise, you may want to leave this option unchecked until after you have gone through the Advanced Configuration (which is described a little later in the chapter). You can also choose to ignore requests from client PCs that have not been pre-staged in Active Directory. If you wish to enforce this option, choose the option titled "Do not respond to unknown client computers." Figure 4.5 shows these two options.

Figure 4.5 Allowing RIS to respond to client requests.

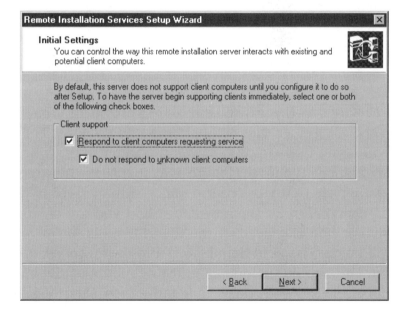

The next screen in the wizard asks for the location of the Installation Source Files. The source files are located on the Windows 2000 Professional CD or on a network share. By default, the wizard looks in the i386 directory on your CD-ROM. If your Windows 2000 source files are located elsewhere, enter that location in the text box, as shown in Figure 4.6.

Figure 4.6 Specifying the location of the Windows 2000 Professional files.

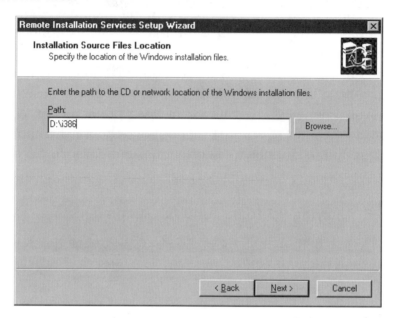

After clicking Next, you will be asked to provide a name for the folder on the RIS server that will hold the initial image. The wizard suggests that you use win2000.pro as the folder name, but you can give it any name you choose. Figure 4.7 illustrates this screen.

The last choice that you need to make in the wizard is to enter a name and description for the new image that you are creating. This information will be displayed by the Client Installation Wizard (which will be discussed in detail later) and in the server properties dialog box. You should include as much detail about the image as possible in these fields—it helps to identify them later! Figure 4.8 shows the default text entered by the wizard.

You are almost finished. Figure 4.9 shows the Review Settings page of the wizard. Check your settings carefully. If you need to make changes, click BACK. If everything looks OK, click NEXT to begin the configuration and file-copy stage.

Figure 4.7 Choosing a name for the first image folder.

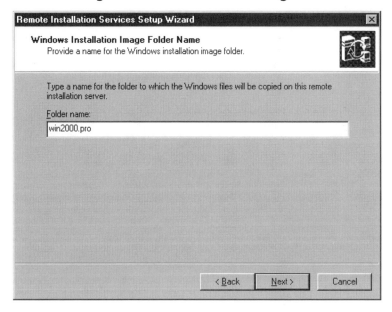

Figure 4.8 Typing a name and description for the first image.

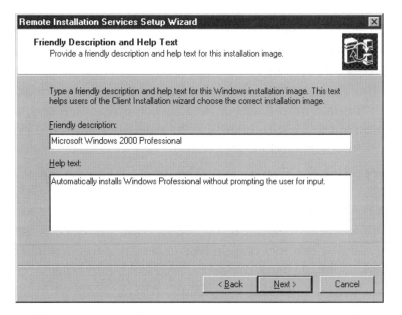

Figure 4.9 Confirming your settings.

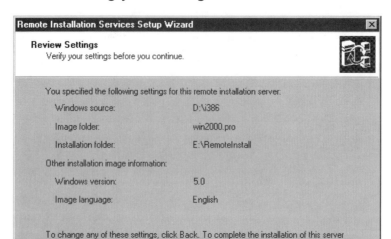

In the final stage, the wizard will create the folders that you specified earlier, copy the template files into the folders, and copy the Windows 2000 Professional source files to the server. Once the file copying is complete, the wizard will start the BINL and SIS services (Figure 4.10).

Once the wizard has restarted the services, your installation is complete. The last step that you need to complete before you can begin delivering images to clients is to authorize your server.

Authorizing RIS Servers in Active Directory

After you have installed the initial CD-based image, your RIS server is ready for action. Well, not quite ready. You still need to perform one more step before RIS can deliver its images to clients. This is the process of authorizing the server in Active Directory.

When it comes to DHCP servers on the network, Windows 2000 has an additional layer of security that its predecessor didn't. In prior releases of Windows NT, anybody could build a new server,

Figure 4.10 Completing the RIS setup.

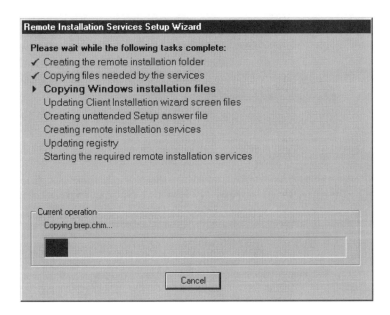

add the DHCP service, configure a scope, and begin causing a night-mare for administrators when it started to give out illegal IP addresses. Windows 2000 requires that DHCP servers (and services such as RIS that listen and reply to DHCP requests) be authorized in Active Directory.

It is easy to authorize your RIS server. Open the DHCP MMC console. At the root of the console is the word DHCP. When you right-click on the root, you will see a menu. Choose the Manage authorized servers option. This is illustrated in Figure 4.11. From the Manage authorized servers dialog box, choose Authorize to bring up the dialog box shown in Figure 4.12. Type in the IP address or NetBIOS name of your RIS server, click OK, and CLOSE.

Now that your server has been authorized, you are truly ready to go. If you want to perform basic OS installation, you really don't need to go any further. However, most organizations will want to modify these default settings. At this point, we will look at the advanced configuration choices you have for RIS.

Figure 4.11 Authorizing your RIS server.

Figure 4.12 Adding your server to the list of authorized servers.

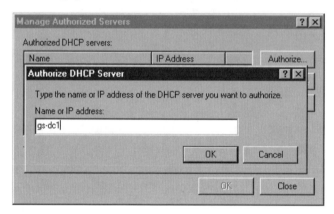

Advanced RIS Configuration

Once you have your Remote Installation server running, you will want to modify the default settings to better meet your needs. There are a number of features that you can change to modify the behavior of your RIS server. Most of them can be found on the Properties page of the RIS server object in Active Directory. There is also a Group Policy Object (GPO) for RIS, which restricts the choices presented by the Client Installation Wizard. We will start by looking at the RIS server's Properties page.

From the Properties page, you can modify a number of the RIS server's features. These include:

- Allowing the server to respond to client requests
- Allowing the server to ignore unknown client computers
- Changing the computer account naming format
- Changing the default computer account location
- Adding and removing images
- Adding and removing tools

To access the RIS server's Properties page, open the Active Directory Users and Computers MMC console. The next section will lead you through the process of opening the Properties page for your RIS server.

The first step is to open the MMC console. On your RIS server, choose Start and Programs. Select Administrative Tools and choose Active Directory Users and Computers. Once the MMC console is open, double-click on the domain that holds your RIS server. This will display all of the Organizational Units in your domain.

It might be somewhat tricky when you try to find your RIS server for the first time. Server objects can be located in one of three locations. Your RIS server could be in the built-in Domain Controller's container, the built-in Computer's container, or an Organizational Unit if you chose to install the server in a different location.

If you installed RIS on a Domain Controller, you will need to look in the Domain Controllers built-in container. If you installed RIS on a member server, and you allowed the Windows 2000 setup routine to choose the default location, you will need to open the Computers built-in container. If you installed the server into an Organizational Unit other than the previously mentioned built-in containers, you will need to look in that OU for your server object.

After you have opened the appropriate container, highlight your RIS server and right-click on the server object. This will bring up a menu. Choose Properties to open the RIS server's Properties dialog box.

Remote Installation servers will have an additional tab at the top of the Properties dialog named Remote Install (see Figure 4.13). Choose that tab to open the RIS Properties page.

Figure 4.13 Remote Installation server Properties dialog box.

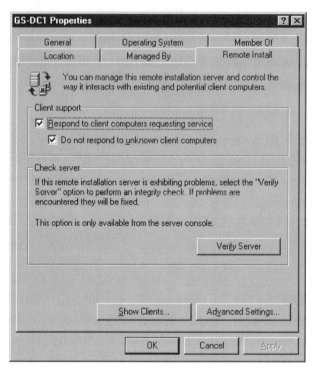

Once you have the Remote Install page open, you have a number of options to choose from. They are separated into four sections:

- Client support
- Check server
- Show clients
- Advanced settings

Let's take a look at each of the four sections and see what effect they have on your server's operations.

Client Support

In the first section, you have two check-box options.

- Respond to client computers requesting service
- Do not respond to unknown client computers

This section should look very familiar to you. It is identical to the settings you made during the initial installation of RIS. If you do not want this RIS server to respond to client requests, uncheck the box next to the first option. If you want your RIS server to ignore requests from unknown client PCs, place a check next to the second option. As you recall, a known client PC is one that you have pre-staged in Active Directory. Pre-staging will be discussed later in the chapter.

Check Server

The Verify Server wizard is used to test the functionality of your RIS server. It is primarily used as a troubleshooting tool if you are unable to receive images on your client PCs. By choosing this button, you will start a wizard that checks the BINL service. At the end of the routine, you will receive a report showing the status of the server.

Show Clients

SHOW CLIENTS will open a dialog box that is preconfigured for searching Active Directory for RIS clients. This is a useful troubleshooting tool, especially when you are trying to determine which client PCs have been installed using RIS. You can search for client PCs by their GUID, by specific RIS servers, or by using a combination of the two.

Advanced Settings

ADVANCED SETTINGS opens another area of the Remote Install page that contains RIS server advanced settings. On this page, you will see three tabs. These tabs correspond to the following sections:

- New clients
- Images
- Tools

We will now examine each of these sections of the Advanced Settings page in more detail.

New Clients

The New Clients tab gives you the opportunity to define a computer naming format and set a location for the computer account to be generated. When the Client Installation Wizard starts the OS installation process, it will create an account in Active Directory for the new computer. It uses the information that is defined in this section to create the computer account name and to choose which container or Organizational Unit to put the account. The first item you can modify is the Computer Naming Format.

Computer Naming Format

This section allows you to set a default computer naming format for the new client PCs that you are creating with RIS. When you choose the Automatic Setup option in the Client Installation Wizard, it will use this format to create the computer account name. There are a number of formats to choose from in the drop-down list, including a Custom format. Figure 4.14 shows the New Clients tab.

In the first section of the New Clients tab you will see the drop-down list, and directly below it, an example of a computer name using the chosen format. Here are the built-in computer naming formats:

Figure 4.14 RIS Advanced Settings page, New Clients tab.

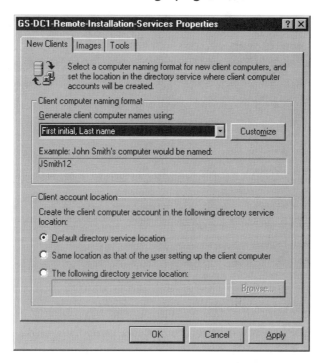

- First Initial, Last Name
- Last Name, First Initial
- First Name, Last Initial
- Last Initial, First Name
- Username
- NP Plus MAC
- Custom

If you do not want to use one of the existing formats, you can click CUSTOMIZE to open the Computer Account Generation dialog box. This dialog box is shown in Figure 4.15.

Creating a custom naming format is relatively easy. By following the examples in the dialog box, you can assemble practically any format that you can imagine.

The second item that you can modify is the Client Account Location.

Figure 4.15 Computer Account Generation screen.

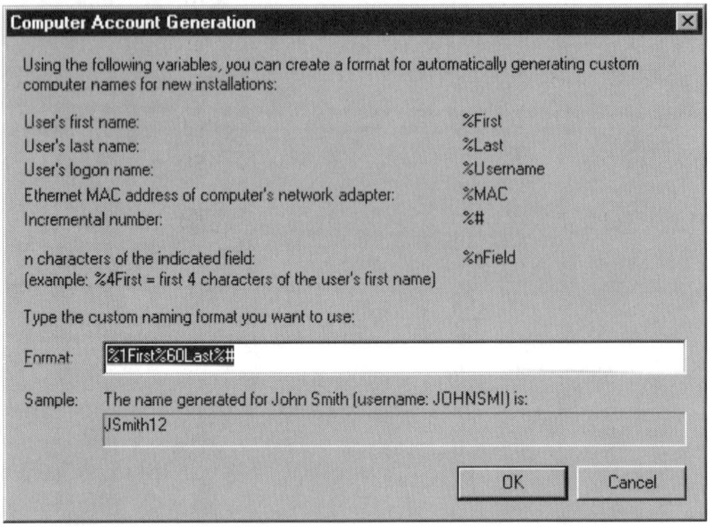

Client Account Location

You are also able to specify which Organizational Unit you want to place your RIS clients in. You have three choices of where your computer accounts are to be created. You can choose to have the computer accounts created in the default OU that is defined for the domain. Your second choice is to create the RIS computer account in the same OU of the user who is setting up the computer. The third option is to define a specific location in the directory. This may be a good option if you want all of your RIS clients to be created in the same OU.

Once you have set your default Computer Naming Format and Account Location, you may wish to work with the images that are installed on this server. The next section will discuss the Images tab.

Images

The Images tab lists all of the CD-based and RIPrep-based images that have been installed on this RIS server. You can view the properties for each image by highlighting one of the images and then choosing Properties. You can also add and remove images from the server from this dialog box. To add a new image, click ADD. This will launch the Add Image Wizard, as shown in Figure 4.16.

With this tool, you can associate a new answer file to an existing image or you can create a new CD-based image. By choosing the

Figure 4.16 Adding a new image to the RIS server.

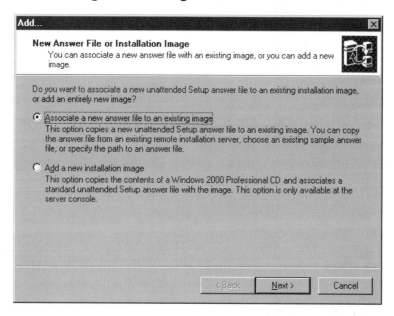

first option, you will be asked to provide the name and location of a .SIF file (that was created with the Setup Manager). Next, you will specify which CD-based image this answer file will be associated with. Once you have completed these steps, you will have an additional image to choose from.

If you choose to add a new installation image, you will need to have your Windows 2000 Professional source files handy. This option copies the source files into a new folder on the server, and creates a new default answer file for that image. Once the file copy stage is complete, you will have an additional CD-based image to deliver to clients.

NOTE

SIS will work to reduce the number of redundant files that get copied to your RIS server. For example, every RIPrep-based image will have the same Windows 2000 Professional source files. SIS will only keep one copy of each duplicate file, and place pointers to the SIS copy in the image directory for each RIPrep-based image.

You are also able to remove images using this interface. To remove a RIS image from your server, highlight the image name, and choose Remove. This will only remove the answer file that is associated with the image you selected. To completely remove the image, use Windows Explorer to delete the folder that contained the image files.

Tools

Finally, the Tools tab lists the OEM Tools that you have installed on your server. These tools, provided by vendors such as AMI and ON Technology, allow you to perform various functions on the client PC utilizing the PXE technology. For example, you may have a tool from your BIOS vendor that allows you to make BIOS changes to the machine remotely.

As mentioned earlier, there is also a Group Policy Object for Remote Installation Services. We will look at how that affects your server's operation in the next section.

Group Policy Settings

RIS has a Group Policy Object (GPO) that can be modified to restrict which options are presented by the Client Installation Wizard. The CIW can present up to four choices:

- Automatic Setup
- Custom Setup

- Restart a previous setup attempt
- Maintenance and Tools

By default, domain users are only given the Automatic Setup option. Domain administrators are given the Automatic and Custom Setup options. The wizard will not display the final two options unless you enable them with the GPO.

WARNING

Be careful when working with Group Policy Objects!

To modify the GPO for RIS, open the Active Directory Users and Computers MMC console. Right-click on the Domain name and choose Properties. Choose the Group Policy tab. Choose the Default Domain Policy and choose Edit. The Group Policy Object for RIS is under User Configuration, Windows Settings, as shown in Figure 4.17.

Figure 4.17 Modifying the RIS Group Policy Object.

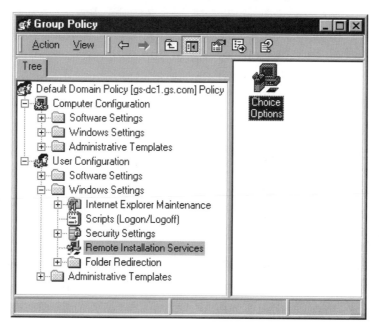

Double-click on Choice Options to open the Choice Options Properties page, as shown in Figure 4.18.

Figure 4.18 Client Installation wizard screen choices.

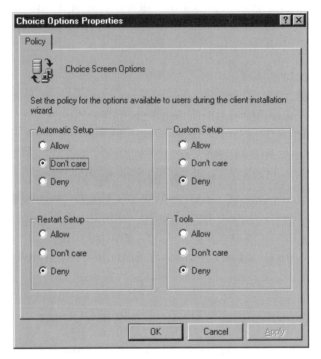

You will see the four choices, and you will see three radio button options for each:

- Allow
- Don't Care
- Deny

The Allow button specifies that every user affected by this GPO will be able to see this option in the Client Installation Wizard. The Deny button indicates that the user will not see this option. If you choose the Don't Care button, a user will get the setting defined in a GPO at a higher level. For example, let's assume you have a GPO set for the domain and a GPO set for an OU. The domain GPO allows the Automatic Setup, but denies the other three. The OU GPO allows the Automatic Setup option, but doesn't care about the remaining three options. If a user belonging to the OU runs the wizard, he or she will only see the Automatic Setup option. That is because the GPO for the Organizational Unit deferred to the domain GPO for those three options, and since the higher-level GPO denies those options, the user cannot see them.

While it is very easy to make changes to the Screen Options on the Default Domain Group Policy, you will need to create several GPOs in order to present different choices to different users (or groups of users). However, the process of creating multiple GPOs is outside the scope of this section.

In the next section, we will discuss the process of creating new images, restricting those images, and pre-staging client PCs in Active Directory.

Remote Installation Services Administration

At this point, our server is ready to provide OS images to your client PCs. In this section, we are going to look at how to create new images, as well as the process of restricting images to certain groups of users. Finally, we will look at pre-staging your client PCs in Active Directory.

You now have one OS image available for download by your clients. In most cases, this will not be enough to satisfy your business requirements. You will need to create additional images for your clients to choose from. There are two types of RIS images that can be delivered by RIS:

- RIPrep based
- CD based

Your first image is CD based—that is, the image starts with the base Windows 2000 Professional CD files, and an answer file

customizes the installation. RIPrep-based images are created by taking a snapshot of a PC with Windows 2000 that has been customized with business software or modified desktop settings. We'll
start this section by looking at RIPrep-based images.

Remote Installation Preparation Wizard

RIPrep stands for the Remote Installation Preparation wizard. This
tool will allow you to take an existing build of Windows 2000,
including any customizations that you have made, and create an
image for RIS to deliver to client PCs.

WARNING

Choose your Reference PC carefully. When you run RIPrep on a PC, the
process removes the unique identifiers from the machine and configures
the mini-Setup program to run on the next boot. If you choose to run
RIPrep on your production PC, you may find yourself unexpectedly sitting
through the setup process.

To start the process of creating an RIPrep-based image, you will
need to have a PC with a base installation of Windows 2000. This
machine is also referred to as a Reference PC. Microsoft recommends that you use a machine that was created from an RIS image,
but you can also use a CD installation. Once you have your
Reference PC prepared, start customizing it for the intended audi-
ence. This may include installing a number of standard software
applications, or you may just need to make changes to the network
settings. Whatever the case may be, now is the time to get the
machine set for your environment.

Once you have finished the customizations, you can run the
wizard. From the Reference PC, choose Start and Run, and type the
following command:

```
\\ris-server\reminst\admin\i386\riprep.exe
```

where *ris-server* is the name of your Remote Installation server. The RIS installation process created the REMINST share on the RIS server by default. When you have entered this command, click OK to start the program.

NOTE

You can only run RIPrep on a Windows 2000 Professional PC.

Click NEXT to go past the Welcome screen for the wizard. Figure 4.19 shows the screen for specifying the server that should receive the new image. You can choose any RIS server in your enterprise.

Figure 4.19 Specifying an RIS server to receive the image.

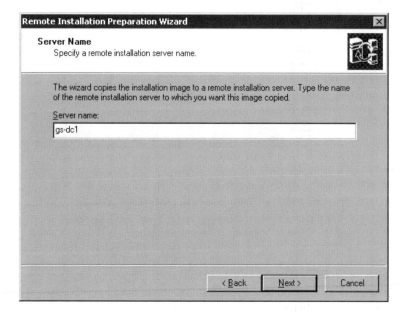

Click NEXT to proceed to the next screen in the wizard. The next three screens are identical to the Remote Installation Services Setup wizard. On the first, you will type the name of the folder for the new image. After you type the name, click NEXT. The second screen asks for the friendly name and description of the image. As we saw earlier in the chapter, this text is displayed during the Client Installation wizard. The final screen asks you to confirm your choices. If everything looks OK, click NEXT. Figure 4.20 shows the last screen of the wizard, which gives a few tips about the image process.

Figure 4.20 Completing the RIPrep Wizard.

After you have read this dialog box, click NEXT. The wizard will begin the process of cleaning the UIDs from your reference PC. Once that is complete, the files will be copied to the RIS server.

TIP

Make sure your applications can find their source files. When you build your reference PC for duplication, install applications from their network locations, rather than from CDs or a temporary location. If a user needs to make changes to the installation or needs to get additional files, the application will look in the correct location for its files, rather than the temporary location used during the build process.

If you want to make additional RIPrep-based images, you will need to create another Reference PC.

CD-Based Images

You do have an alterative to building a Reference PC if you are only making changes to the base Windows 2000 Professional settings. RIS will allow you to create additional answer files (SIF) and then associate them with Image names. This is helpful if you need to deploy images with minor cosmetic changes, such as graphic resolutions or network settings.

Although the creation of answer files is discussed in another chapter, it is helpful to point out the areas that you need to focus on during the process. When you run the Windows 2000 Setup Manager, you will choose to create a new answer file and specify that it is for Remote Installation Services. The remaining portions of the Setup Manager are identical to the stand-alone answer file process, except that you will have the opportunity to add a friendly name and description to the answer file for advertisement by RIS. Once you have created the new file, instruct the Setup Manager to copy the answer file to your Remote Install directory. It is recommended that you place the new .SIF file in your original CD-based folder (which is named win2000.pro by default).

Restricting Access to the Images

Once you install the RIS images on the server, you may want to restrict which images are offered to your users. This is done by setting an Access Control List (ACL) on the image folders and on answer files (in the case of CD-based images).

For example, the initial CD-based image is installed in the win2000.pro folder under Images. If you navigate into the win2000.pro folder, you will find a folder called i386, and in that folder you will find a Templates folder. This is where the answer files are located. The default answer file for a CD-based image is called ristndrd.sif. To restrict access to this image, you merely need to set an ACL that allows/denies Read access to that SIF file for the appropriate user/group.

In the case of an RIPrep-based image, you should set the ACL on the image folder, rather than the SIF file. There is usually only one answer file associated with an RIPrep-based image, while you can associate multiple answer files with a single CD-based image.

Pre-Staging Computers

The last feature that we'll discuss on the server side is the process of pre-staging computers in the Directory. By pre-staging your computers, you can specify the exact location for the computer account in the Directory, and specify the computer name. If your environment uses complex computer names, this method is much easier than the custom-naming format. Another reason for pre-staging is for load balancing among multiple RIS servers. This is an advanced topic, and is not within the scope of this section.

In order to pre-stage a computer, you will need to have its Global Unique Identifier (GUID). The GUID is a 16-byte (128-bit) hexadecimal number that is guaranteed to be unique. System manufacturers use an algorithm to create the GUID. This algorithm uses the MAC address of the network card and the current date/time stamp to generate the GUID. An example of a GUID would be {761FF923-AB42-11BE-ABCD-00CA0034B177}. This number is then stored in the BIOS and posted on the outside of the client PC on a label for your convenience. If you cannot locate the GUID on your PC, you may need to refer to the *For IT Professionals* section for a shortcut to pre-staging the client PC.

TIP

Another name for the Global Unique Identifier is UUID, or Universal Unique Identifier.

Once you have the GUID, you will need to open the Active Directory Users and Computers MMC and open the container into which you wish to pre-stage your PC. Right-click on the container and choose New and Computer. Type the computer name and click NEXT.

Figure 4.21 shows the second screen that allows you to specify that this computer is a managed computer. When you check the box for "This is a managed computer," you will be allowed to enter the GUID for the computer. When you have finished, click NEXT to complete the operation.

Figure 4.21 Entering the GUID for a managed PC.

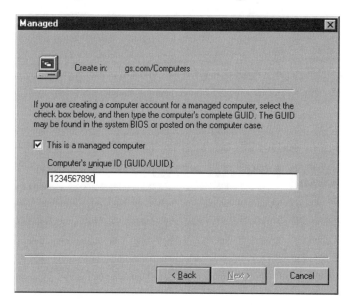

We have looked at the setup and configuration of the RIS server. We have examined the process of creating images to distribute to the client PCs and discussed pre-staging computers. We are now going to turn to the processes that run on the client computer.

For IT Professionals

Pre-staging Shortcuts

Here is a simple way to pre-stage a computer in the Active Directory if the GUID is not easily accessible. Set up your new computer for network boot, and boot into the Client Installation wizard. Log in to the Directory using an account with Administrator permissions. Choose the Custom option. Type in the computer's name and the name of the container into which you want to pre-stage it (if different from the Computers container). Choose any of the available OS images, and at the last screen, which allows you to verify the information that you have just entered, power off the system. You have just created a pre-staged computer account with the GUID properly recorded. You can now assign the appropriate permissions for the new user to the computer account and deliver the system to the desktop.

Remote Client Installation

Up until this point, the majority of the discussion has been focused on the server side of RIS. The final section of this chapter will examine the client-side process of Remote Installation Services.

Before you attempt to boot from the network, you need to verify which type of network card you have in your client PC. If it is equipped with a NIC that has the Remote Boot ROM, you will need to change a setting in the BIOS. You will need to set the network as the first boot device if you want the network card to control the boot sequence. If your client PC does not have a NIC with a Remote Boot ROM, but the NIC is supported by the RIS process, you will need to create a Remote-Boot Floppy Disk. Once you have the disk, you can boot from it to start the RIS process.

Remote Boot Disk Generator

The Remote Boot Disk Generator is a program that creates a floppy disk containing a Universal Network Device Interface (UNDI) driver. Using this universal driver, you can enable a client PC to download the Client Installation wizard to start the RIS process. The only drawback to this method is that the list of supported PCI drivers is rather short. Table 4.1 lists the supported adapters of the final version of Windows 2000.

Table 4.1 Compatible PCI Network Adapters

Manufacturer	Model
3Com	3C900B-Combo
	3C900B-FL
	3C900B-TPC
	3C900B-TPO
	3C900-Combo
	3C905B-Combo
	3C905B-FX
	3C905B-TX
	3C905C-TX
	3C905-T4
	C905-TX
AMD	PCnet Adapters
Compaq	NetFlex 100
	NetFlex 110
	NetFlex 3
DEC	DE450
	DE500
HP	DeskDirect 10/100 TX
Intel	Pro 10+
	Pro 100+
	Pro 100B
SMC	8432
	9332
	9432

To create a Windows 2000 Remote Boot Disk, you will need a formatted floppy disk. Start the program, choose Start and Run, and type the following command:

`\\`*ris-server*`\reminst\admin\i386\rbfg.exe`

where *ris-server* is the name of your Remote Installation server. As Figure 4.22 shows, you insert the floppy disk into the drive and click CREATE DISK. Once the operation is complete, you are ready to start the RIS process.

Figure 4.22 Running the Remote Boot Disk Generator.

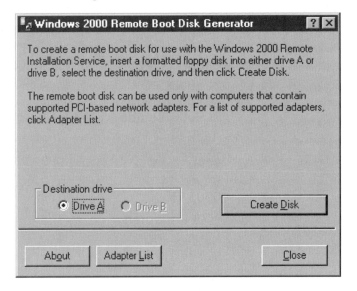

The Client Installation Wizard

When you initiate the remote boot process, the RIS server downloads the Client Installation Wizard to the client PC via TFTP. You can break down the Wizard into seven steps:

1. Press F12 for network boot.
2. The Welcome screen appears.
3. User logs on.

4. Image selection takes place.

5. Disk-format warning appears.

6. The GUID is confirmed.

7. OS installation takes place.

Let's walk through each of these steps and see what is happening.

Press F12 for Network Boot

When you initiate a network boot, you see a few messages on the screen from the PXE process. These messages indicate the NIC is requesting an IP address and the location of the boot server. Once the BINL service responds and sends the boot image down to the client PC, you will see a message similar to:

```
Press F12 for Network Boot
```

You will have three seconds to press F12 to start the Client Installation wizard. If you aren't quick enough, the PXE process will time-out and your client PC will attempt to boot from the next device in the BIOS list.

The Welcome Screen Appears

After you press F12, the Client Installation wizard's Welcome screen appears. This screen presents basic information about the process, and asks the user to press ENTER to continue.

User Logs On

The next screen in the wizard asks the user to type his or her Active Directory credentials. These include the username, password, and domain. If the user's domain is the same as that of the server, you can omit the domain during logon. The wizard assumes you are in this domain. If you successfully authenticate into the Active

Directory, you will go to the next screen. Otherwise, you will receive an error message and be asked to reenter your credentials.

Image Selection Takes Place

The next screen is presented differently based on the credentials you presented during the log on. The Client Installation wizard compares your credentials against the ACLs that have been set on the images, as well as comparing your credentials against the Domain's Group Policy. Based on these results, this screen may show a number of different options.

Up to four choices can be presented at this point:

- Automatic Setup
- Custom Setup
- Restart Setup
- Tools

If you remember from the section on setting Group Policy Objects, the default choice for domain users is Automatic Setup. The following section discusses each of the choices that could be presented by the wizard.

Automatic Setup

When you choose the Automatic Setup, you will see all of the images for which you are authorized (by the ACLs set on the images). The computer name will be set according to the naming format, unless it has been pre-staged, and in this case, it will be given the name from the pre-stage process. In addition, the computer account will be created in the default Directory container.

Custom Setup

When the Custom Setup option is selected, you will be able to choose from any images that you are authorized to download, and you will be able to override the computer name and location information. A good use for this option is for the Help Desk employee setting up a PC for another user. The ability to override the default information would be helpful in this instance.

Restart a Previous Setup Attempt

This option is available if a previous Remote Installation process failed. By selecting this option, the RIS process will start over using the information that the user entered on the failed attempt.

Maintenance and Troubleshooting

The final option presents a list of tools that can be used in the pre-boot environment. When you choose this option, you will receive a list representing the tools that have been installed on the RIS server. By choosing one of these tools, you will be able to use this functionality in the pre-boot stage.

Disk Format Warning Appears

Once you have chosen a setup method and have selected an image to install, you will see a warning screen. This warns you that the RIS process will format the hard disk and anything on the disk will be erased.

The GUID Is Confirmed

The last screen of the Client Installation wizard allows you to confirm the information that you have chosen in the earlier screens. You will see the GUID and computer name of the client PC, as well as the container in the Active Directory in which the account was created. If you are pre-staging the computer, you can turn off the client PC at this time, and it will be pre-staged in Active Directory. If you are ready to begin the OS Installation, press ENTER to continue.

OS Installation Takes Place

The Client Installation wizard passes control to the Windows 2000 Professional setup program at this point. It will take approximately 30 minutes for the client PC to receive the new OS (based on network and PC speed).

This wraps up the discussion on the Client Installation wizard. It is a fairly simple routine, and when all the pieces of Remote Installation have been properly configured, it is very easy for a user to install Windows 2000 Professional on a PC.

Summary

Remote Installation Services is the latest tool to help reduce the total cost of ownership for deploying the operating system to client PCs. By using Remote Boot ROM technology, RIS enables the administrator to deploy Windows 2000 Professional without having to visit every workstation in the enterprise.

In this chapter, you learned about the technology that is behind the Remote Installation server. We walked through the installation of the RIS components, and discussed the advanced options that are available on the RIS server.

We also learned about the differences between the CD-based and RIPrep-based images. The Remote Installation Preparation Wizard is used to create images containing the base Windows 2000 Professional source files, as well as business software and customizations from the administrator.

Finally, we looked at the Client Installation wizard, and examined the steps necessary to start the RIS process from the client PC.

RIS is a great technology for deploying Windows 2000 Professional. It should definitely be examined as an alternative to visiting each workstation to install the operating system.

FAQs

Q: Can I use RIS to install Windows 2000 if my client PC has a Token Ring NIC?

A: No. At this time, RIS does not support Token Ring or PCMCIA network cards. Future updates from Microsoft may allow these devices to take advantage of RIS technology.

Q: Can I use RIPrep to clone a PC with multiple partitions on the primary hard disk?

A: No. RIS will only install Windows 2000 on a single-disk, single-partition PC.

Q: Can I use RIS to upgrade my Windows 98 PCs to Windows 2000 Professional?

A: No. RIS only supports the clean installation of Windows 2000 to a PC. It does not support upgrading from any prior version of Windows.

Chapter 5

Deploying Software with Group Policy

Solutions in this chapter

- Deploying Software
- Managing Software
- Planning for Software Deployment

Introduction

Significant changes in the way that computers are used in the work-place have heralded an increased focus on the support and maintenance of computing platforms. Information technology has ushered in an era characterized by high availability, high productivity, and increased support levels. Most of these attributes can be leveraged through software that effectively combines the intellect of the user with the raw processing power of the computer.

The tools and applications that leverage the power of operating systems are the real lifeblood of modern businesses—without them, the most powerful computer would be nothing more than an expensive paperweight. Software is to computers what gasoline is to automobiles—it is the element that makes the vehicle truly useful. Without fuel, a car can provide no real function. The expensive and complex engine (operating system) housed in the sleekly contoured body (computer) is very pleasing to the eye, but useless without gas (software).

As a consequence, the management and delivery of software to workstations has taken on increased importance. Software deployment has over the years achieved a prime position in the IT administrator's problem space. Current deployment strategies and technologies are beginning to creak under the strain of increasing software complexity, greater distribution sizes, and inhouse initiatives by management to drive the cost of ownership lower.

Much has been said about the complexity and size of Windows 2000, but what is Windows 2000 but a very large piece of software? The modern-day software malady of ever-increasing size and complexity is not confined only to operating systems, but is a reflection of current trends in software development. Unfortunately, these increases usually translate into software that is more expensive to deploy and support.

It's no secret that network clients are also becoming more complex, harder to manage, and geographically dispersed. Network managers lost in glassy-eyed reverie often regale their younger colleagues with tales of the wonder years, when men were men and terminals were dumb. With the advent of the more intelligent and flexible client workstation, the specter of increased maintenance costs arose. As client workstations became more intelligent, the software followed suit with increasing complexity and size. A glaring omission in the Windows technical strategy was the lack of a cohesive infrastructure to manage client configuration changes and administration. With the release of Windows 2000, Microsoft provides a number of symbiotic technologies that enable users to be productive under a variety of circumstances and allows the administrator to deploy software from a central location.

Remote administration and maintenance are key factors in the fight to lower Total Cost of Ownership (TCO). Allowing increased control and manageability over client workstations provides administrators with an effective method of reducing the time required for configuration and problem resolution. Centralized remote administration can also provide a scalable way to deploy software to a burgeoning user base. Microsoft has recognized this as an essential requirement to redress the imbalance in software deployment and ownership, and has provided a tool set and infrastructure that eases the rocky road traveled by administrators as they attempt to deploy and maintain software within the business.

Software deployment in Windows 2000 relies on a number of powerful technologies that are new to the Windows family. Before deployment of software, an administrator must understand these new concepts and technologies. Within the context of Windows 2000, software deployment can be considered to be a change and configuration management issue. Software deployment leverages the power and scalability of a technology called Group Policies that allows you to define the users' computing environment . This chapter provides an insight into a particular change and configuration management issue—software deployment—and how IntelliMirror addresses it using Group Policies.

Change and Configuration Management

A great deal of attention has been focused on the cost of owning computing platforms and, in particular, client workstations. Microsoft has often, quite correctly, been criticized for a lack of native infrastructure aimed at lowering the cost of owning Windows-based computers. Microsoft has aggressively addressed this issue by providing a series of technologies for Windows 2000 that supports change and configuration management. Change and configuration management encompasses all of the corrective, configurable, and preventive tasks that an administrator must perform to keep his user base productive, including the deployment of software to the desktop.

After consulting customers and the IT sector, Microsoft realized that its change and configuration management feature set needed to meet at least the following requirements:

- The capability to store user data centrally.
- Support of a personalized computing environment; that is, data and applications should follow the users as they roam around the network.
- The capability to allow the user to work on- or offline.
- Reduction of administrative overhead by providing the capability to centrally configure clients by policy, including software deployment by policy.
- Self-healing desktops that reduce support-call incidents.
- Add or replace desktops without pre-staging.

Two complementary technology sets support change and configuration management (see Figure 5.1) in the Windows 2000 environment—Remote Operating System Installation and IntelliMirror.

The first technology set, Remote Operating System Installation, provides the administrator with the ability to install Windows 2000 from a remote location using a variety of deployment tools and techniques.

Figure 5.1 Change and configuration management in Windows 2000.

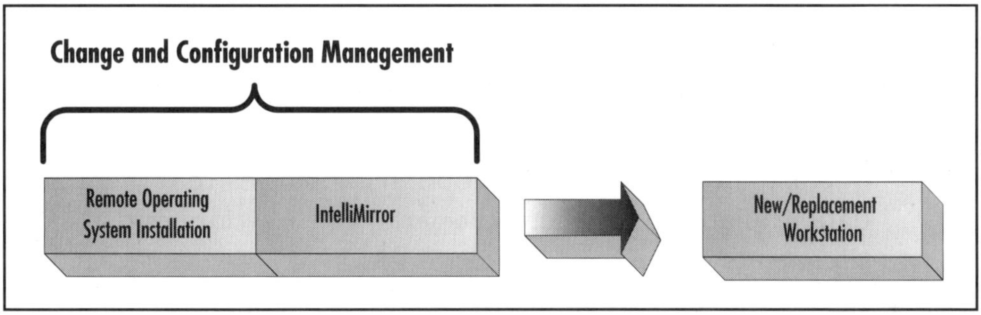

Tools such as Sysprep, Setup Manager, and automated installation files provide the mechanisms to generate a Windows 2000 Professional workstation without user intervention. Techniques such as Remote Installation Services, Disk Imaging, and Automated Setup Scripts describe the methodologies. Remote Operating System Installation has a variety of applications such as machine recovery and the speedy automation of setup. The first few chapters of this book provide a detailed discussion of the use and implementation of this technology.

IntelliMirror

The second and most complex change and configuration management technology set is IntelliMirror. While Remote Operating System Installation involves the deployment of operating system to computers, IntelliMirror involves managing computers after deployment. By using a comprehensive array of supporting technologies, IntelliMirror provides the user with the same personalized working environment regardless of which Windows 2000 computer is used. User data is made consistently available, whether online or offline, while being simultaneously maintained on the server. Policy-based user and computer configuration settings ensure a consistent and personalized workspace. In short, IntelliMirror ensures the high availability of personal computer settings, software, and user data by combining centralized administration with distributed-client computing. Three major features support the IntelliMirror technology:

- **User Data Management** Users can have access to their data whether they are online or offline. This feature includes the Active Directory, Group Policy, folder redirection, disk quotas, and file synchronization, technologies that increase data availability. In Microsoft parlance, *"My data and documents follow me."*

- **User Settings Management** Allows preferences to follow the user. The user's personalized settings, such as desktop arrangements and software and operating system settings, follow the user. This feature includes the Active Directory, Group Policy, roaming profiles, and particular shell enhancements, technologies that increase computer availability. In Microsoft parlance, *"My preferences follow me."*

- **Software Installation and Maintenance** Ensures that users have access to their required software. Software can be advertised to install on demand or be installed by default. This feature includes the Active Directory, Group Policy, self-repairing software, and application deployment, technologies that increase application availability. In Microsoft parlance, *"My software follows me."*

Each of these features is supported by an array of technologies (see Figure 5.2) that have two common threads, Active Directory and Group Policy. With Active Directory, Microsoft provides an extensive and scalable directory service that is a well-structured information source and a tool for centralized administration. Group Policy centrally manages and configures user and computer settings for specific groups or individuals.

IntelliMirror is not an all-or-nothing technology. Administrator can choose the features that best meet the needs of the organization. By identifying the particular features required, the relevant technology can be implemented without having to configure a host

Figure 5.2 Technologies used by IntelliMirror.

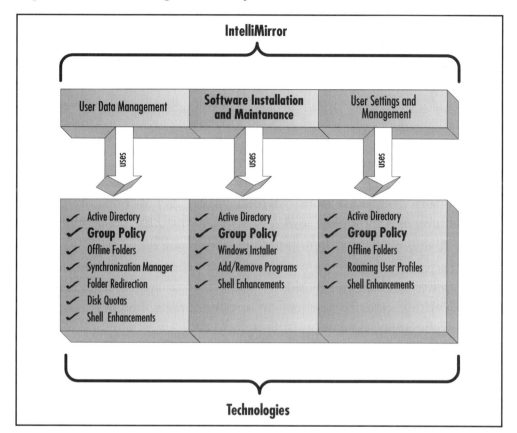

of supporting technologies. IntelliMirror uses Active Directory in conjunction with Group Policy to manage the user's desktop, though it is important to note that Group Policy and Active Directory are not required to leverage each of the IntelliMirror features. For example, local policies (as opposed to Group Policies) can be used to determine the configuration of individual computers even when offline.

The *"follow me"* model of IntelliMirror ensures the high availability of a user's personalized computing environment, including data, settings, and software. The design of IntelliMirror is intended to please both the administrator, by offloading some of the work to the supporting infrastructure, and management, by reducing the cost of change and configuration management.

The three features of IntelliMirror are scalable, from the small business to the global enterprise. With the support of Active Directory and policy-based management, features can be assigned a granularity defined by the administrator.

A brief summary of some of the technologies used with IntelliMirror includes:

- **Active Directory** A scalable directory service that stores information about the network that can be accessed by users and administrators alike. It can act as both an information source and a centralized administrative tool.

- **Group Policy** A technology that enables administrators to precisely define the configuration of the user's computing environment. It can satisfy such diverse requirements as setting security settings, to application deployment. Group Policy can control both user- and machine-based configuration settings.

- **Offline Files and Folders** A technology that accesses defined files and folders while offline. Accessing files or folders offline may be necessary when the network is unavailable, or when the user is mobile. Entire mapped drives can even be accessed while offline. The Synchronization Manager can be used to determine what files to make available offline and when they should be updated.

- **Folder Redirection** The capability to point a folder, such as My Documents, to another (network) location.

- **Distributed File System (DFS)** This service can build a single namespace consisting of multiple shares on different servers. DFS provides the capability to load share and increase data availability.

- **Roaming User Profiles** A centrally stored user profile that follows the user around the network.

- **Windows Installer** A standardized, scalable installation service that is customizable, consistent, and provides diagnosis and self-repair functionality.

- **Disk Quotas** A technology that enables administrators to monitor and limit disk space usage on a per-volume, per-user basis.

One of the features of IntelliMirror is Software Installation and Maintenance. This feature embraces the *"follow me"* model and allows applications to follow users or computers. A user roaming from computer to computer will always have his required software available since IntelliMirror technologies track his movement from workstation to workstation and make the relevant applications available to him at logon. The Software Installation and Maintenance feature allows the administrator to force the installation of applications for certain users or computers, or to provide an option to users to install specific applications as desired. This feature is mainly supported by Active Directory, Windows Installer, and Group Policy. One of the most important tools for managing a Windows 2000 environment is Group Policy. It is a key component in all of the features, but is particularly important for software deployment and maintenance.

Group Policy is a detailed and sometimes complex technology that requires that the administrator understand certain essential concepts relevant to all Group Policy features. Understanding how Group Policy relates to Active Directory, and what rules govern its behavior, are fundamental concepts when learning how to deploy software using Group Policy.

Group Policy

At times it seems as soon as your back is turned, more clients attach themselves to the network. The growing hunger of businesses to technologically enable their work force can create a mounting headache for the administrator of today's networks. Maintaining and enforcing a standardized configuration while allowing the users freedom to work unhindered is a juggling act that sometimes requires the administrator to have too many balls in the air at once. The only way to ensure that the configuration of possibly thousands of workstations is maintained in a consistent manner is by allowing the network to enforce the rules for software deployment and other change and configuration issues. Policy-based management is one answer to Windows 2000 change and configuration management issues.

The Windows 2000 platform is the largest operating system that Microsoft has developed to date, and it goes without saying that the number of configurable options have grown proportionately. Obviously the danger is that this can lead to a profusion of confusing and risky configuration options, with some under management and some not. To counter this, Microsoft has ensured that most of the configuration options can be defined and maintained from central locations through the Group Policy. A policy can be considered to be a set of configuration data describing the settings of computers and users.

The vast array of configurable settings ensures that there is a wealth of usage scenarios for Group Policy, such as:

- Install the accounting package on all computers in Finance.
- Run acclogon.cmd when users in the Accounts department log on.
- Do not save settings on exit for all consultants.
- Disable the RunAs service for the whole organization except administrators.
- Launch this Web page at user logon.

User and computer configuration settings compiled and detailed in a policy can be applied to workstations and the user's personalized computing environment and enforced automatically. These configuration settings can range from hiding certain icons on the desktop for a small group of users, to deploying a major software package to the entire organization.

Policies can be divided into local and Group Policies. In a large network, the operating environments of particular groups of people or resources often have to conform to certain requirements. By placing these users and resources into logical groups or containers, policies can be applied *en masse*. The logical and physical groupings that can be utilized by Group Policy are Sites, Domains, Organizational Units (known as SDOUs), and Security Groups. This implies that certain Group Policies with particular settings can be associated with particular containers in the Active Directory. This association is often called linking. Security Groups cannot be linked with Group Policies, but can be used to further refine the scope of a Group Policy within the container with which the Group Policy is associated (see Table 5.1).

Table 5.1 Entities that Can Affect the Scope of Group Policies

Entities that Can Affect the Scope of Group Policies	Description
Site	A site can be considered to be a number of subnets that have reliable and fast network connectivity (sites do not usually extend over wide area links). Sites may cross domain boundaries. *Group Policies can be associated with a site.*
Domain	A domain can be considered to be a security, administrative, and partitioning boundary. *Group Policies can be associated with a domain.*

Continued

Entities that Can Affect the Scope of Group Policies	Description
Organizational Unit	An Organizational Unit can be used to logically group Active Directory objects. Organizational Units are child containers within domains. *Group Policies can be associated with an Organizational Unit.*
Security Group	Windows 2000 supports three types of Security Groups: local, global, and universal. *Group Policies groups cannot be associated with Security Groups.* Security Groups can filter the effects of Group Policy settings. The Discretionary Access Control List (DACL) details the permissions for which Security Groups have access to a particular policy.

Simply put, Group Policies enable the administrator to define the state of the user's computing environment and use the network to enforce that definition according to the required scope. Group Policies can be used throughout Windows 2000 to define user and computer configuration settings such as scripts, software policies, security settings, application deployment, user settings, and document options. Since Group Policy is a common thread in all three of the features of IntelliMirror, it is of prime importance in change and configuration management.

Using Group Policies opens up new avenues of centralized administration and provides a number of advantages, such as:

- **Capitalizes on Active Directory** By leveraging the groupings within Active Directory, Group Policy can be applied with the required amount of granularity throughout the business. Management of the Group Policies themselves can also be controlled and delegated.

- **Flexible, scalable, and extensible architecture** Group Policy scales with Active Directory and can be used in companies of all sizes. The varied amount of management configurations for Group Policy provides a great deal of flexibility.

- **Management tools** Management tools within Windows 2000 are hosted by the Microsoft Management Console (MMC), which provides a consistent set of management interfaces. Group Policies are no exception to this rule and are modified through the Microsoft Management Consoles.

- **Reliable and secure policy application** Features within Windows 2000 ensure that the Group Policies are reliably applied.

- **Feature rich** Provides additional functionality such as slow-link detection.

Group Policy is one of the most important technologies in the Windows 2000 administrator's armory, but, as is usually the case, there are certain infrastructure gotchas. The Windows 2000 platform supports group policies, but:

- Active Directory must be in place to use Group Policies.

- Even though Windows NT and Windows 2000 are close relatives, Windows NT only provides limited support of Group Polices through the use of Administrative Templates.

- Windows 9*x* and Windows 3*x* do not support Group Policies.

Unlike Active Directory, Group Policies only work with the Windows 2000 platform. Existing or alternative strategies have to be employed to manage non-Windows 2000 desktops. This means that software deployment using Group Policy will only work for Windows 2000 computers. The relationship between the Active Directory and Group Policies is one way; meaning that Group Policies require the presence of Active Directory, but Active Directory can be used without implementing Group Policies.

System Policies vs. Group Policies

Are Group Policies for Windows 2000 really an improvement over System Policies for Windows NT 4.0? First, they are very different animals, and the lessons learned from the shortcomings of the original System Policies have been incorporated into Group Policies. Centralized management of the user's computing environment has come of age with Group Policies, unlike System Policies. Table 5.2 lists a few of the differences between Group Policies and its poorer relation.

Components of Group Policy

The Group Policy namespace consists of two components: user and machine configuration. Policies can be created that take advantage of user settings only or the machine settings only. These settings can then be subdivided into five main areas of configuration:

- **Software settings,** which allow software to be managed centrally, including application deployment and removal

- **Scripts,** which contain configuration information for scripts, such as startup and shutdown scripts and logon or logoff scripts. These scripts can take advantage of new technologies such as the Windows Scripting Host.

- **Security settings,** which contain configurable settings relating to security for a particular machine or user

- **Administrative Templates,** which are registry-based settings that configure a number of components from disk quotas, to printers, to the user's desktop. These settings are written to the registry each time the Group Policy is applied.

- **Folder Redirection,** applicable only in the user-based configuration of the policy. Folder redirection allows well-known folders, such as My Documents, to be located centrally instead of on the local machine.

Table 5.2 Group Policies vs. System Policies

Windows 2000 Group Policies	Windows NT 4.0 System Policies
Group Policies provide a comprehensive collection of configuration settings that can be used to manage and maintain the user's computing environment, such as software deployed using Group Policy.	System Policies offer a much more limited spectrum of configuration and maintenance settings—they consist purely of registry settings. For example, there are no software distribution policies. The policies are mainly limited to controlling the user's desktop.
Group Policies can be associated with sites, domains, and Organizational Units. Additional filtering can be performed by using Discretionary Access Control Lists (DACLS).	System Policies are associated with domains only. Access is controlled by Security Group membership.
Configuration and maintenance settings are confined to specific areas in the registry and are appropriately cleaned after a specific Group Policy Object no longer applies. The registry locations (in both HKEY_LOCAL_MACHINE and HKEY_CURRENT_USER) where settings are written in are: \Software\Policies \Software\Microsoft\ Windows\CurrentVersion\ Policies	Registry settings persist when applied by System Policies until some form of negating action is taken. This usually implies deleting the registry keys in question or reversing the policy.
Provide easy and intuitive management.	System Policy tools are not as flexible or as powerful.

How Group Policies Work

Group Policy settings are contained within Group Policy Objects (GPOs), which are associated with Active Directory containers (see Table 5.1 for information on the entities that can affect the scope of

Group Policies). GPOs can be linked to Sites, Domains, and Organizational Units (SDOUs). To provide a tight level of management, multiple GPOs can be associated with a single SDOU. The GPOs associated with a particular container can easily be prioritized to determine how the Site, Domain, or Organizational Unit is affected by the policies.

NOTE

Group Policy Objects are stand-alone objects that can be associated with multiple Sites, Domains, and Organizational Units (SDOUs). GPOs by default affect all the users and computers in a container. Group Policies are only inherited from the Domain that the computer or user belongs to, and not from higher-level Domains. Conversely, Group Policies are inherited down the Organizational Unit tree within a Domain.

As discussed earlier, we noted that there are two components to Group Policy Objects—user- and computer-specific settings. Computer-based settings in the Group Policy Object are applied when the computer is booted up followed by the startup scripts. When a user logs on to the workstation, the user-based settings are applied, followed by the logon scripts. Examples of computer settings include how the operating system is configured, how applications are deployed, and what startup scripts should run. GPOs can be configured to just execute the user- or computer-based configuration settings.

WARNING

Group Policy Objects (GPOs) work only for users and computers, not groups. If an Organizational Unit only contains groups of users, the users will not receive the GPOs linked to that container.

Since Group Policy objects can be associated with a number of Active Directory containers it is very possible that Group Policies could be associated to Sites, Domains, and Organizational Units. The application, or inheritance, of policies follows the SDOU order: First, the site Group Policy is applied, followed by the Domain, then the Organizational Unit. The Group Policy associated with the container closest to the user or computer determines the final settings, overriding settings in containers "further away."

Group Policy provides a great deal of flexibility in the manner with which settings are applied using the SDOU scheme, but additional tailoring can be undertaken by using the No Override (also known as Enforce Policy) and Block Policy options. Using No Override for a Group Policy prevents other GPOs from overriding a policy. If you enforce the Site GPO by setting the No Override option, Group Policies in lower containers (Domains and Organizational Units) are not able to change the settings of the Site GPO. On the other hand, blocking policy inheritance prevents GPOs in higher-level containers from applying their policies to the blocked container and its children. It should be noted that enforced GPOs always take precedence over blocked containers.

Some Group Policy components require a certain amount of code on the client workstations to implement the Group Policy. This code is packaged in DLL format and is called a client-side extension. The workstation gets a list of all GPOs and determines if any of the GPOs contain data that requires the client-side extensions to be loaded. Client-side extensions are then loaded on a demand basis to process the settings in the GPOs.

Group Policy Objects

A Group Policy Object is a virtual container that stores information in the Group Policy Container and a Group Policy template. Group Policy Containers are Active Directory objects that store the GPO properties. The Group Policy template is stored in the Sysvol\ Policies folder on domain controllers and contains information such as Administrative Template policies, what applications are ready for deployment, and script files.

TIP

User-based configuration settings in the Group Policy Object (GPO) are applied at logon and include software deployed to the user, desktop configuration, security settings, and logon scripts. By default, the CTRL+ALT+DEL screen will not be displayed until the computer settings of the GPOs have been applied, and the user's desktop will not be displayed until the user settings of the GPOs have been applied. This behavior can help with troubleshooting.

The option to apply GPOs synchronously (default) or asynchronously can be configured through the policy, though applying GPOs asynchronously is not recommended.

Slow-Link Detection

Group Policy can determine if it is running across a slow connection. Using a standard algorithm, it determines ping times and compares them to a threshold. The threshold can be configured by Group Policy in the Administrative Templates\System\Group Policy folder. See the section later in this chapter on using Group Policies to modify this setting.

If a Group Policy detects a slow link, certain user and computer settings are not applied by default. The default settings are:

- Software settings are disabled
- Scripts are disabled
- Security settings are enabled
- Administration settings are enabled
- Folder Redirection is disabled

The basic Active Directory structure of the XYZ Company is detailed in Figure 5.3. Administrators for the company have created nine Group Policies, GP1 through to GP9, each associated with a different SDOU.

Figure 5.3 Group Policy inheritance.

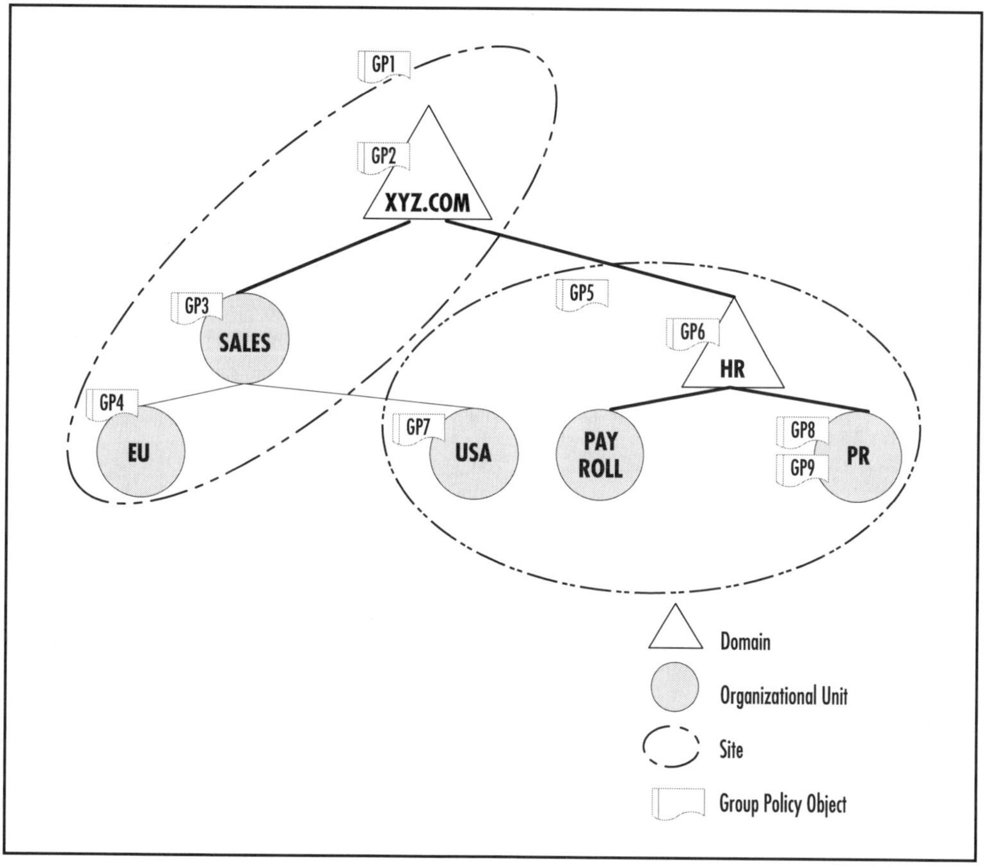

The Group Policies for each Organizational Unit are applied in a specific order:

- SALES—GP1, GP2, GP3
- EU—GP1, GP2, GP3, GP4
- USA—GP5, GP2, GP3, GP7

- PAYROLL—GP5, GP6
- PR—GP5, GP6, GP9, GP8 (assuming that GP8 has been given a higher priority than GP9)

To complicate matters even further, No Override and Block Policy Inheritance could be used to manipulate how policies are inherited. If the HR Domain Administrator sets the Block Policy inheritance for the HR domain, then the order of Group Policy application for the HR domain and its child containers would be:

- HR—GP6
- PAYROLL—GP6
- PR—GP6, GP9, GP8 (assuming that GP8 has been given a higher priority than GP9).

Assume that the Block Policy Inheritance option did not provide the results expected, and the Domain Administrator for the HR domain uses the No Override policy option for GP6 instead of the block policy option for the HR domain. Effectively, this would mean that the GPOs application order would be:

- HR—GP5, GP6
- PAYROLL—GP5, GP6
- PR—GP5, GP9, GP8, GP6

The actual application of the GPOs for the PR Organizational Unit would still be GP5, GP6, GP9, then GP8, but since GP6 is being enforced by the No Override option, it logically implies that the GP6 GPO is applied last.

Security groups in tandem with Discretionary Access Control Lists (DACLS) provide an additional layer of control over who receives Group Policies. To receive a Group Policy, a security group must have Apply Group Policy and read access to the GPO. Authenticated users have Apply Group Policy and Read permissions by default for all policies. It is not recommended to use the DACLS and the No Override and Block Policy Inheritance attributes too freely, as it can lead to overly complex administration. This feature is discussed in greater length later in the chapter.

NOTE

Policies can be configured for stand-alone computers using Local Group Policy Objects. The Local Group Policy Object is located in \%SystemRoot%\System32\GroupPolicy. When using LGPOs, note that:

- Software settings are not loaded by default.
- Security settings are loaded by default.
- Scripts are loaded by default.
- Folder Redirection is not loaded by default.
- Administrative Templates are not loaded by default.

Group Policy Filtering and Security

Much like a normal file on a hard drive, each GPO has an access control list that determines who can do what to it. For example, for a group to receive a Group Policy, the Read and Apply Group Policy Access Control Entries (ACEs) need to be enabled for the specific group. The process for editing the ACEs for GPOs is described later in this chapter. The default ACEs for new GPOs are:

- Authenticated Users have Read and Apply Group Policy ACEs.
- Domain Administrators, Enterprise Administrators, and Local System have all permissions except Apply Group Policy.

Since Authenticated Users have Read and Apply Group Policy ACEs, it is not necessary to modify the security of GPOs if no additional filtering is required. Domain Administrators, Enterprise Administrators, and Group Policy Administrators have the authority to create new GPOs in Domains and Organizational Units. You should be a member of Enterprise Administrators if you want to create a Site GPO. Administrators can allow other groups (and other administrators) to manage GPOs by additionally enabling the specific security group to write to the Group Policy.

In Figure 5.3, the XYZ Company could further refine how Group Policies apply by using security groups as a filter. Let's assume that the group of users, called PR Assistants, does not require the settings in GP9. The inheritance of GPOs for all users in the PR Organizational Unit prior to applying any filtering is GP5, GP6, GP9, GP8. By removing the Apply Group Policy ACE associated with GP9 for the security group PR Assistants (whose members are leaf objects in the PR Organizational Unit), the inheritance of Group Policies would be changed to GP5, GP6, GP8 for PR Assistants only.

Deploying Software

Software versions seem to change as quickly as odometer readings, with new releases of major applications a monthly occurrence. Compound this with the incredible variety of software available and you have the potential for nightmare software management scenarios. Large organizations may require hundreds of applications to be supported on thousands of machines—an impossible task without some form of supporting infrastructure. Unfortunately, software deployment does not stop there—administrators also have to contend with patches, revisions, and minor updates. Administrators cannot keep pace with the rate of change of software, or meet the requirement to deploy software to numerous users without offloading some of the work to an application deployment infrastructure. Allowing the deployment of software to be enforced by the infrastructure provides a scalable solution that can reduce the workload and eliminate a certain amount of human error.

We have discussed how Group Policy, a part of the IntelliMirror technology set, is used to address change and configuration management issues. Since change and configuration management encompasses software distribution, it follows that Group Policy has a well-defined software deployment component. Understanding Group Policy and its relationship to the Active Directory is integral to being able to develop a flexible and scalable software deployment strategy.

Microsoft has developed the software management capabilities of Group Policies and supporting technologies to help in four key areas:

- **Preparation** To provide additional value, and to leverage the advantages of Group Policy, software has to be prepackaged into a certain format.

- **Distribution** Software that has been packaged needs to be made available at distribution points. These distribution points can later be accessed by client workstations.

- **Targeting** Not all client workstations require all packaged software, and as a result, certain clients have to be grouped together as recipients of the particular software. This is known as targeting client workstations or users.

- **Installation** Once the software has been prepared in the correct format, made available at distribution points, and the clients have been targeted, the installation of the software can take place.

Software deployment using the set of technologies that support the software installation and maintenance features of IntelliMirror provides an administrator with centralized control over the following tasks:

- Installation, upgrade, or removal of applications
- Installation of service packs and software updates
- Assigning applications to computers or users
- Publishing applications to users
- Appearance of applications on the Start menu or in Add/Remove programs

Software is deployed using Group Policies by creating a Group Policy Object that contains the details for installing the packaged software on client workstations. The targeting of clients is achieved by linking the GPO to a container and using the rules for Group Policy inheritance. Additional control can be gained by using filtering and DACLs.

There are three methods of deploying software using Group Policy:

- Assigning applications to users
- Assigning applications to computers
- Publishing applications to users

Assigning Software

Group Policy allows software to be assigned to users or computers. Assigning an application to a computer or user implies that the application is available for use at all times, even though the files and installation resources to run it may not be present. The assigned application appears as a shortcut on the desktop or an entry in the Start menu.

User Assignments

The entry point for applications that are assigned to users follows the user to every Windows 2000 computer on the network. The application is made available for the user on every machine by the advertisement of a shortcut on the desktop, or by inserting a menu item in the Start menu. If a user is assigned an application and logs on to another workstation then an entry point on the desktop or in the Start menu will advertise that the assigned program can be run. Clicking on the shortcut for the first time seamlessly installs the application in the background, requiring no user interaction. The only difference the user will notice is a delay in the amount of time the program takes to launch. An assigned application will also install and launch if a user clicks on a file that has an association to a specific application.

Applications can be configured to be persistent. In other words, even if the user deletes them using the Add/Remove Programs applet, they will be readvertised at next log on.

Computer Assignments

Computers that have a certain function due to their location are prime targets for applications assigned to computers. If the requirement is that anyone logging on to a specific computer should have access to a certain application, then the application should be assigned to the computer.

Computer-assigned applications are installed when the computer settings of the Group Policy are first applied at startup. This is slightly different from user-assigned applications that are installed the first time the user launches the application.

Every user who logs on to that specific computer will see the desktop shortcut or entry in the Start menu for the assigned application. Since the application is linked to the computer, the user will not be able to remove the application using Add/Remove Programs. This restriction does not apply to administrators or other accounts with similarly high privileges.

Publishing Software

Applications within the business that are not mandatory but may be necessary to some users can be published. Using Add/Remove Programs, users install the applications themselves. Double-clicking on a file associated with a published application can also initiate the installation process. Using Add/Remove Programs displays a list of published applications that can be optionally installed. Figure 5.4 shows a published application called Balancing Act.

Figure 5.4 A published application in Add/Remove Programs.

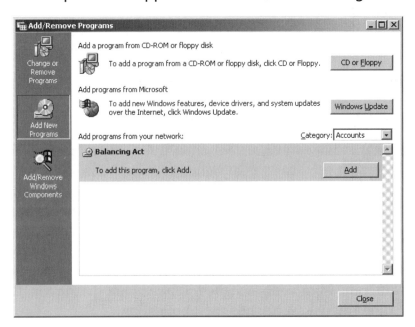

Enhancements within Add/Remove Programs

The Add/Remove Programs applet is designed to help users add and remove Windows components, as well as add, remove, repair, and modify other Windows programs. The Windows 2000 Add/Remove Programs applet has seen considerable improvement over its Windows NT counterpart. As Figure 5.4 shows, there are three buttons in a column on the far left of the Add/Remove Programs applet: Change or Remove Programs, Add New Programs, and Add/Remove Windows Components.

Clicking on Change or Remove Programs lists the set of applications currently installed on the Windows 2000 computer. Clicking on a specific application lists additional details of the installed application, such as the last time the application was used, how often the application has been used, and its size.

Applications that support the new method of packaging for distribution, which is discussed in the next section, can also include support information such as Web addresses and phone numbers

(Figure 5.5). The Support Info screen also provides a button to allow the application to repair itself.

NOTE

The Change or Remove Programs portion of the Add/Remove Programs applet displays information about currently installed applications. The Sort by: drop-down box provides a means of ordering the list by name, size, frequency of use, and date last used. The size displayed is only an estimate, while the frequency of use is determined by measuring the number of times the application has been run in the last 30 days.

Figure 5.5 Improved functionality in Add/Remove Programs.

The Add New Programs portion of the Add/Remove Programs applet allows users and administrators to install a program from CD or floppy, to retrieve updates from Microsoft using the WINDOWS UPDATE button, or to add programs that have been published on the network. Programs published on the network can be viewed by category, allowing departmental or functional delimitation of programs.

Packaging an Application

For software to be assigned or published, it needs to be packaged in a form that can be distributed using Group Policy. Windows Installer provides a packaging format that answers many of the questions posed by IT professionals regarding the setup process and application packaging.

There has been a great deal of dissatisfaction regarding the installation and setup process on the Windows platform. To address the problems faced on an almost daily basis by support staff, Microsoft developed a new installation mechanism called the Windows Installer. The native format of a Windows Installer package is the preferred format for packaging software for distribution by Group Policies.

Windows Installer

When administrators imagine software being installed on client workstations, they sigh and begin to dread the imminent raft of commonly experienced problems. Will installing this software break another piece of currently functional software? Will the software uninstall properly? What DLLs will change? No standardized setup process existed that developers could follow, which led to each application having its own setup routine. Installing applications turns into a software version of Russian roulette—each time an application is installed, you were left wondering if another application would be shot with a magic bullet.

The Windows Installer Service was developed to resolve these issues and provide a method of enforcing setup rules, managing shared resources, diagnosing and repairing problems, and easing customization. The Windows Installer is a service that resides on client workstations and is installed automatically during Windows 2000 setup. To leverage the advantages of the Windows Installer Service, an application needs to be described in a standard way. The Windows Installer Service is comprised of an installation service, a component management format, and a management API for applications and tools.

Installation Service

Windows 2000 includes the Windows Installer Service as a standard operating system component that runs under the local system account. Using the local system account ensures that applications can be installed regardless of who is currently logged on. When presented with an application described in the standard Windows Installer format, the service installs the application—negating the need for a separate installation program for each application. The Windows Installer Service is saddled with the responsibility of enforcing the installation process rules.

Component Management Format

The Windows Installer Service divides applications into components, features, and products. A Windows Installer component is a set of installable resources such as files or registry keys that are installed together. Components are visible only to the developer and not the user. The smallest entity that the Windows Installer Service can manipulate is a component. Files and registry settings are installed by installing components, and as a result, interdependent resources can be grouped together in a component to ensure that they are always installed and uninstalled together. Applications can be easily uninstalled because information is maintained at the component level, which ensures no installable resources are left behind after application removal.

NOTE

An installable resource can only be in one Windows Installer component. Two components cannot contain the same registry keys or files, whether they are part of the same product or not. Components are unique and will be identical, regardless of what application they are shipped with. Each component has a Globally Unique Identifier (GUID) called the component code.

A feature is a part of the application that is available for installation. During a custom installation, the user-definable options are often comparable to features. A feature can be viewed as a way of selecting a group of components for installation. Windows Installer features provide a much more flexible set of installation types, and can be set to be:

- **Installed on Local Hard Disk** All the relevant components are installed on to the local machine.

- **Installed to Run From Source** The application files are fetched from a source location, such as a CD.

- **Advertised** The application is not installed but appears to be available. The first time the user attempts to invoke the application, the relevant installable resources are installed.

- **Not Installed** No files are copied.

A product is comprised of one or more features described by a single package file. The package file, which has the extension MSI, describes the relationship between features, components, and resources, as shown in Figure 5.6. Packages have a database format optimized for installation performance. A Windows Installer product usually represents a full product, such as the Balancing Act accounting software for the XYZ Company.

When the package file is executed, the Windows Installer interrogates it to determine what installation actions must be completed. A package file can contain the application files internally using cabinet files (.CAB files), or the application files could be placed in the same directory as the package file itself.

An example of an application that uses the MSI format is Office 2000. Word, Excel, Access, and PowerPoint are features, while Office 2000 is the product.

Figure 5.6 Windows Installer component format.

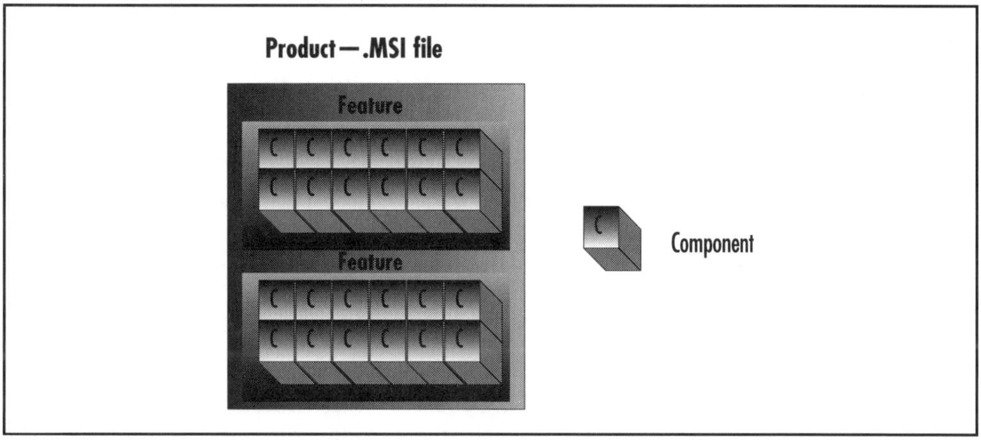

Management API

The management API allows applications to programmatically detail what products, features, and components are installed on a computer, to install and configure products and features, and to establish the path to Windows Installer components. The API manages file paths for the application so that the Windows Installer application can query the Windows Installer service for a path to a component. This eliminates the need for hard-coded paths. Applications that use the management API are enabled to:

- **Support roaming users** Paths are not hard coded and the management API allows for the installation and configuration of the application.

- **Provide on-demand install at the feature level** If a user requested a feature not currently installed and the application has been designed to use the management API, the Windows Installer Service would install the necessary feature without intervention. When a feature is available, but has not been installed, it is said to have been advertised. Since the technology required to invoke the management API is part of the application, feature-level demand installs work on Windows 9x and Windows NT.

- **Provide on-demand install at the product level** Products can be advertised in a similar way to features, except it is the operating system, not the application, that uses the abilities of the management API. Advertising a product creates an entry point on the client to install the product. This can be in the form of a shortcut, a file extension association, or OLE registration. When these entry points are activated, it is the operating system that calls the Windows Installer Service to install the product. Since the operating system must be designed to call the Windows Installer management API, product-level on-demand installs only work on Windows 2000. After installation has been completed, the Windows Installer service launches the application.

- **Runtime resource resiliency** Applications designed to use the management API can be enabled to repair themselves. The Windows Installer Service performs two checks when resolving a path requested by an application. First, it determines if the feature or component has already been installed, and then it verifies that the components are installed correctly. If the Windows Installer Service determines that a component is missing or corrupt, it performs an on-demand repair in a similar fashion as an on-demand install.

Additional Features

- Windows Installer provides a transacted rollback facility. During an install, the Windows Installer records an undo operation for every action it performs, and saves replaced or deleted files and registry settings in a temporary location. If at any time the installation fails, the machine can be reverted to its original state.

- Windows Installer can interrogate multiple sources for the installation files if required for an operation such as an on-demand install.

- Windows Installer includes functionality to upgrade and patch applications. Support is included to determine if an application should be upgraded by using Upgrade Codes. Applications can also be patched using the Windows Installer.

- Transforms can modify the Windows Installer package when it is executed and provide a way to dynamically influence the installation process.

- Windows Installer can run under the Local System Account, which has elevated privileges, or the user account. This caters to environments that do not provide the users with high privileges on their local workstations.

Creating a Package

The Windows Installer Service provides a means of installing packages, but does not include a tool to package applications into the format it uses to describe the installation process. To create a package that takes full advantage of the Windows Installer Service, component management format, and management API, a third-party authoring tool from vendors such as InstallShield and WinINSTALL should be purchased.

Repackaging

Though Microsoft has not bundled an authoring tool for Windows Installer packages, it has bundled a copy of the repackaging tool WinINSTALL LE on the Windows 2000 Server CD. Repackaging tools record the changes that an application makes to the computer during its installation process. A snapshot, which is a description of the computer's configuration, is taken before the application is installed (before snapshot) and after the application is installed (after snapshot). The two snapshots are compared, and the differences are then packaged into a set of files and a Windows Installer description (.MSI file) of the steps to follow to install the files. Repackaged applications provide many of the same benefits as applications that have been packaged using third-party authoring tools, and can be published, assigned, and repaired. However, since applications that are repackaged were not initially designed to leverage Windows Installer, they are viewed as a single feature, and do not therefore support feature-level install on demand. WinINSTALL LE is located on the Windows 2000 Server CD in the VALUEADD\3RDPARTY\ MGMT\WINSTLE directory.

ZAP Files

An alternative to using authoring or repackaging tools is to use ZAP files. These files allow an administrator to publish the setup program that is bundled with the application itself. Since the original setup program from the application itself is being published, the application can only be installed with the options available to the original setup program. So, if the setup program has no silent option, the user will have to go through whatever setup screens are presented. Many of the benefits of using the Windows Installer are not available when using ZAP files. Applications using the ZAP file format can only be published. These applications are still available for installation and uninstallation from Add/Remove Programs, but cannot be installed using elevated privileges. Additional benefits of using Windows Installer files (.MSI), such as the rollback and repair features, are not available when using ZAP files.

A ZAP file is a clear-text file similar in format to an INI file. To create a ZAP file, you should know what the commands are to install the program, what the application properties are, and what entry points the application should automatically install. An example of a possible ZAP file used to distribute Balancing Act within the XYZ Company could be:

```
; ZAP File for Balancing Act accounting software from the XYZ Company

[Application]

; The first two lines, FriendlyName and SetupCommand, are the only required
entries

; FriendlyName is the name that is used by Add/Remove Programs and the
software

; installation Group Policy snap-in

FriendlyName = "Balancing Act"

; SetupCommand is used to launch the application installation

SetupCommand = "setup.exe /q"

; DisplayVersion is the version that is used by Add/Remove Programs and the

; software installation Group Policy snap-in

DisplayVersion = 3.2

Publisher = XYZ Company

URL = http://www.xyzcompany.com/support

[ext]

;File extensions that cause the application to install

ACC=
```

Customizing a Package

It is often the case that different groups of users require the same application customized for their environment. Transforms allow you to modify a Windows Installer package to create custom installations. The transform file (.MST file) is applied to the package file (.MSI file), resulting in a customized version of the application.

A commonly encountered scenario is that departments need different features of a particular product. For example, the accounts department requires Microsoft Word and Microsoft Excel (both features of the product Microsoft Office 2000), while the marketing department only requires Microsoft Word. Microsoft Office 2000 is supplied with a utility (Office 2000 Customization wizard) that allows you to generate transforms for the generic package file that is shipped with the CD. The generic package file is then transformed for each department without having to have two full installation sets.

Creating Distribution Points

Once the software has been packaged appropriately, it needs to be made available on the network. This usually implies copying all the relevant files to a suitably named directory on a network share called the distribution share, or distribution point. The files could include application files, MSI files, MST files (transforms), and ZAP files. Rights need to be set on the shared directory to allow the appropriate groups access.

Allowing Everyone Read access ensures that issues regarding access to files are negated. The obvious downside to this is that users can navigate directly to the share and install applications. Administrators, or an equivalent group, could be given Full Control or Modify rights to administer the distribution point. In large organizations, the distribution share can become a warren of files and directories. Since Windows 2000 does not supply any dedicated tools to facilitate the creation and management of distribution points, maintaining the distribution points on the corporate network can become problematic. Decide on a directory structure that provides a certain level of organization. Examples of organization schemes for the distribution share include creating departmental folders and adding applications to the appropriate departmental directory, or organizing applications along functional lines. It is imperative to maintain tight change and access controls on the distribution point. Distributed File System (DFS) can be used to increase availability of the distribution point.

Targeting Software and Using the Software MMC Snap-In

Software deployment is a feature of IntelliMirror configured using Group Policy and Active Directory. The introductory topics on Group Policy tackled at the beginning of this chapter provide us with an understanding of how Group Policies work and how Group Policy Objects are associated with SDOUs. Software can be assigned or published to groups of computers or users by creating GPOs with the relevant packaged applications configured in the Software settings section, and linking these GPOs to Active Directory containers. The applications are then deployed to groups of users or computers according to the inheritance rules of Group Policy in the Active Directory. The Microsoft Management Console (MMC) is the common host for most administrative functions within Windows 2000, and is used when creating or modifying GPOs.

Using the Group Policy MMC Snap-In

Group Policies can be accessed in two ways, both of which involve using the Microsoft Management Console. The first method uses the stand-alone Group Policy snap-in to launch a Microsoft Management Console with the focus on a particular Group Policy Object. The second method uses the Group Policy snap-in from within the Active Directory Users and Computers snap-in, or the Active Directory Site and Services snap-in.

Using either of these allows administrators to browse to containers to which they wish to link GPOs. Launch the Active Directory Users and Computers snap-in and right-click on the container you wish to associate a Group Policy with (or to edit an existing Group Policy Object). Click on Properties toward the bottom of the pop-up list. Approximately five tabs will be displayed in the Properties window. Clicking on the far right tab, Group Policy, provides a window that displays any GPOs associated with this particular container, as shown in Figure 5.7.

Six buttons on the left side of the window detail management actions for the GPOs. If there is more than one GPO associated with a container, Up and Down are activated, allowing the administrator to specify the order of priority of the GPOs for that container.

GPOs are processed from the bottom up as they are displayed on the Group Policy tab, with the topmost GPO overriding settings in

Figure 5.7 Group Policy tab in the Properties window.

the lower GPOs. In Figure 5.7, the Default Domain Policy would be applied first, followed by Corporate Settings.

The management buttons allow you to:

- Create a new GPO by clicking NEW
- Associate an existing GPO with this container by clicking ADD
- Edit the currently selected GPO by clicking EDIT
- Enforce a policy (GPO settings cannot be overridden) or disable a policy by clicking OPTIONS
- Delete a GPO, or delete its link to the current container by clicking DELETE
- View summary information, disable computer or user settings, find what containers are associated with this GPO, and set additional filtering security by clicking PROPERTIES

Double clicking on the Group Policy Object, or selecting the Group Policy Object and clicking EDIT launches the Group Policy console. The tree pane in the Group Policy management console contains two main components, Computer Configuration and User Configuration, each with child nodes containing particular configuration policy settings. The Default Domain Policy for the XYZ Company is displayed in Figure 5.8.

Figure 5.8 Default Domain Policy.

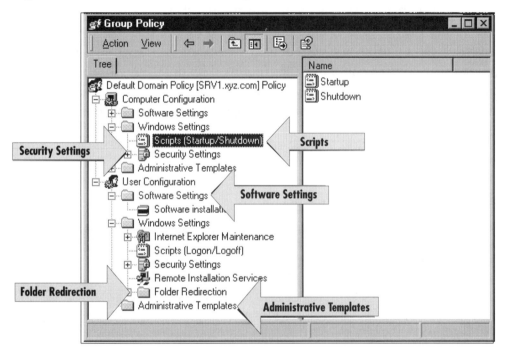

Specific settings can be configured by double-clicking the subtrees and the appropriate settings. Some policy settings also provide helpful explanations on the exact function or consequences of applying a policy setting in the Explain tab.

Using the Software Policy MMC Snap-In

The software settings subtree in the Computer Configuration and User Configuration nodes is actually an extension to the Group

Policy snap-in. This means that an MMC console can be configured with only the software settings visible for a particular Group Policy Object, as shown in Figure 5.9.

TIP

The Microsoft Management Console provides features aimed at easing the job of the administrator. The Favorites tab can be used to store frequently accessed or modified policy settings, or frequently modified GPOs. Fast access can be gained simply by adding frequently used GPOs to Favorites and saving the console. The next time the console is opened, the list of Favorites can be used to navigate to the relevant object you wish to modify. The console can be further modified by detailing what extensions should be displayed in the snap-in. For example, an administrator could create a specific console that only displays the Software Settings node of specific GPOs.

Figure 5.9 Software Settings snap-in.

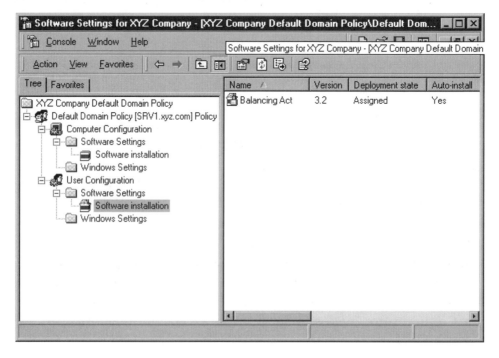

Follow these steps to create a custom console with only the software settings node visible:

1. Launch the Microsoft Management Console by running MMC.EXE.

2. Click on the Console menu item and select Add/Remove snap-in. CTRL-M can be used as a shortcut to this window.

3. Click on ADD.

4. Select the Group Policy snap-in and click ADD.

5. The snap-in then requires that you focus on a particular Group Policy Object. By clicking BROWSE you can select the required Group Policy Object. Click FINISH and then CLOSE after the focus has been set.

6. Select the Extensions tab. This page provides a list of all the available extensions for Group Policy. Deselect the Add all extensions check box. Deselect all available extensions except Software Installation (Computers) and Software Installation (Users).

7. The Console Root can be renamed to provide a more detailed description of the GPO whose software settings you are modifying.

8. Click CONSOLE and select SAVE AS to save the console to the Administration tools folder.

Using Group Policy to Assign or Publish an Application

Both the Computer Configuration and User Configuration nodes have software settings folders. This folder branches into software installation. Before deploying an application, decide whether you wish to assign or publish the application to a computer or to a user. To assign or publish an application to a user or computer, right-click on Software Installation in the tree pane of the relevant computer or user configuration node. Select NEW and then select PACKAGE. The common open dialog box allows you to navigate to the distribution point that contains the .MSI file for the application you wish to deploy. If you are publishing an application to a user, you can also open ZAP files. It is important that you navigate to the .MSI or .ZAP file using a network path, even if the files are local to the computer you are working on. This ensures that clients on the network have the correct path to the installation files.

The next window, Deploy Software, as shown in Figure 5.10, provides three deployment options, Published, Assigned, and "Advanced published or assigned."

Figure 5.10 Software deployment methods.

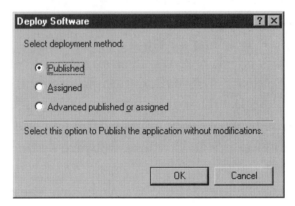

Selecting Published or Assigned will publish or assign the application you have provided without additional configuration information. After selecting either of these two options, the Group Policy window will reappear, displaying the entry for the newly assigned or published application.

Selecting "Advanced published or assigned" allows you to configure additional properties for deployment. The application properties sheet includes six tabs. The General tab displays the Name of the application and product and support information. The Deployment tab, shown in Figure 5.11, provides the options to change:

- Deployment type from Published or Assigned.

- If the application automatically installs using document associations.

- If the application uninstalls when the GPO no longer applies.

- Whether to display the application in Add/Remove Programs.

- The installation interface options. Developers can choose to provide a basic interface that provides predetermined options, or a maximum interface that requires user interaction to customize the installation.

Figure 5.11 Advanced Published or Assigned Deployment options.

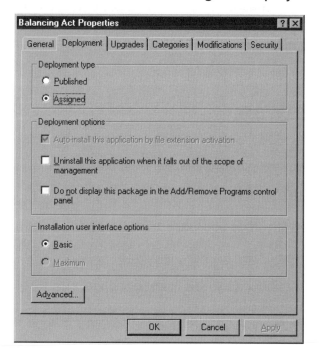

Managing Software

So far, we have suggested that applications should be packaged in the Windows Installer format to leverage all the benefits of the new installation architecture. If applications cannot be packaged into a

.MSI file, a ZAP file can be used (taking note of inherent limitations such as the inability to roll back or assign ZAP files). Once the software has been packaged, it needs to be made available for distribution. The location of the package and related files is called the distribution point or distribution share. GPOs containing Group Policy settings detail what applications to install, and if they are to be assigned or published. The GPOs are then linked to Sites, Domains, or Organizational Units. Linking GPOs to SDOUs allows the administrator to effectively target the deployment of applications by using GPO inheritance.

We now understand the framework for deploying software, but what about maintaining and managing the software once it has been deployed? What happens when an application is upgraded? How is an application removed? Who should be allowed to manage the Group Policy software distribution settings? Managing the software once it has been deployed is as critical as the deployment process itself.

Upgrading Software

Software applications have over the years become business critical, resulting in shorter cycles between new versions of products. Managing the process of upgrading to the latest release has always been problematic. The process of upgrading existing software has been integrated into the software installation and maintenance feature of Group Policy. To upgrade an existing application, a .MSI file needs to be created for the updated version of the application. Group Policy then needs to be instructed what to do during the upgrade process. Should it remove the previous version, or install directly over it? Upgrades can also be classified as:

- **Required** Upgrades are automatically installed.
- **Optional** The upgrade process allows the user to choose whether to upgrade or not.

To upgrade an existing application, create a new package and select the Advanced Published or Assigned deployment option (Figure 5.10). The properties for the application are displayed with six tabs. Select the Upgrades tab. The tab is divided into two, with the top half indicating what package this package upgrades. The bottom half of the tab indicates what packages can upgrade the current package. This tab can be used to examine existing packages to determine if they are targeted for upgrade by other packages.

The Required Upgrade for existing packages check box determines whether the package is a required or optional upgrade. If the check box is ticked, it is a required upgrade. Click ADD to progress to the Add Upgrade Package window, as shown in Figure 5.12.

WARNING

Software upgrades should always be piloted first to provide enough time to evaluate the changes that the new version provides.

Figure 5.12 Add Upgrade Package.

The Add Upgrade Package window provides the ability to choose a package that the current package will upgrade. The package can upgrade a package from the current GPO, or the administrator can browse for a specific GPO. Highlight the packages that are to be upgraded in the "Package to upgrade" box and select whether the existing package should be uninstalled first, or if the package should upgrade over the existing package. Click OK and return to the Upgrades tab. The packages you selected in the "Package to upgrade" box should now appear under "Packages that this package will upgrade." Under Software Installation in Group Policy, the packages' icon should now include a small upward-pointing arrow.

Upgrading Windows 2000

The option to upgrade software using Group Policy is extremely versatile. Earlier in the chapter, Windows 2000 was described as just a very large and very complex piece of software. So it follows that since Windows 2000 is just a piece of software, it, too, can be upgraded to later releases (including Service Pack releases) using Group Policy. Obviously, Group Policy cannot be used to upgrade a non-Windows 2000 computer, since Group Policy requires that the client already be a Windows 2000 computer.

Microsoft ships Windows 2000 with a Winnt32.MSI file in the \i386 directory of the Windows 2000 CD. This can be used to prepare an upgrade package that can be Assigned or Published. If the Windows 2000 upgrade were assigned to a user, every machine the user logs on to would receive the upgrade. A more sensible option is to assign the upgrade to computers or publish it to users.

Removing Software

Two options exist for removing software:

- **Forced removal** The next time the Group Policy is applied, the package is removed.

■ **Optional removal** The software can be uninstalled when desired, but no new installations are allowed.

Right-clicking on the package that you wish to remove, selecting All Tasks and then Remove, displays the Remove Software window shown in Figure 5.13. The option to immediately uninstall the software can be considered to be forced removal, while the second option to allow users to continue using the software is optional removal.

Figure 5.13 Removing software.

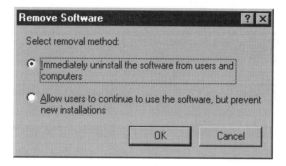

Redeploying Software

Most software will require a patch or an update to fix problems or to provide additional functionality during its lifetime. Group Policy allows for the distribution of patches and updates by providing a redeployment option.

Redeploying applications involves copying the patched or up-dated version of the package to the distribution point, opening the original GPO, and right-clicking on the patched application and selecting All Tasks and then Redeploy Application. A warning dialog box then informs you that the application will be reinstalled every-where. Applications are redeployed the next time the GPO is applied. This means that applications assigned or published to a user will be redeployed at the next logon, while applications assigned to computers will be redeployed at the next reboot.

For IT Professionals

SMS and Software Deployment Using Group Policies

On the surface, there seems to be a great deal of overlap between SMS and the change and configuration management features of Windows 2000, but they are in fact very distinct. However, parallels can be drawn between them when considering operating system upgrades and software deployment. While Windows 2000 can use Remote Installation Services to install Windows 2000 on a new computer, SMS can only upgrade clients with existing operating systems. Software deployment with SMS relies on agent software resident on the client, but there are similarities and differences, including:

- IntelliMirror is a technology set aimed squarely at Windows 2000, while SMS works across a number of clients.

- SMS provides good support for remote sites and is a mature product suitable for large organizations.

- SMS provides hardware and software inventory, network diagnostic tools, software metering, and remote control functionality.

- SMS also provides a greater degree of help when distributing applications to distribution servers.

- SMS groups clients into collections based on inventory details, and allows a more flexible approach to targeting clients.

- SMS can compress applications between sites and thus maximize the usage of scarce slow-link resources.

- SMS does not require the hard coding of distribution points. SMS will know which server is the closest.

Continued

> SMS provides a great deal of functionality not found in the Windows 2000 change and configuration management technologies. IntelliMirror technologies compliment the features found in SMS, and at times provide features that are not necessarily included with SMS.

Software Installation Options

Additional software installation options are available on a per-Group-Policy-Object basis and facilitate the management of deployed applications. Most of these settings can be unique to each GPO, allowing for a great deal of flexibility. The software installation options include:

- **General deployment options** The default package location can be specified. Whenever a new package is created for a GPO, it uses this location as the default. This location is the distribution point.
  - When adding a new package, the default deployment method can be specified.
  - The default installation user-interface level. When a Windows Installer package is added, this setting determines the default interface option.
  - Removing the application when the GPO no longer applies to that user or computer.
- **File extensions** Lists the file extensions, which application should be invoked, and the precedence of these applications per GPO.
- **Categories** Allows you to add categories for installed applications. Categories are not local to the GPO, but are established for each Domain. This provides a method of organizing applications by function or department, making it easier to navigate to relevant applications in Add/Remove Programs. As shown earlier in Figure 5.4, the Balancing Act

accounting package is displayed in the Accounts category. Applications, which can be in more than one category, will only be displayed if they have been published to a particular user.

The software installation options can be modified by right-clicking on the software installation node, then selecting Properties. Three tabs labeled General, File Extensions, and Categories, provide the software installation options (Figure 5.14).

Figure 5.14 Software installation options.

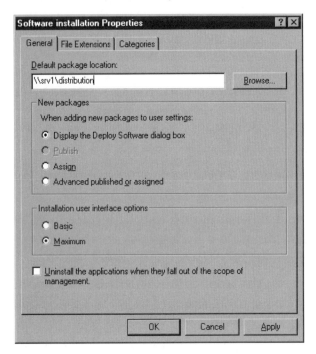

Group Policy Settings

The deployment and management of applications can be further refined and controlled using Group Policy settings. Group Policy settings of particular interest for software deployment and management are divided into those that affect Group Policy itself (see Table 5.3) and those that affect Windows Installer (see Table 5.4).

Table 5.3 Group Policy Settings

Computer Configuration\ Administrative Templates\ System\Group Policy	User Configuration\ Administrative Templates\ System\Group Policy
■ **User Group Policy loopback processing mode.** Forces the application of the GPO for the computer to users who log on to the computer affected by this policy. ■ **Group Policy slow-link detection.** Determines the threshold for links to be classified as slow links. Software is not deployed over slow links by default. ■ **Software Installation policy processing.** This allows you to specify if software installation policies should be processed even across slow links. Also allows you to process the GPO, even if it has not changed.	**Group Policy slow-link detection.** Determines the threshold for links to be classified as slow links. Software is not deployed over slow links.

Using the loopback processing mode is particularly useful for computers that have a special function, such as those in public places. Loopback processing has a replace mode and a merge mode. The replace mode forces the application of the user policies of the computer's GPO on any user who logs on to that particular machine. Merge mode combines the user policies of the computer's GPO and the user policies associated with the user.

Group Policy can restrict the use of snap-ins by setting the User Configuration\Administrative Templates\Windows Components\ Microsoft Management Console\Restrict Users to the explicitly permitted list of snap ins. This Group Policy could be used to restrict Group Policy snap-ins to just the Software Settings snap-in for either the user or computer configuration node.

Another useful Group Policy setting is Computer Configuration\ Administrative Templates\System\Verbose versus normal status messages. Using verbose messages will echo certain actions to the user when starting up or during logon (such as the installation or removal of packages).

Windows Installer also has several options that are configurable by Group Policy that help with the maintenance and management of applications (as in Table 5.4). Logging off Windows Installer events is particularly useful in helping to troubleshoot installation problems. An important feature of the Group Policy settings in the Administrative Templates folders is that a detailed explanation is included on the Explain tab of all the settings.

Table 5.4 Windows Installer Group Policy Settings

Computer Configuration\ Administrative Templates\ Windows Components\Windows Installer	User Configuration\ Administrative Templates\ Windows Components\Windows Installer

■ Always install with elevated privileges
  ■ Disable rollback
  ■ Disable browse dialog box for new source.
  ■ Disable patching
  ■ Disable IE Security prompt for Windows Installer scripts
  ■ Enable user control over installs
  ■ Enable user to browse for source while elevated
  ■ Enable user to use media while elevated
  ■ Enable user to patch elevated products
  ■ Allow admin to install from Terminal Services session
  ■ Cache transforms in secure location on workstation
■ Logging
	■ Always install with elevated privileges
	  ■ Search order
	  ■ Disable rollback
	■ Disable media source for any install

Delegating Control of Group Policy

As is the case with many tasks associated with the Active Directory, Group Policy management (and as a consequence, software deployment) can be delegated. Tasks that can be delegated include:

- Managing Group Policy links
- Creating GPOs
- Editing GPOs

To delegate the management of Group Policy links, right-click on the container for which you wish to delegate authority, and select Delegate Control. The Delegation of Control wizard then guides you through the process of determining which users or groups require delegated authority. The next window provides a list of tasks to delegate with an option to Manage Group Policy links (Figure 5.15) toward the bottom of the list. Select this task and proceed to the next screen, which provides a summary of who is receiving the delegated authority. Click FINISH, and the users or groups you selected previously now have the authority to manage GPOs linked to the specific container. The user, or group of users, can now add, delete, or reorder GPOs linked to the specified container to which the user has delegated authority.

NOTE

Using the Delegation of Control wizard to allow users to manage linked Group Policies does not allow the user to edit or create new Group Policy Objects. Delegating the managed linked Group Policies grants the user read-and-write access to the gPLink and gPOptions properties of the container.

Figure 5.15 Delegating the management of Group Policy.

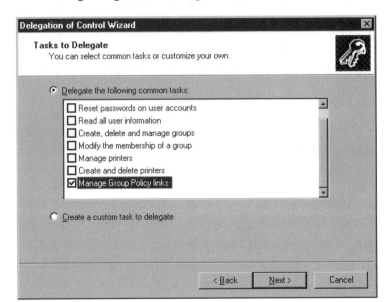

To delegate the creation of GPOs, a user must be added to the Group Policy Creator Owners security group. This security group will allow users to create new GPOs, but edit only the ones created by that particular user or delegated to that user. Another restriction is that members of the Group Policy Creator Owner security group cannot link GPOs to a container.

A user can edit a GPO if he or she is granted all permissions on the GPO except Apply Group Policy. Providing the user with the ability to edit a GPO does not provide the ability to link the GPO with a container.

Application Deployment Walkthrough

In previous sections we covered a great deal of ground on IntelliMirror, Group Policy, Software Deployment, Software Management, and the Windows Installer. The following list summarizes what we currently know about software deployment.

- Deploying software can be considered part of change and configuration management.

- Change and configuration management is addressed by IntelliMirror and Remote Operating System Installation.

- One of the features of IntelliMirror is Software Installation and Maintenance.

- To prepare applications for deployment, Windows Installer files (.MSI) and ZAP files (.ZAP) can be used. The Windows Installer format (.MSI files) is the preferred format for distributing applications. WinINSTALL LE can be used to repackage applications.

- Once applications are prepared, they need to be made available for distribution. Associated files and installation information is stored on a distribution share located on a distribution server.

- Group Policy is used by the Software Installation and Maintenance feature to deploy software.

- GPOs are linked to containers within the Active Directory to target the deployment of applications.

- Applications can be assigned or published.

- While Group Policy with Active Directory delivers the application to the right user or computer, the Windows Installer Service installs the application itself.

Let us assume that the Balancing Act accounting package needs to be published to all staff in the accounts department. An Organizational Unit called Accounts is a child of the XYZ.COM domain. The process to deploy and effectively manage the application using Group Policy could be as follows:

1. After investigating development costs associated with designing a version of Balancing Act for Windows Installer, the XYZ Company decided to save and repackage the application using WinINSTALL LE. ZAP files were not

considered because of their lack of functionality when compared with the Windows Installer format.

2. WinINSTALL LE generated a Balancing Act.MSI file and associated installation files. These files were placed in a directory called Balancing Act on the distribution share (\\srv1\distribution).

3. The accounts department of the XYZ Company has only just been migrated to Windows 2000 and as a result, certain configuration options need to be set. Launch the Active Directory Users and Computers snap-in, right-click on the Accounts Organizational Unit, and select Properties. In the Accounts Properties windows, select the Group Policy tab and click NEW. Enter the name Accounts for the Group Policy Object, and then click EDIT. Expand the Software Settings folder in the Computer Configuration node and right-click on Software Installation. Select Properties, then:

   ■ Set the default package location to \\srv1\distribution. This is done at the Default Package Location prompt. This should also be done for the Software Installation node in User Configuration.

   ■ Categories for published applications need to be established. This is done by selecting the Categories tab and adding categories suitable to the entire Domain (the category need only be added at one node). A category called Accounts is added. Click OK to return to the Group Policy snap-in.

4. Select Software Installation in the Software Settings folder of the User Configuration node. Right click Software installation, and click NEW, then select PACKAGE. The default open dialog box is then displayed, pointing at the default package location. Navigate to the Balancing Act directory and select the Balancing Act.MSI file. The Deploy Software window then provides you with deployment methods. Select Advanced Published or Assigned, and click OK.

5. In the Balancing Act Properties window, check that the Name, Product Information, and Support Information are all correct. Click on the Deployment tab and ensure that the deployment type is set to Published. Check the "Auto-install this application by file extension" activation box and the "Uninstall this application when it falls out of the scope of management" box. This ensures that if the user leaves the accounts department, then the package will no longer be available to him or her. Check that the Installation user-interface option is set to Basic.

6. Click the Categories tab, Select the Accounts category, and click SELECT.

7. Click OK to complete the configuration.

8. Users in the accounts department can now install the application by launching Add/Remove Programs and selecting the Accounts category in the Add New Programs section.

Planning for Software Deployment

An often overlooked aspect of software deployment is planning. A great deal of effort should be invested in determining the requirements for effective software distribution within the organization. Just some of the areas that require consideration include the Active Directory design, network bandwidth and network usage patterns, deployment methods, and contingency planning.

Application Deployment Performance

Before deploying applications, take the time to review your infrastructure to understand the constraints on performance. Application deployment can be optimized by:

- **Making a member server, not a domain controller, the distribution server** Additional consideration could be given to the configuration of the server (such as RAID levels and memory) to further increase performance.

- **Implementing Distributed File System**. DFS can provide load-balancing features for distribution servers.

- **Not installing or advertising software over links that do not provide acceptable performance** Consideration should be given to putting distribution servers at sites with slow links.

- **Educting users on the process of installing published applications** Since users conduct installations at different times, it may be easier to educate users on the process of installing published applications than increasing infrastructure capacity and assigning software.

Active Directory and Group Policy Design

The design of the Active Directory within an organization impacts many areas of functionality within Windows 2000, including software deployment. What should be considered while designing the Active Directory for your organization is how this will affect software deployment, and are there possible ways of modifying the design to optimize application deployment. Software should be deployed as high in the Active Directory tree as possible, though the depth of the Active Directory structure does affect Group Policy design. If the directory is deep, then it is easier to deploy software to tightly targeted groups, but inheritance rules become more of an issue. If the directory structure is shallow, filtering may have to be used to achieve a degree of granularity, but inheritance rules are not as likely to cause confusion.

When designing a Group Policy infrastructure (which is the foundation for application deployment), there are several variables that can affect your design. It is important to consider the effect of Group Policies while doing the initial brainstorming for your Active Directory structure. A recommended option is to create

Organizational Units for computers along functional lines. For example, create an individual Organizational Unit for member servers, domain controllers, and normal workstations. Group Policy administration can then be simplified by linking a GPO to each of the Organizational Units.

The number of GPOs associated with computers and users has a direct impact on performance and administration. The greater the number of GPOs linked to a container, the longer the download time will be. It also adds complexity to any Group Policy troubleshooting. Other factors that influence the design include at what speed subnets are connected, and what is the preferred administration model (i.e., is administration delegated).

Fewer GPOs with larger numbers of applications per GPO shorten the logon time, decrease the number of GPOs to manage, but make achieving the desired granularity an issue. A larger number of GPOs allows applications to be targeted more accurately without filtering, but increases the logon time and the number of GPOs to manage.

Deployment Methods

The differences between assigning and publishing packages are detailed in Table 5.5. These differences provide a means of determining if software should be assigned or published to users or computers.

Summary

Microsoft has developed a cohesive strategy for addressing change and configuration management issues. IntelliMirror and Remote Operating System installation are technology sets designed to address change and configuration management. One of the features of IntelliMirror is software installation and maintenance, which leverages technologies such as Group Policy, Active Directory, and the Windows Installer. Group Policy is used to satisfy software deployment requirements within a Windows 2000 environment.

Table 5.5 Software Deployment Methods

Application Deployment Method	Description	Examples
Assigning Applications to Computers	Applications are assigned to a computer when everyone who uses a particular computer will require a specific application. Applications are available after next reboot. Generally, all applications that are bound to the specific location of computers should be assigned to computers.	Information kiosks that require an inhouse developed guide to the company. Call Centers that require the call center incident-logging application.
Assigning Applications to Users	Applications are assigned to a user when a user requires the application. This often can be used with job/functional specific applications. Applications are available at next logon. Generally, all applications that are mandatory should be assigned to users.	Project Managers that require project management software for time and resource planning.
Publishing Applications to Users	Applications are published to users when a user may require an application. This provides the user with the option of installing an application. Can use ZAP file format. Applications are available at next logon.	Support Engineers that may need certain diagnostic tools to help facilitate troubleshooting.

Group Policies enable the administrator to define the state of the user's computing environment and uses the network to enforce that definition according to the required scope. A Group Policy has a computer configuration and user configuration namespace. Group Policy Objects (GPOs) are virtual containers for Group Policy settings. GPOs can be linked to Sites, Domains, and Organizational Units (SDOUs). Multiple GPOs can be linked to a single SDOU. The application of GPOs follows a strict inheritance order: site GPOs first, then Domain GPOs, then Organizational Unit GPOs. The inheritance order can be modified by using Block Policy Inheritance and Enforce Policy. The application of GPOs can also be modified by using Discretionary Access Control Lists (DACLs) as filters.

Deploying software can be broken down into preparing packages, distributing packages, targeting clients, and installing the package on the designated clients. Software is packaged for distribution by either using a third-party authoring tool or the WinINSTALL LE repackaging tool located on the Windows 2000 Server CD. These tools create a Windows Installer package. Windows Installer is a resident installation service that is installed by default with Windows 2000. It enables applications to roll back, self-repair, and install on demand. ZAP files, which are similar in format to INI files, can also be used to describe how an application should be installed. It is important to note that ZAP files have considerably less functionality than programs described by the Windows Installer format. Once applications have been packaged, they are placed on distribution servers that are available to network clients.

Groups of computers and users are targeted for software deployment by the linking of GPOs to SDOUs and filtering. Software is then assigned or published to users and computers. Software that is assigned to a computer is installed when the computer is rebooted, and is always present on the machine, while software that is assigned to the user installs an entry point at user logon. This entry point is then used to install the application when it is first run. Published applications are visible in Add/Remove Programs and can be installed at the user's discretion. The Group Policy console used to manage software deployment can be customized to include specific GPOs, and only to display settings relevant to software deployment.

Group Policy provides for software management by allowing applications to be removed, redeployed, patched, and upgraded. Applications can be optionally upgraded, or the upgrade can be forced. Removals can also be forced or optional. Group Policy can even be used to upgrade Windows 2000 to a later version. Categories can be used to organize applications into departmental or functional groups when published to the user. These categories are visible when the Add/Remove Programs is used to install published applications. Group Policy settings can be used to configure Group Policy itself and the Windows Installer to aid in management and troubleshooting functions. Group Policy administration can be delegated by using the Delegation wizard.

Before commencing with deploying applications using Group Policies, proper planning should be completed. This includes investigating software deployment optimization, Active Directory and Group Policy design considerations, and which deployment methods to use.

FAQs

Q: Can I use Local Group Policies to help with software deployment?

A: No. Local Group Policies do not provide a Software Installation subtree in the Group Policy namespace.

Q: When my users go home, they lock their Windows 2000 workstations. How do I force the application of the Group Policy?

A: Software can only be installed if a machine is restarted or if a user logs on. Ways to solve this problem include using a forced logoff or forcing a reboot.

Q: How does software distribution work in a distributed environment?

A: If subnets are connected by slow links (dial-in, WAN), then Group Policies do not by default apply Software Installation settings, or scripts of folder redirection. The threshold for what constitutes a slow link can be modified in the Group Policy settings. By default, link speeds slower than 500 Kbps are deemed to be a slow links.

Q: How does software deployment with Group Policy support roaming users?

A: To support roaming users, applications can be assigned or published to the roaming users.

Q: How does software deployment with Group Policy support mobile users?

A: Applications targeted for mobile users can be published to the user. This ensures that if the user is targeted for software deployment, but is connected over a slow link, he or she can install the software if required. By default, software is not deployed over slow links. The threshold for what determines a slow link can be configured using Group Policy.

Chapter 6

Managing User and Computer Settings

Solutions in this chapter:

- Group Policy for Users and Computers
- Roaming Profiles
- Folder Redirection and Offline Folders
- Managing Personal Settings
- Configuring User and Computer Policies
- Creating a Roaming Profile
- Setting Up Folder Replication
- Sample Group Policy Setting
- Offline Folders
- Replication Cache Setup

Introduction

Imagine, if you will, the first time your users sit down to work at their PC after it has been upgraded to Windows 2000. Despite looking similar to its predecessors, Windows 95 and Windows 98, your users will notice the differences in the Windows 2000 user interface and begin to explore them. They will look to see what new desktop patterns, fonts, sounds, and themes are available. They will check to see if Solitaire is still there and what other games have been added. They will, in fact, go exploring their new computer, changing features and settings to suit their whims, doing exactly the things that used to give you headaches and heartburn.

This is where Windows 2000 tries to be the best of both worlds. It has the ease of navigation of Windows 95 or 98, while keeping users from being able to delete key system files and crashing the computer. It has the stability and security of Windows NT without the clunky user interface. But both sides of the computer team, users and support staff, will have to make compromises for a full implementation of Windows 2000 to be effective. Users must understand that administrators don't want them editing system configuration files on the fly. Administrators must understand that users don't want to be completely locked down in their workspace, but rather, want to have flexibility. The effective system administrator or support manager will understand how to manage the deployment and migration process to keep both sides happy in the new world of Windows 2000. Fortunately, Microsoft has provided a number of features and tools to help make this goal a reality. One of the most useful features for managing the user environment is Group Policy. An effective Group Policy configuration can successfully manage a myriad of individual user and computer settings. Other tools helpful in maintaining the user environment include roaming user profiles, which allow a user's environment to follow him or her from computer to computer, and offline folders, which allow a user to access files when the network is down or when he or she is away from the office. The remainder of this chapter will focus on these three tools and how they can best be put to use in your environment.

Group Policy for Users and Computers

Group Policy is similar to System Policy under Windows NT in that it is a set of configuration settings that control the work environment for Windows 2000 users. Group Policy is different from System Policy in a couple of key ways. First, Group Policy can affect a broader range of system settings than could System Policy. Second, Group Policy can be applied to one or more Active Directory objects at any layer in the Directory, and the administration of Group Policy for an object is done by the administrator of that object. As a result, Group Policy is more powerful and much more complex than System Policy.

NOTE

Group Policy does not manage settings for Windows NT, Windows 95, or Windows 98 clients. By default, Windows 2000 will not process Windows NT 4.0 System Policies.

What Exactly Is Group Policy?

A Group Policy is a set of configuration information that determines how Active Directory objects perform. A Group Policy administrator can configure Group Policy to govern a user's computer environment, including default desktop and application settings, installation and configuration of applications, and system and file settings. Group Policy settings are contained in a Group Policy Object (GPO), which can be applied to a Site, Domain, or Organizational Unit (SDOU) within Active Directory. Multiple GPOs can be applied to a SDOU, and vice versa. The settings in a GPO apply to the associated SDOU and all objects in the branch beneath the SDOU, unless the GPO is configured to block inheritance of its settings down the tree, or there is another GPO lower in the tree that overrides the parent GPO.

The information contained in a GPO is stored in two locations, Group Policy Containers (GPC) and Group Policy Templates (GPT). The GPC is the Active Directory object that contains the GPO properties. Policies that change infrequently and are relatively small in size are stored in the GPC. For instance, information used by the Software Installation snap-in, data for the applications and other interfaces that control the publishing and assigning of software, are stored here. The GPC has the following properties:

- **Version information** Information that it used to ensure that GPC information is synchronized with GPT information.

- **Status information** Information that indicates the status of the GPO, enabled or disabled.

- **List of components** Information about the policies that have been configured in the GPO.

The Group Policy Template is a file structure located on a domain controller. The files are stored on the system volume (Sysvol) of the controller in the Policies folder. It contains applications available for software installation, security settings, scripts, folder redirection, and Administrative Template policies. The globally unique identifier (GUID) of the associated GPO is also the name of the directory where the GPT files are stored. The GPT directory contains several subfolders, and the contents of some of these folders are described below.

- **adm** Stores the .adm files for the GPT.

- **Scripts** Contains the script files for the GPT.

- **User** Stores the Registry.pol file that contains the registry settings to be applied to the user upon login. These registry settings are stored in the HKEY_CURRENT_USER portion of the registry.

- **User\Applications** Stores the scripts associated with the applications that are advertised to the user by the GPT.

- **Machine** Stores the Registry.pol file that contains the registry settings to be applied to the computer when it joins the domain. These registry settings are stored in the HKEY_LOCAL_MACHINE portion of the registry.

- **Machine\Applications** Stores the scripts associated with the applications that are advertised to the computer by the GPT.

The policy settings for Group Policy are broken down into two logical categories, computer and user. The specifics of each of these categories are detailed later in this chapter, but a general summary of Group Policy types is listed in Table 6.1.

Table 6.1 Types of Group Policies

Type of Group Policy	Description
Application deployment	Governs user access to applications in two ways: application assignment creates a non-removable instance of an application on a client computer, and application publication advertises an application's availability through Add/Remove Programs in Control Panel, so users can choose to install or uninstall the application.
File deployment	Specifies files to be copied into special folders on the client computers, such as placing a link to a New Employee Handbook in a user's My Documents folder.
Scripts	Specific scripts and batch files that are to be run at specific times, or during logon and logoff.
Software	Configures settings in the user profile for default application, Start menu, or desktop settings.
Security	Configures user access to files and folders, password restrictions, and other security-related settings.

Group Policy Inheritance

Since Group Policy can be applied at the Site, Domain, or Organizational Unit level, it is important to understand how objects in the Active Directory inherit Group Policy settings. The order of inheritance for Group Policy is Site, then Domain, then OU. Windows 2000 will apply Group Policy to an object starting with the highest level of policy defined, then traverse down the directory to the level where the object is located, applying any additional policy on the way. Knowing this, a system administrator could set generalized policy settings for all objects at the site level, then allow lower-level object administrators to set more specific settings for their areas. For instance, if an administrator within a particular OU wanted to prevent users within his OU from changing their default screensaver, but the rest of the company did not have this restriction, the administrator would set that policy at the OU level, not at the Domain or Site level. In doing so, the administrator helps to keep policy settings minimized (and simplified!) for the remainder of the company.

The same method applies to conflicting policies. The policy closest to the object (the most recently applied policy) overrides other policy objects when there is a conflict between policies. For example, if a policy is set at the Domain to prevent user accounts from changing their network passwords, but another policy is set at an OU within that domain that specifically allows user accounts to change the network password, any user object within the OU will be allowed to change its password.

In cases where a user policy and computer policy conflict, the user policy setting usually takes precedence, but there are exceptions. For instance, the Disable New Task Creation policy exists for both users and computers. If this policy is disabled for the user, which would allow the user object to create new tasks in the task scheduler, but enabled for the computer, which would prevent users from creating new tasks, the computer setting overrides the user setting. Therefore, any user who logged on to that computer would be unable to create new tasks in the scheduler, even if Group Policy allowed the user to do so on another computer.

Windows 2000 has two additional options that can change the default processing paradigm for policy settings. The Block Policy Inheritance setting prevents any GPO setting in a parent container from being applied. This option would be useful in cases where a subordinate object requires significantly different settings than supplied by a parent container.

The No Override option prevents subordinate containers from overriding policy settings at a higher-level GPO. In the previous example, the OU policy setting would not apply if the Domain policy was set to No Override, meaning that all user objects in the subordinate OU would be prevented from changing their passwords, as are all user objects within that Domain. In cases where a container has the No Override option set, the Block Policy Inheritance option in all subordinate containers has no effect.

Group Policy can also be filtered by security settings. The policies in a GPO are only applied to an object that has Read permissions on the GPO. This approach could be used to apply different policy settings to objects within the same container. Revisiting our previous password example, two policies could be applied to a container, one that prevents user objects from changing network passwords, and another that allows the change. User objects within that container would then belong to one of two groups in the container. One group would have Read access to the GPO that denies a password change and no access to the GPO that allows the change. The other group would have Read access to the GPO that allows the change and no access to the GPO that denies it. In that way, a container could be set up to have different policies applied to subsets of its objects without having to create additional OUs or subordinate containers.

Group Policy Editor

There are two ways to access the Group Policy Editor. One is through Active Directory Users and Computers on a domain controller. When open, click on the Domain or Organizational Unit (OU) desired, then open the Properties for that object (see Figure 6.1).

Figure 6.1 Selecting the GPO for a Domain or OU in Active
Directory Users and Computers.

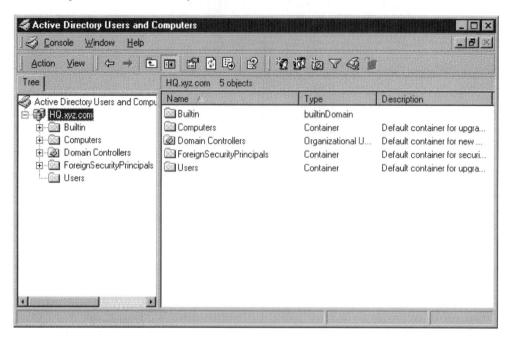

Clicking on the Group Policy tab will show which GPOs are active
for that object (Figure 6.2). To open the editor for a particular GPO,
select the GPO from the list, then click EDIT. This will open the
Group Policy Editor (GPE) for that policy, shown in Figure 6.3. The
Block Policy inheritance check box in Figure 6.2 will, when checked,
prevent any policy settings from a parent container from being
applied at this level.

From the Group Policy tab of the Properties dialog box of the
Site, Domain, or OU object, you can also view the options and properties associated with the GPO.

Clicking OPTIONS will open the Group Policy Options dialog,
shown in Figure 6.4. The No Override: check box, when selected,
will prevent any peer or subordinate GPO from overriding any policy
specified in this GPO. The Disabled: check box, when selected, will
prevent the selected GPO from applying to the current container.

Figure 6.2 The Group Policy tab of a Domain Properties dialog.

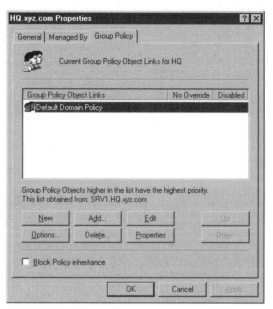

Figure 6.3 Group Policy Editor window for GPO.

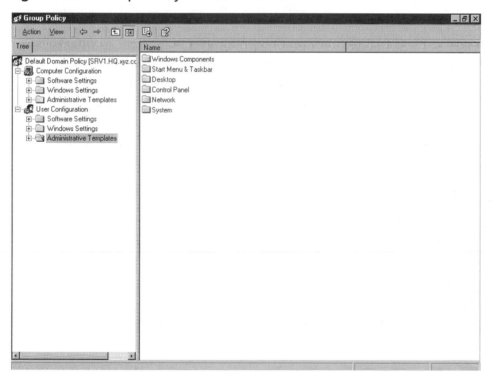

Figure 6.4 Group Policy Options dialog.

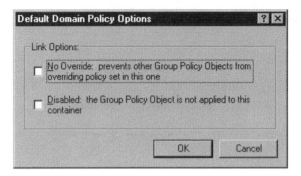

Clicking PROPERTIES in the Group Policy tab of the object Properties dialog box will bring up the Group Policy Properties dialog, shown in Figure 6.5. This dialog presents information about the GPO, and allows the system administrator to disable the Computer or User configuration settings for this object. If the Active Directory object that the GPO is being applied to contains either no user or computer objects, turning off the settings for that type of object will speed up the processing of the GPO for that container. Disabling both sets is effectively the same as removing the GPO from the container, but should only be done in testing or transition, as the objects will still examine the GPO even though no settings are to be applied. To remove the settings of a GPO, always remove the GPO to reduce processing time and avoid confusion. More information about the GPO settings for user and computer objects appears later in this section.

Another method for opening the Group Policy Editor is through the Management Console (MMC) Group Policy snap-in. Using MMC to edit Group Policy can be performed by the Group Policy administrator from any computer on the network that has MMC installed. This tool is accessed by selecting Add/Remove Snap-in inside MMC, clicking ADD in the Standalone tab of the Add/Remove Snap-in dialog box, and selecting Group Policy from the list in the Add Standalone Snap-in dialog (see Figure 6.6). Clicking ADD will open the Select Group Policy Object wizard, and clicking BROWSE will open

Figure 6.5 Group Policy Properties dialog.

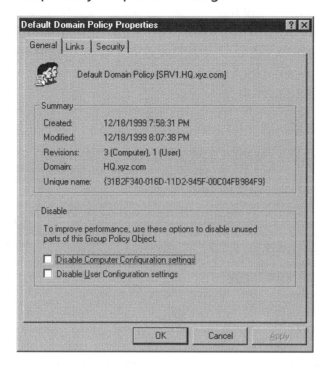

Figure 6.6 Selecting Group Policy from the list of snap-ins.

the Browse for a Group Policy Object dialog. Select the desired GPO (see Figure 6.7) and click OK. Then click Fɪɴɪsʜ in the Select Group Policy Object wizard, click Cʟosᴇ in the Add Standalone Snap-in dialog, and finally click OK in the Add/Remove Snap-in dialog. This will add the Group Policy information to the MMC window, as shown in Figure 6.8.

Figure 6.7 Selecting a Group Policy.

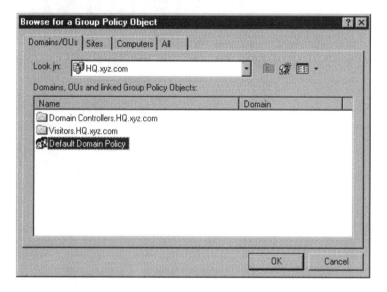

In the Group Policy Editor, it is clear to see that the GPO is divided into two categories: Group Policy settings that apply to computer objects in the container, and settings that apply to user objects in the container. Both of those categories are further divided into three identical subcategories: Software Settings, Windows Settings, and Administrative Templates. The policy settings in the subcontainers differ between user and computer objects. The following sections describe some of the settings for each category and show some of the interface differences between the two Group Policy Editor tools.

Figure 6.8 Group Policy snap-in added to Console window.

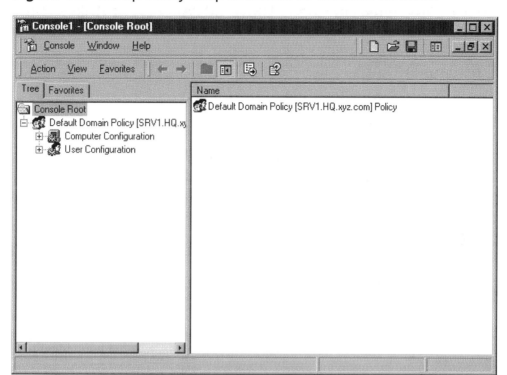

Computer Configuration

Group Policy settings for computer objects in Active Directory are applied when the computer boots and joins the Directory. The settings under Software Settings, Windows Settings, and Administrative Templates generally apply to the way the computer interacts with the Active Directory, or the way in which a user interacts with the local computer. There are some settings, however, that are mirrored from the user policies that govern specific user interface issues, settings that could force interface objects to be presented the same way to any user who logs on to the computer, regardless of his or her own policy information. Any conflicting policies between computer and user settings usually default to the user settings. The computer policy settings are stored under the HKEY_LOCAL_MACHINE key of the registry.

Software Settings

The Software Settings section of the Computer Configuration governs software packages that will be installed or available on computers belonging to the GPO. Information for the Software Settings policies are stored in both the Group Policy Container and Group Policy Object. The Windows Installer package definition is stored in the GPO in Active Directory, and the actual script files are stored in the GPT in the Sysvol folder. Though a thorough description of the complete software maintenance process is beyond the scope of this chapter, the basic process will be outlined here. To add a package for installation, right-click on the Software Installation object under Software Settings, then select New Package. Browse to the location of the installer package, select it, and then click OPEN. For the Computer Configuration settings, you can only select Assign or Advanced Publish and Assign in the Deploy Software dialog. Click OK, and the GPE will inspect the installer package. If you selected Advanced Publish and Assign, the Properties dialog (see Figure 6.9) for the package will be displayed immediately; otherwise, the package will be added to the GPE, as shown in Figure 6.10.

Application packages can only be assigned to computer objects in Group Policy. As shown in Figure 6.9, some deployment options are grayed out, as they do not apply to Computer Configuration. Once the package is configured in the GPO, it will be advertised to all member computers and installed on the computers when it is safe to do so. This usually occurs the next time the computer is restarted. Once the software is installed, it is available to all users on the computer, but no user will be able to remove the software from the computer.

Figure 6.9 Application Package Properties dialog.

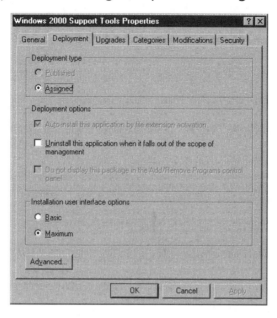

Figure 6.10 Group Policy Editor with software installation package installed in Computer Configuration.

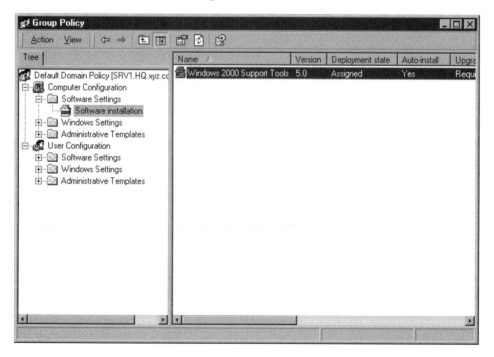

Windows Settings

Figure 6.11 shows the Windows Settings branch of the Computer Configuration Group Policy tree expanded in the MMC. This contains policy settings for scripts and security on the computer. The scripts area governs settings related to scripts that will run at startup, shutdown, or other times on the computer.

Figure 6.11 Expanded view of Computer Configuration, Windows Settings in GPE.

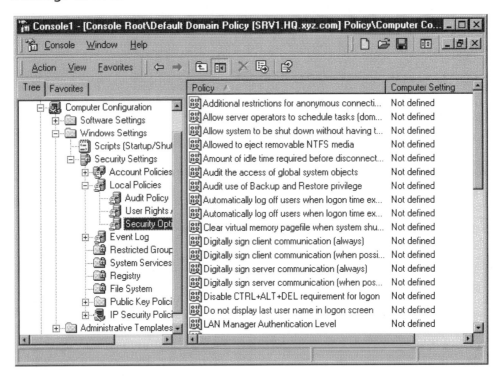

Security Settings cover a wide range of system security options for Windows 2000 Professional or Windows 2000 Server. The settings in this extension complement internal system security tools, such as Local Users and Groups and the Security tab in the Properties dialog of an object. Some of the security options that can be set for Windows 2000 clients include:

- **Account Policies** Settings for password policies, lockout policies, and Kerberos policies.
- **Local Policies** Settings for audit policies, user rights policies, and security options.
- **Event Log** Settings for the Application, System, and Security logs viewable through Event Viewer.
- **Restricted Groups** Settings for determining which objects can be members of a restricted group, and which restricted groups can belong to other groups.
- **System Services** Settings for services like network services, file and print services, etc.
- **Registry** Settings for providing security to such registry keys as access control, auditing, and ownership.
- **File System** Settings for controlling security on file system objects.

If you wanted to hide the username in the login screen, you would locate the "Do not display last user name in logon screen" property in Computer Configuration, Windows Settings, Security Settings, Local Policies, and Security Options of the GPE, and set it to Enable. This will make that option active and hide the username in the login box. This option is a Computer Configuration option because it governs the behavior of the machine, not the user account that logs on to the machine.

Administrative Templates

Figure 6.12 shows the expanded Computer Configuration Administrative Templates tree in the GPE. The Administrative Templates section has four main nodes: Windows Components, System, Network, and Printers. These nodes contain the following additional settings:

- **Windows Components** Settings for NetMeeting, a real-time voice/data conferencing application; Internet Explorer; Task Scheduler, a tool that can initiate the execution of a program, script, or document at specified times; and Windows Installer, a new tool that helps to manage the installation and removal of applications on a workstation.

- **System** Settings for Logon, Disk Quotas, DNS Client, Group Policy, and Windows File Protection.

- **Network** Settings for Offline Files, a mechanism for keeping local copies of network files available for use when a client is not on the network, and Network and Dial-up Connections.

- **Printers** Settings for printer functions.

Again, the settings described here apply more to the computer environment than the user environment, but some settings will have a direct impact on the user environment. For example, if you set a computer policy that disabled the Windows Installer for a computer, the application of the setting would not alter the user's interface to the computer, but it would prevent the user from running the Windows Installer on the affected computer.

Additional template files are available with Windows 2000 and can be added by right-clicking the Administrative Templates node and selecting Add/Remove Templates. You can then choose from the additional templates available by default, or browse to a location with additional templates. Windows NT 4.0 System Policies can be added to the Administrative Templates node in this manner, but great care must be used in doing so. Since Group Policy with Windows 2000 is broader and much more powerful than Windows NT System Policy, any System Policy settings should be applied through the Group Policies, not by using the old policy files. This ensures that the correct policies are set for the environment modifications you wish to make.

Figure 6.12 Administrative Templates policies for Computer Configuration in MMC.

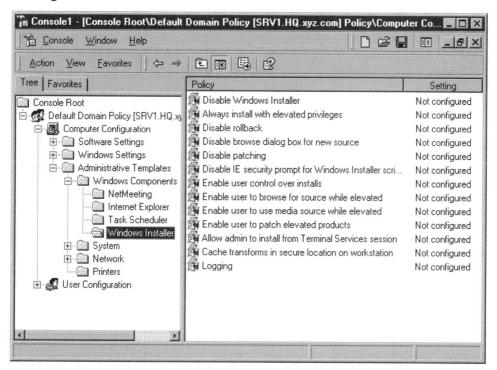

User Policies

Group Policy settings for user objects in Active Directory are applied when the user object logs on to the network. The settings under Software Settings, Windows Settings, and Administrative Templates generally apply to the user-interface environment with which the user interacts when logged on a Windows 2000 computer. User Configuration policies are stored in the HKEY_CURRENT_USER key in the Windows registry.

Software Settings

Figure 6.13 shows the User Configuration Software Settings branch expanded in GPE. As with the Computer

Configuration policies described in the previous section, the
Software Settings policies allow an administrator to make software
available to users across the network. Unlike the Computer
Configuration policies relating to software installation, the settings
here apply directly to the user object, and thus are available to the
user no matter with which machine the user logs on.

Figure 6.13 Software installation object in the User Configuration
of GPE.

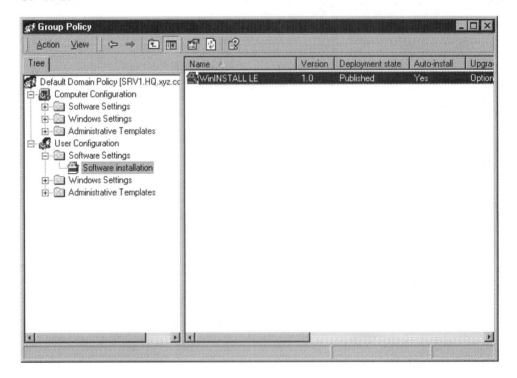

Another key difference is that software can be advertised to
the user object in two ways: Assigning and Publishing. When an
application is assigned to a user, the user is notified the next
time he or she logs on and information is added to the local computer's registry that will automatically install the application
when the user tries to access it. Depending on the application
that is configured, the policy may add file extension information
to the registry so the application will install and run when the

user tries to open a file of that type. Another option is to place a shortcut on the desktop or in the Start menu, and the application will install when the user selects it.

If an application is published to a user, information about the application is not configured on the local workstation as when the application is assigned. Instead, information about the application is placed in Active Directory, which can be read by the user object. The user can install the application on the computer through the Add/Remove Programs Control Panel. The application will also be installed when the user tries to open an associated file. In addition, the user can remove the application from the computer in the Add/Remove Programs Control Panel. If the application is removed, it will be reinstalled the next time the user tries to open a document belonging to that application. Since the file association with the application is stored in Active Directory and not on the local computer, the association information is not removed when the application is uninstalled.

Windows Settings

Figure 6.14 shows the expanded User Configuration Windows Settings Group Policy branch. The settings in this node are divided as follows:

- **Internet Explorer Maintenance** Settings for Browser User Interface, Connection, URLs, Security, and Programs.

- **Scripts** Identifies scripts to be run by the user object at logon and logoff.

- **Security Settings** Settings for user Public Key Policies.

- **Folder Redirection** Settings for specifying network locations for special Windows system folders.

Figure 6.14 User Configuration Windows Settings in GPE.

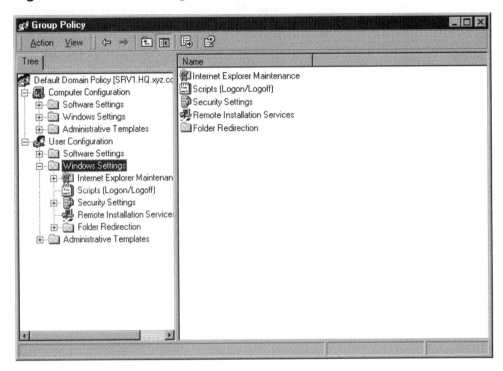

Administrative Templates

Figure 6.15 shows the expanded User Configuration Administrative Templates section of the GPO. The Administrative Templates section has settings for Windows Components, Start Menu & Taskbar, Desktop, Control Panel, Network, and System. The Windows Components section contains settings for NetMeeting, Internet Explorer, Windows Explorer, Microsoft Management Console, Task Scheduler, and Windows Installer. Start Menu & Taskbar contains policies that modify the settings for these objects. The Desktop section contains settings that govern the appearance and function of the user's desktop, as well as settings for interacting with Active Desktop and Active Directory. The Control Panel section has settings for Add/Remove Programs, Display, Printers, and Regional Options. Network contains options for Offline Files and Network and Dial-up Connections. System contains policies for Logon/Logoff and Group Policy.

Figure 6.15 User Configuration Administrative Templates Settings in GPE.

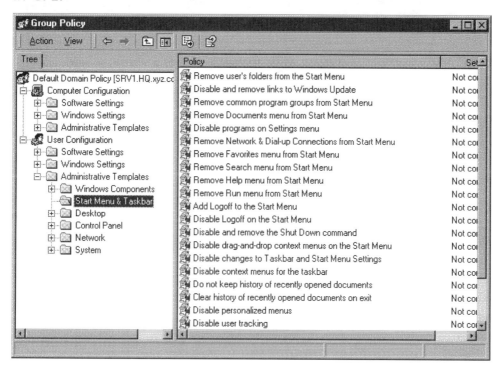

Example: Modifying User Policy Settings

In this example, we will walk through the process of modifying a user policy setting and give additional detail about the policy interface. Let's suppose that you have a group of user objects for which you want to disable the screensaver when they are logged on. This could be an account that operates a stand-alone kiosk or has some other function where the computer screen needs to be visible at all times. Figure 6.16 shows the location of the "No screen saver" policy in User Configuration, Administrative Templates, Control Panel, Display section.

Figure 6.16 Location of the "No screen saver" policy in GPE.

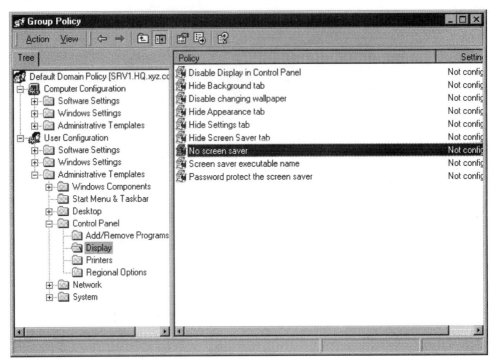

Double-clicking the "No screen saver" property will open the Properties dialog as seen in Figure 6.17. The Properties dialog has two tabs: Policy and Explain. Choosing the Enabled radio button will activate the "No screen saver" policy for this container. Choosing DISABLED will disable this policy from this container, possibly overriding an enabled setting from a higher container. Selecting Not Configured will allow this container to simply inherit the "No screen saver" policy from a higher container, if it is set. Two additional buttons allow you to navigate through the other policies in the current section, if desired. Clicking PREVIOUS POLICY will take you back one policy in the list, and clicking NEXT POLICY will move you forward one policy in the list.

The Explain tab of the Properties dialog, seen in Figure 6.18, gives a description of the policy and how the application of the policy will affect objects within the container. The Explain tab can be

Figure 6.17 Policy tab of Properties dialog of "No screen saver" policy.

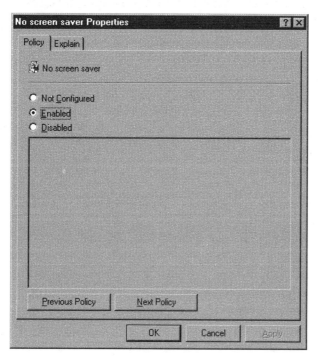

very useful in making sure you know how a policy is going to impact the container. Some policy names are not very clear, and their expected impact can be a little foggy as a result. As with the Policy tab, Previous Policy and Next Policy will navigate you through the list of policies in the current section.

Apply will become active when a change is made in the Policy tab. Making a change in the Policy tab and then moving to another policy without clicking Apply or OK will remove the change made to that policy. Once a policy change is applied, it becomes immediately active within Active Directory and is applied to all objects the next time the object joins the network or logs on. In this example, all user objects within this container will be unable to activate a screen saver after they log back on.

Figure 6.18 No screen saver Properties Explain tab.

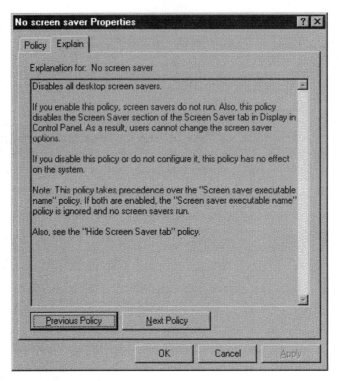

Roaming Profiles

Roaming profiles are a special type of user profile implemented in Windows 2000. A user profile contains settings for the user, such as color scheme, screen resolution, or items in the Start menu. With Windows 95 and Windows 98, these settings apply to the computer, no matter who logs on. With Windows NT, users could store unique settings that applied only to their sessions and would not impact the settings of other users on the box. Roaming profiles were introduced with Windows NT, and their functionality has carried forward into Windows 2000. Table 6.2 summarizes the basic types of user profiles.

Table 6.2 User Profiles

Type of User Profile	Summary
Local User Profile	Created on the local computer when a user logs on for the first time. Contains profile information specific to that computer only.
Roaming User Profile	Created by a system administrator and stored on a network server. This profile is applied to any computer on the network when the network account logs on. All changes made to the profile are stored back on the network server and are available the next time the account logs on to any workstation.
Mandatory User Profile	A roaming profile that is used to designate specific settings for a network account or a network group. Only changes made by the system administrator are stored back on the network server—the individual accounts cannot save changes to the profile.

There are a few key differences between the implementation of user profiles in Windows NT and Windows 2000. For local profiles, the user information is stored in the system partition root\Documents and Settings\userid folder, usually C:\Documents and Settings\userid. Contained within the profile is a My Documents folder, placed on the user's desktop by default, which is the default folder for opening and saving documents.

A roaming user profile differs from a local user profile in that it is available to the user no matter which computer is used to log on to the network. When the user logs on, his or her profile settings are copied from a network server to the local computer where the settings are applied. The profile settings are still stored on the local machine, but the local copy is compared to the network profile, and any differences are copied down to the local machine during the logon process. One of the setbacks of using roaming profiles with Windows NT, namely, only being able to use a roaming profile on computers with identical hardware configurations, has been eliminated with Windows 2000. Windows 2000 will do its best to match the profile settings to the hardware used by the local computer.

Creating Roaming Profiles

There are two steps in creating a roaming profile for user accounts. First is to set up the network share where the profile information will be stored, such as \\server_name\Profiles. The server used to store roaming profiles should be accessible by all computers where a roaming profile could be used, and, for performance reasons, should be a member server instead of a domain controller or other heavily used server.

Second is to enable the user account for a roaming profile. In the Profile tab of the Properties dialog box of the user account, enter the path to the server share where the profiles are stored, as in \\server_name\Profiles\userid. Figure 6.19 shows the path where the profile for user jsmith is stored. As a shortcut, you can use the %username% variable when entering the path, as in \\server_name\Profiles\%username%, and Windows 2000 will automatically substitute the actual account name.

The next time the user account logs on, the account will be enabled with a roaming profile. If the account already had a profile on the local computer, that profile information will be copied to the server profile folder when the account logs off. Otherwise, the account will inherit the default profile settings for the local computer, and those settings, along with any customizations, will be saved on the server at logoff. By default, several folders will be created in the roaming profile folder, including Start Menu, Desktop, and My Documents. In addition, several hidden files will be created, including Ntuser.dat and Ntuser.ini. The Ntuser.dat file contains the unique information for the user account.

Another way to get profile information set for a user account is to preconfigure the account before letting the user log on. This way, the account profile can be set for any default customizations needed to operate in your network environment. The next section details methods for setting up profile templates to configure multiple user accounts with the same environment.

Figure 6.19 User Properties dialog for John Smith.

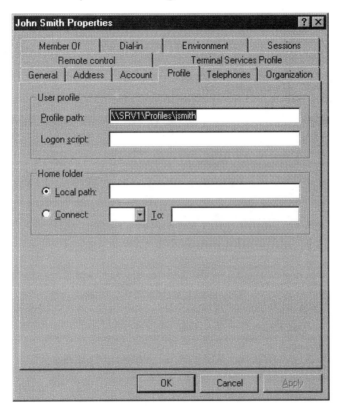

Administering Roaming Profiles

As described earlier, the most straightforward method for establishing a user profile is to enable the user account for roaming, log on as the account, and configure the account environment. However, this method is not very efficient when dealing with large numbers of user accounts. One way to simplify this process is to create profile templates to apply to new accounts as you create them. An example of this follows.

Exercise: Creating an Account and Roaming Profile Template

Follow these steps to create a template account and its associated profile.

1. Open Active Directory Users and Computers.
2. Click on the Users folder in the left pane, and then select New→User from the Action menu.
3. Enter information for first name, last name, and account name as desired (scc Figure 6.20), then click NEXT.

Figure 6.20 Sample setup for a template account.

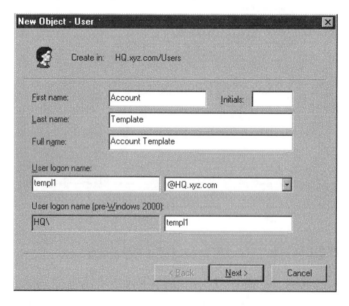

4. Specify a password for the account, and then click NEXT.
5. Review the account information, and click FINISH.
6. Log on as the new account on a computer most like the computers that will be used by the new accounts, and configure the user environment.

7. Log off of the account to save the profile settings.

8. From the computer used to configure the account, log on to the network with an administrator account.

9. Open the System control panel (or right-click on My Computer and select Properties), and click on the User Profiles tab.

10. Select the template profile and click COPY TO... (Figure 6.21).

Figure 6.21 Selecting the template profile.

11. Type the path to the roaming profiles folder for the destination account in the "Copy profile to" text field, then click CHANGE... (Figure 6.22).

12. Select the correct account from the account list, and then click OK (Figure 6.23).

13. Verify that the information is correct in the Copy To dialog and click OK (Figure 6.24).

Figure 6.22 Specify roaming profile destination.

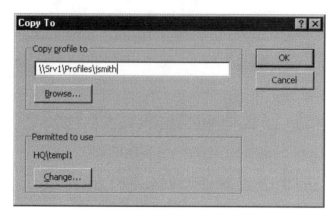

Figure 6.23 Select destination account.

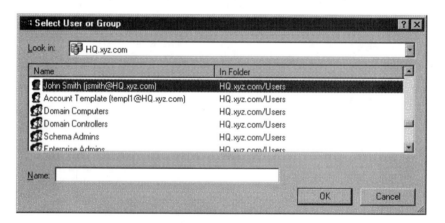

14. If the destination account already has a roaming profile on the server, a warning dialog will appear (Figure 6.25).

15. Modify the destination account to activate its roaming profile if it has not been enabled already.

16. Log off as Administrator and log on with the destination account to make sure the profile copied correctly.

Now the template profile can be copied to the roaming profile folder for any account, and that account will use the roaming profile once it has been enabled.

Figure 6.24 Verify profile information.

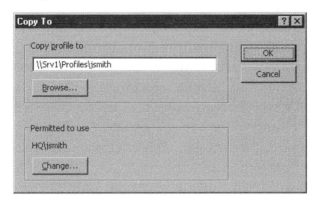

Figure 6.25 Confirm Copy dialog.

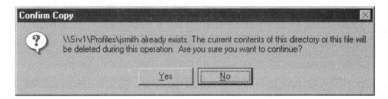

TIP

When configuring a profile as a template, you should verify the settings on multiple computers. However, make sure not to log on to the account on more than one station at a time, since profile settings are not saved to the server until logoff. If you log on Workstation1 and Workstation2 at the same time, all changes you made to the profile will be saved to the server when you log off Workstation1. But when you log off Workstation2, its current settings will be saved back to the server, overwriting the settings saved when Workstation1 logged off. One easy way to avoid this scenario is to limit the template account to one simultaneous logon connection.

Mandatory and Group Profiles

There are times when you may want to prevent an account from modifying its profile or have a group of accounts use the same profile. To do this, you would change a roaming profile into a mandatory profile. A mandatory profile, described earlier in this chapter, is a roaming profile that is read-only, preventing the account from saving any profile changes back to the server. To change a roaming profile into a mandatory profile, simply change the name of the Ntuser.dat file in the account's roaming profile folder to Ntuser.man. Windows 2000 will treat this file as a read-only file, preventing any changes from being made.

It is also possible to have several accounts use the same profile. In the Profile tab of the account object's Properties dialog box in Active Users and Computers, enter the network path to the shared profile folder in the Profile Path: text field. For example, if you wanted all the members of a marketing group to share the same profile, you could create the profile, save it to \\Srv1\Profiles\Marketing, and then enter that profile path for each account to use the profile. In addition to locking down the user environment, which can greatly help in troubleshooting (not to mention in keeping the ugliest color scheme from appearing on desktops all over the company), this approach also makes it much easier to implement changes in the user environment. If you wanted to add a new application, for instance, you would convert the profile from mandatory back to roaming, make the changes to the environment, then convert the profile back to mandatory. The next time an account logged on with the shared profile, the changes you made would automatically appear in the user's environment.

Folder Redirection and Offline Folders

Folder redirection and offline folders are necessary counterparts when using roaming profiles. After all, how productive can someone be if his or her documents are not available when logging on to a computer?

Even if not making use of roaming profiles in a Windows 2000 environment, the use of folder redirection and offline folders makes good business sense from a data integrity and security standpoint. Plus, it can make a network administrator's life much simpler when arranging for data backups.

For Managers

Where to Store User Data

When PCs were first networked together with file and print servers, it was a common practice to store all applications and data on the file server. This was easy to do, and made a lot of sense in a DOS-based environment. As operating systems and applications have become more complex, running applications off a file server has fallen largely out of practice, especially with so many applications installing components in system directories within the OS. In the same way, user data has seen a migration from server to local disks. Since laptop PCs have become so prevalent in the business world, servers have provided little more than e-mail and printing services.

Many support professionals have witnessed the anguish this practice leads to when a laptop hard drive crashes. Restoring the operating system and application packages is a fairly straight-forward, albeit time-consuming, process. But not so for the data the user kept on the disk. Even if a company provides remote data backups, the integrity of the data is not guaranteed. Many factors can interfere with even the best-designed backup system, such as network outages, power outages, backup software configuration, and not having a laptop connected to the network during its sched-uled backup window. Not knowing where user documents are stored means that the majority of the computer hard drive must be backed up to provide the best chance at getting the user's data backed up, an approach that is very costly in terms of equipment, time, and management.

With the advent of Windows 95, Microsoft began to provide a location for user data in a folder called My Documents. While the default location of this folder has changed in almost every version of the operating system, most mainstream applications are now designed to look for and use a My Documents folder as the default storage location for data. Educating users to store all their files in the My Documents folder can cut down on the amount of data needing to be backed up, but the process is still susceptible to the conditions described above.

Storing user data on a file server addresses most of these data integrity issues. In the event of a hard drive crash, only the OS and applications are lost and need to be reinstalled; the data is still intact on the server. Backup times are reduced, as files are not being copied across the network from each client. Network outages do not interfere with the backup process, provided the backup device is connected to the server where the data is stored. And only data files are copied, as no applications are stored in the user's server space.

The challenge, then, is to reeducate users to use file servers for data storage. Interfaces that are counterintuitive or just plain difficult to use present a significant barrier to this end. The remainder of this section discusses new tools available with Windows 2000 that make this objective easier to achieve.

Folder Redirection

Folder redirection is an extension of the Group Policy object used to redirect Windows 2000 folders to a network location. The folders that can be redirected are listed in Table 6.3.

Table 6.3 Windows 2000 Redirection Folders

Windows 2000 Folder	Comments
Application Data	Applications that use this folder to store user preferences, temporary files, or other settings will benefit from using a network location, as the user will receive the same application data storage from anywhere on the network.
Desktop	Any files, folders, and shortcuts placed on the user's desktop will be stored in the remote folder so the items are accessible by the user no matter which computer is used.
My Documents	The default folder used by newer applications as the place to store user documents. Placing this folder on a remote server will make the files available to the user anywhere on the network. As user data can be quite large, the remote location for storage of this data should have ample disk space, or there should be multiple storage locations broken down by Sites, Domains, Organizational Units, or special groups.
My Pictures	This folder, normally contained within the My Documents folder, can have a separate network location specified. As picture files tend to be large, the comments about network storage space above apply here as well.
Start Menu	Customizations to the Start menu can be stored on a network location so the user's Start menu appears the same no matter where he or she logs on.

Folders can be set to point to a globally shared resource for all users or to a unique location for each account. To uniquely identify a user's folder on the network, use the %username% environment variable in the network path, such as \\server\share\%username% \foldername. Other environment variables could be used to point to network locations for other subsets of your user population. A folder redirection configuration example appears later in this section.

Your approach to establishing redirected folders will be influenced by several factors. While none of these approaches are mutually exclusive, the techniques for one may not work as well as for another.

NOTE

Folder redirection only works for Windows clients on a Windows network. Even though other computer types can be served by a Windows network, such as the Apple Macintosh, folder redirection and other advanced file maintenance features are not supported on these other platforms.

Redirection for Data Integrity

This approach, which provides better integrity for your users' data without a complex setup, focuses on the My Documents folder. Moving a user's My Documents folder to a network location protects the data from a local disk crash and could make the data easier to back up, as it would be in a centralized location. Depending on the size of your organization, you may need to spread out the storage across several servers. For instance, members of the Accounting group could have their My Documents folders stored on one server (\\SRV1\Home\%username%\My Documents), and the Marketing group could be on another (\\SRV2\Home\%username%\My Documents). Or, if the two departments have separate volumes on the same server, the redirection could be pointed to \\SRV1\ Accounting\%username%\My Documents and \\SRV1\Marketing\ %username%\My Documents.

If your organization is making heavy use of the My Pictures folder in the My Documents folder, you may want to set up a separate redirection policy for that folder. By default, Windows 2000 will include the My Pictures folder and its contents inside the redirected My Documents folder. However, the My Pictures folder can redirect to a separate location on the network, and a shortcut to the My Pictures folder will be placed inside the My Documents folder.

Example: Redirecting the My Documents and My Pictures Folders

While it is possible to set folder redirection on a per-user basis administratively, this can quickly become a management headache. Using Group Policy to manage folder redirection greatly simplifies the process and aids in future troubleshooting. This example will show how to configure the My Documents and My Pictures folders to redirect to separate locations on the network.

The configuration for folder redirection is in the User Configuration, Windows Settings, Folder Redirection section, shown in Figure 6.26. To specify settings for the My Documents folder, right-click on the My Documents icon and select Properties. This will bring up the Properties dialog shown in Figure 6.27.

Figure 6.26 Policy settings location for Folder Redirection in GPE.

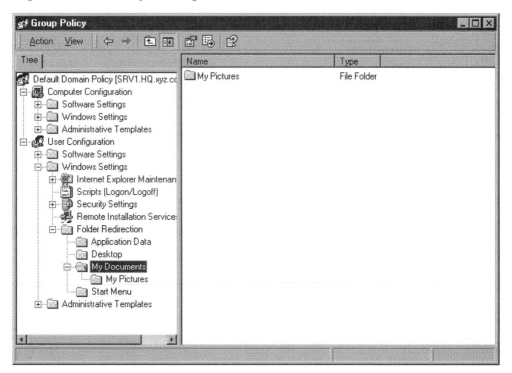

Figure 6.27 Properties dialog for folder redirection of My Documents.

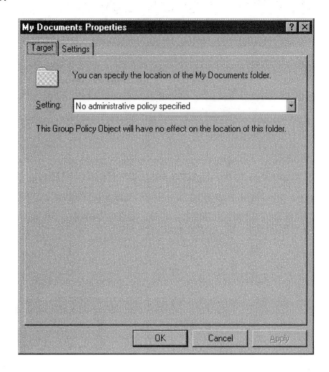

In the Setting: pull-down menu of the Target tab are three options. The default option is "No administrative policy specified." This setting means that there are no Group Policies governing the redirection of this folder. The next setting, the one used for this example, is "Basic–Redirect everyone's folder to the same location," shown in Figure 6.28. Selecting this option adds a new area to the dialog, a place to specify the target location for the redirected folder. This target can specify a share that every user object will use to store documents for this folder, or you can use the %username% variable to create unique subfolders in the target path for each user. As indicated in Figure 6.28, the %username% variable does not have to be the last item in the path. A complete subfolder path can be specified within the folder created with the user's name.

Figure 6.28 Basic redirection setting for My Documents folder.

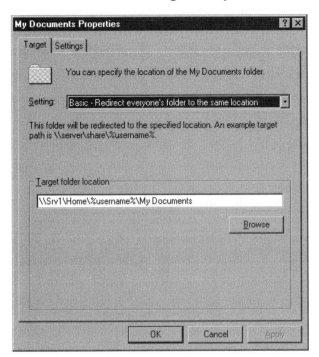

The third option for the target folder setting is "Advanced–Specify locations for various user groups." This option brings up a larger window in the Target tab where the administrator can specify a group object and the target folder associated with that group object. As with the Basic setting, the target path can, and probably should, include the %username% variable to generate a unique folder for the user. However, this Advanced option lets the user specify different folder settings for groups within a container without creating a separate OU for the different settings.

When the Basic or Advanced setting is selected, the options in the Settings tab become active, as shown in Figure 6.29. By default, the "Grant the user exclusive rights to My Documents" and "Move the contents of My Documents to the new location" check boxes are checked, and the "Leave the folder in the new location when policy is removed" radio button is selected. When the user is granted exclusive rights to the folder, the permissions on the folder are set so that only the user has rights to access the folder, and administrators do not. If the option to move the folder contents is set, the contents of the user's My Documents folder will be moved to the redirected folder at the next logon. To avoid massive confusion, this policy should be applied when the affected users are not logged on. If a user object is logged on to one computer before the policy takes effect and then logs on to another computer after the policy has been enacted, the contents of the folder will move, leaving the contents of the data for the user on the first computer in a precarious state.

Figure 6.29 Folder redirection settings for the My Documents folder.

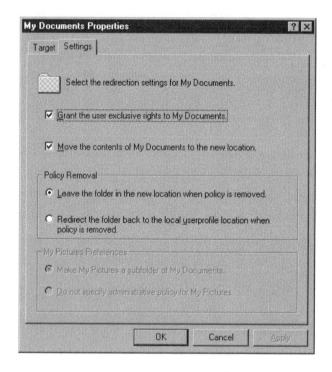

If the "Leave the folder in the new location when policy is removed" setting is selected when the policy is removed, the folder will remain redirected to the remote location, the contents of the remote folder will remain unchanged, and the user will still have full access to the remote folder through redirection. Selecting the "Redirect the folder back to the local userprofile location when policy is removed" is dependent upon how the contents of the folder were handled when the policy was put into effect. Table 6.4 details these actions.

Table 6.4 Effect on data when folder redirection policy is removed

Contents of Folder	Action on Policy Removal
Moved from the local profile to the redirected location	■ Folder returns to the original user profile location ■ Contents of the redirected folder are copied back to the original profile location ■ Contents of the redirected folder are not deleted ■ User object only has access to the local contents of the folder
Not moved from the local profile to the redirected location	■ Folder returns to the original user profile location ■ Contents of the redirected folder are not moved or copied back to the profile location ■ Contents of the redirected folder must be copied back to the user profile location in order for the user to have access to the files

The settings for redirection of the My Pictures folder are slightly different from the settings for the My Documents folder, so they are summarized here. Figure 6.30 shows the Properties dialog for the My Pictures folder. When the folder is set to the default setting, "Follow the My Documents folder," the contents of the My Pictures folder will reside within the redirected My Documents folder.

Figure 6.31 shows the Properties dialog when the folder is set to "Basic–Redirect everyone's folder to the same location." Here, the target is a different network share than with the My Documents folder, but the %username% variable is still used to generate separate folders for each user. There is also an "Advanced–Specify locations for various user groups" setting that behaves the same as with the My Documents folder. There is also a "No administrative policy specified" setting that will allow the user profile to determine the location of the folder.

Figure 6.30 Default setting for redirection of My Pictures folder.

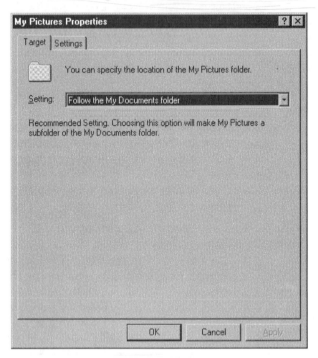

Redirection for Laptop Users

General practices for setting up folder redirection are straightforward and easy to implement, as long as your organization is made up entirely of desktop computers. Once PC laptops are thrown into the mix, however, the guidelines change. Though goals of data integrity and management still apply to laptop users, the new issue of productivity comes into play when a laptop user is not connected to the network. Files stored on a network share become inaccessible when the user goes home for the night or weekend, or when the user is traveling away from the office. Even though the user may be able to connect to the network via a modem, working with large sets of files, or just large files, becomes problematic with slow connections and bothersome with good ones.

Figure 6.31 Target folder location for My Pictures folder.

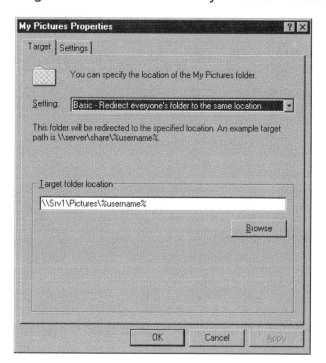

In general, and no offense is intended, laptop users tend to be rather insistent that all their data is kept on their laptop hard disk so they can have access to it at all times. This is advantageous for the users because they always have their data with them. At the same time, it is a nightmare for the support team when a hard drive crashes or when files are lost in other ways. At the same time, having a laptop is essentially pointless if the user has access to his or her data only when sitting at the desk, which is costly both from a productivity perspective and in terms of hardware costs, since laptops tend to be more expensive than their desktop counterparts.

Fortunately, a compromise is available that will allow the laptop user to access his or her data, whether on or off the network, while keeping the data stored on a network share for security and backup benefits. This solution comes in the form of offline folders.

Offline Folders

Redirecting user data folders to a network location, while greatly beneficial to the network administrator, does have its drawbacks to the user. If the network goes down, how do users work with their data? Or what happens when a VP forgets to copy a presentation file to his laptop before he leaves town for a sales meeting? Folder redirection in itself is not a complete data storage solution, but becomes a powerful tool when combined with offline folders. When offline folders are set up on a Windows 2000 computer, the OS keeps a local copy of files from a network folder that can be accessed when the network is not available. This is different from a user manually copying an important file to a local folder, which can become confusing quickly. When a folder is configured as an offline folder, the user has access to the folder and its data from the same interface, whether the network is available or not.

Users can individually set a folder to be available offline by right-clicking on the desired network folder and selecting Make Available Offline from the pop-up menu. This will start the Offline Files wizard. The wizard first asks if the user wants to synchronize the contents of the folder at every logon and logoff, as in Figure 6.32. The user has the option, in the next page of the wizard, of enabling reminders when the computer goes online or offline. The user can also specify if he or she wants a shortcut to the offline folder created on the desktop, as seen in Figure 6.33. When the user clicks FINISH, the folder is marked for offline use and a synchronization is done immediately.

Windows 2000 has several methods of synchronization to keep the local and network copies of the files up to date. Files and folders can be synchronized manually, or a synchronization schedule can be configured in the Synchronization Manager. The Synchronization Manager can synchronize files several ways:

- At logon and logoff
- During computer idle time
- At specific times

Figure 6.32 Automatic synchronization setting in Offline Files wizard.

Figure 6.33 Reminders and shortcut settings in Offline Files wizard.

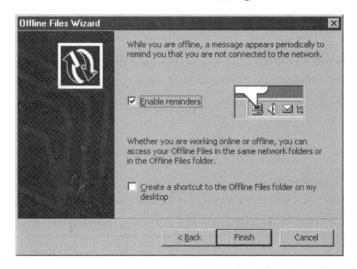

Different synchronization schedules can be set for different files and folders. In addition, there are two types of automatic synchronization, which are described in Table 6.5. It should be noted that a manual synchronization on a file or folder transfers the complete contents so the files are identical on both ends.

Table 6.5 Methods of Automatic Synchronization

Synchronization Type	Action
Full Synchronization	Copies all files on the network path to the local disk, making sure that every file is the latest version. Can be time consuming for large amounts of data.
Quick Synchronization	Checks to make sure that a copy of every file on the network path is available locally, but may not provide the latest revision of every file. Takes much less time than a full synchronization.

TIP

Offline file configurations are not available in a Novell NetWare environment. However, any system that supports Server Message Block (SMB) File and Print Sharing can be used for offline folders.

Configuration settings for offline files can be managed in the Offline Files tab of the Folder Options dialog, which can be found under the Tools menu in an Explorer window. The settings in this dialog, shown in Figure 6.34, define the synchronization and reminder settings, as well as the option to place a shortcut to the Offline Files folder on the desktop. In addition, the user can specify the time interval between reminder notices and how much local disk space to use for offline files.

TIP

When creating an Offline Files folder on the desktop, be aware that the shortcut only points to the folder where the local copies of the offline files are stored. It does not contain the folder structure of the network folders that have been made available offline. Since the network path to the offline folders will still seem to function normally when offline, to avoid confusion on the user's part, a shortcut to the Offline Files folder should not be placed on the desktop.

Figure 6.34 Offline Files tab of the Folder Options dialog.

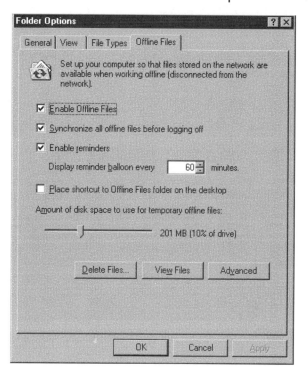

In addition to synchronization options, offline file configuration specifies how to react when a network location becomes unavailable. The Offline Files–Advanced Settings dialog box (see Figure 6.35) allows the user to select which of two actions take place when a network disruption occurs. Selecting "Notify me and begin working offline" will display a dialog box indicating that the network connection has been lost and will allow the user to begin working with the offline version of the affected files. Selecting "Never allow my computer to go offline" will prevent the user from being able to use the offline files when the network connection is lost.

Different actions can be specified for different network locations in the lower portion of this dialog. For instance, if you want to specify that files from only one network location are to be made available offline, you could set the workstation's default behavior to be "Never allow my computer to go offline," and then add a separate rule to make files from the network location available when offline. To do this, click ADD in the Offline Files–Advanced Settings dialog, specify the network location, then select "Notify me and begin working offline." Figure 6.35 shows the Advanced Settings dialog configured to only allow connections to server SRV1 to be available offline.

Figure 6.35 Options in Offline Files–Advanced Settings dialog.

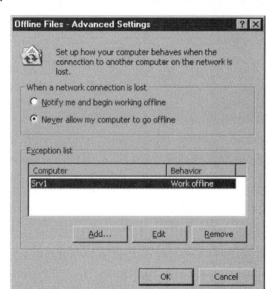

Managing Offline Files with Group Policy

Even though a great deal of customization for offline folders can be handled at the user level, managing a larger set of user settings for offline folders is more easily achieved with Group Policy. Settings for offline folders are located in the Administrative Templates, Network, Offline Files section under both Computer Configuration and User Configuration. The policies govern which offline files settings can be controlled by the user. Unfortunately, the default policy settings do not allow the administrator to specify which user folders are made available offline, but only how the user can configure them. Administrators can, however, set network folders as offline folders, and when users access these folders, they will inherit the policy settings for offline folders and the system will behave accordingly.

One of the key policy settings for offline folders is the "Disable user configuration of Offline Files." When enabled, this will prevent the user from being able to modify any of the settings related to offline files. If the administrator has already configured offline files for the user, he or she will be able to interact with the system normally, but will not be able to alter the offline files configuration. This policy locks down the offline files configuration from the user perspective and allows the administrator to control the complete offline files environment through Group Policy.

Figures 6.36 and 6.37 show the policies for offline files for Computer Configuration and User Configuration, respectively. In general, offline files policy settings should only be set for one configuration or the other, not for both. For the majority of the offline files policies, if a conflicting policy is encountered, the Computer Configuration policy will override the User Configuration policy.

Figure 6.36 Offline Files policies for Computer Configuration.

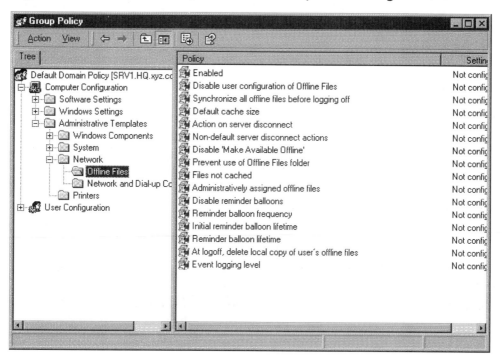

Figure 6.37 Offline Files policies for User Configuration.

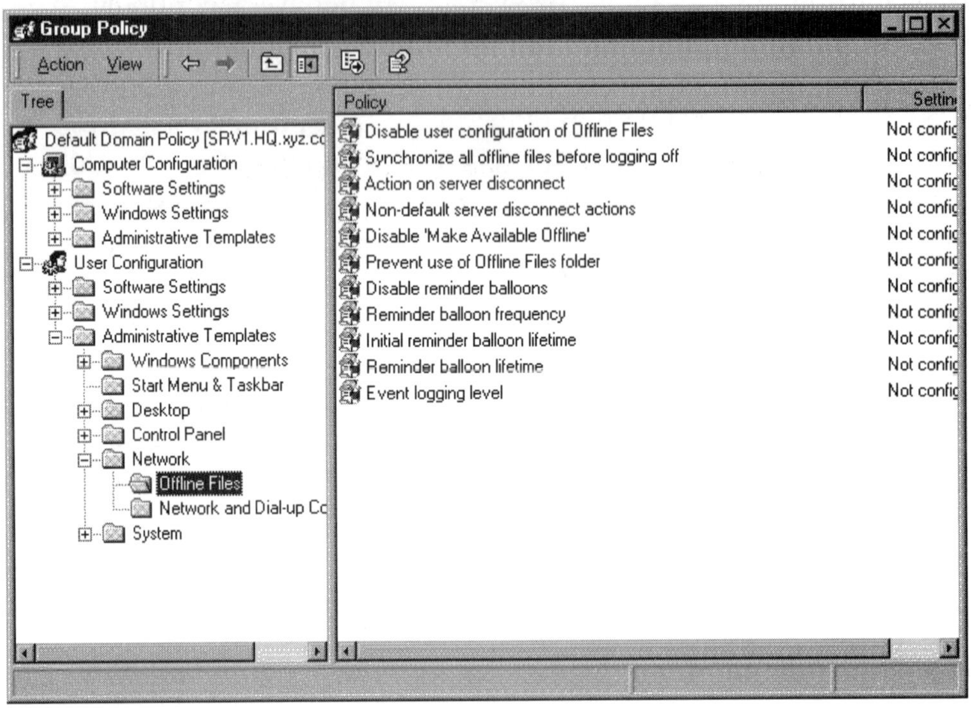

Cache Settings

Obviously, for network files and folders to be available to users while not connected to the network, the files have to be stored on the local disk. One important issue that remains to be covered in this chapter is how to control the amount of local disk used for storage of offline files. Without some form of limitation, a user could try to synchronize several hundred megabytes of data in offline files, and potentially fill up his local disk (at best) or even crash the drive (at worst). Fortunately, there are offline files settings, both in Group Policy and on the local machine, that can limit the amount of offline data to be stored locally.

As we saw earlier in Figure 6.34, the local Folder Options settings for offline files has a slider bar that can be used to specify the amount of local disk space to be used for caching offline files. The default setting for local cache with Windows 2000 is 10% of the total space on the primary drive. This setting can also be mandated in the "Default cache size" policy, shown in Figure 6.38.

Figure 6.38 Default cache size policy dialog.

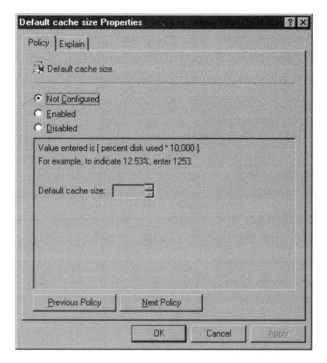

Summary

Windows 2000 provides system administrators with a powerful tool for managing user and computer environments in the new Group Policy. Group Policy is stored in the Active Directory and can be applied at the Site, Domain, or Organizational Unit (SDOU) level. Computer objects within a container managed by Group Policy inherit policies when they join the network at boot time. User objects inherit their policy settings at logon. Group Policy is applied hierarchically: Any policy at the Site level is applied first, followed by policy at the Domain, then at the OUs. If conflicting policy settings are encountered, the policy closest to the object is the one that is applied. User policies generally override computer policies in case of a conflict. Policies can be set to block overrides by subordinate policy objects or to prevent inheritance from parent policy objects, but the block override setting always overrides a block inheritance setting in case of conflict. Group Policy settings are changed in the Group Policy Editor, which can be accessed through Active Directory Users and Computers or with the Group Policy Object snap-in in Microsoft Management Console (MMC).

Group Policy settings are divided into two groups, Computer Configuration and User Configuration, with three subgroups, Software Settings, Windows Settings, and Administrative Templates. Computer Configuration settings are stored in the registry in the HKEY_LOCAL_MACHINE key, and User Configuration settings are stored in the HKEY_CURRENT_USER key of the registry. Software Settings policies control availability and installation of software on a computer or for a user. Applications can be assigned to computer and user objects and published to user objects. Assigned applications for a computer object are installed on the computer when safe to do so, usually at boot time. Assigned applications for user objects are installed when a user tries to access the application. Published applications can be installed by the user through the Add/Remove Programs control panel. Applications governed by Computer Configuration Software Settings are available only on that computer. Applications governed by User Configuration Software Settings are available to the user no matter which computer he or she uses. Windows Settings for Computer Configuration have policies for startup and shutdown scripts, as well as security settings. Windows Settings for User Configuration contains policies for Internet Explorer maintenance, logon and logoff scripts, security settings, and folder redirection. Administrative Templates for Computer Configuration contains policies for Windows components, System, Network, and Printers. Administrative Templates for User Configuration has policies for Windows Components, Start Menu & Taskbar, Desktop, Control Panel, Network, and System. A standard set of Administrative Templates is included in the Group Policy Editor (GPE) by default, but additional templates can be added, and custom templates can be built. Policies can be Enabled, Disabled, or Not Configured. Enabled policies enact that setting for the current container. Disabled policies turn off that setting for that container, assuming that the policy had been enabled in a parent container. A policy that is Not Configured simply inherits the setting from a parent container.

Roaming profiles are user profiles that are stored in a network location instead of on the local computer. A user account that has a roaming profile configured will have his or her personalized settings available, no matter where the user logs on. A mandatory roaming profile is a special type of roaming profile that prevents the user from changing any settings. Roaming profiles can be configured on a user-by-user basis or through policy templates. Roaming profile templates can be created and copied to user accounts if a set of accounts needs a similar profile environment. A roaming profile can be changed to a mandatory profile by changing the name of the Ntuser.dat file in the Roaming Profile folder to Ntuser.man.

Folder redirection changes the location of a special system folder from a local disk directory to a network location. A user's My Documents folder can be pointed to a network path, making the data in the folder available to the user no matter which computer is used to log on to the network. Other folders that can be redirected include Application Data, Desktop, My Pictures, and Start Menu. Folder redirection can be done by the individual user or through Group Policy. Redirecting folders through Group Policy can ease user data administration, as the system administrator can specify the network locations where all user data folders will reside. Using the %username% variable when specifying a network location for folder redirection will create a folder for each user automatically. Offline folders can be used in conjunction with folder redirection to make sure that a user's data is available to him or her in case of network outage or travel. The computer will keep local copies of files in offline folders. Copies of local files can be synchronized with the network source and with a choice of several predetermined schedules. Offline file settings can also be managed locally or through Group Policy.

FAQs

Q: Do I have to use Group Policy if I already have a set of System Policies that work for my organization?

A: While your System Policies may work fine by themselves, you should incorporate them into a Group Policy for your organization. This way, you can take advantage of the additional settings and controls you get with Group Policy, and you can tailor the policy settings to different groups within your organization.

Q: Can I establish policy settings that will apply to only one user or computer object?

A: This can be done through Group Policy filtering, given the creation of a special group object that contains the user or computer object and Group Policy settings that would be used by those objects. You would then set up a discreet access control list (DACL) on the policy for the special group, which would, in effect, apply that policy only to that group. There are a couple of concerns about doing this. If there were any significant conflicts between the special policy and the general policy for the container, you would have to apply a filter to the main policy object to ensure the special group object does not attempt to apply the main policy. If the reason behind the specialized policy changes, however, there will be two places that would need to be modified, something that could be easily overlooked. In addition, setting up a special policy for only one user or computer in a container could lead to troubleshooting difficulties down the line. The purpose of Group Policy is to establish a set of common environment settings for a group of users or computers. Trying to set specific settings for a single user or computer in that group begs the question of the object belonging to that group in the first place. Before taking the time to specify special settings for an object, make sure the object is in the right place in Active Directory.

Q: I have tried to create Group Policy settings for my Organizational Unit, but the settings don't seem to take effect. Why?

A: Depending on the policy set, the computer may need to be restarted, or the user object may need to log off and log back on for the setting to take effect. The Group Policy in a parent OU, Domain, or Site may have been set to prevent overrides in a subordinate policy. Check with the Group Policy administrator for a parental container to see if this is the case. There may be a conflict with another policy setting in your container. User policy settings generally override computer policy settings, except for offline folder policies, where computer policies generally override user policies.

Q: In what order are user and computer policies applied when a workstation boots up and a user logs on?

A: User and computer policies are applied in the following manner during startup and logon:

1. The computer boots and starts network services—RPCSS (Remote Procedure Call System Service) and MUP (Multiple UNC Provider) services must start.

2. The computer reads and applies Group Policy.

3. The computer runs startup scripts, including any software installation scripts.

4. The user presses CTRL+ALT+DEL to log on, and the user's profile is loaded after network authentication is passed.

5. The user's Group Policy is applied in the following order: Local Group Policy, Site, Domain, OU, etc.

6. The user logon scripts are executed. First, the Group Policy scripts are run, hidden from the user, then the user object logon script is run, visible in a normal window.

Q: Can I place a share for roaming profiles on any Windows 2000 server in my site?

A: Technically, yes. However, copying roaming user profiles from the server to the workstation can be a resource-intensive process, especially if you have a lot of roaming going on in your organization. You should avoid putting roaming profiles on a domain controller or any other high-activity server.

Q: I'm trying to set up folder redirection for the My Documents folder in Group Policy. I set the policy to move the contents of the folder to the redirected location. When I logged on, I received a message that the contents of the My Documents folder were unavailable because they had moved or changed. What is going on?

A: Most likely, your account was already logged on to another computer when you changed the policy and tried to log on. The other computer probably also received a similar error message. You need to log off both computers, and then log on to one of them and check the contents of your My Documents folder. Chances are the contents are complete and now stored in the new location. (This has happened to the author more times than he cares to admit!)

Q: I removed a folder redirection policy for one of my groups, and now some users cannot get the data that was in the redirected folder. What happened?

A: The redirection policy setting for policy removal was set to redirect the folder back to the local user profile location when policy is removed. Chances are that the folder contents were not moved to the new location when the policy was enacted. Happily enough, the user data is still in the redirected folder and can be copied back to the user folder.

Q: I set a policy to redirect the My Documents folder for a group of users to a new network server. One of my users complains that some of his files are missing and others have been changed. How did this happen?

A: If you set the policy to point the My Documents folder to a network share and did not use the %username% variable, all user objects affected by the policy are now using the same network folder as their My Documents folder. So, if one user deletes a file from his My Documents folder, it will be removed from all users' My Documents folders. When using Group Policy to redirect folders to a network share, you should always use the %username% variable to create a unique folder in the share for each user, so each person has protected space for his or her data.

Chapter 7

Managing User Data

Solutions in this chapter:

- Planning User Data Management
- Managing User Documents
- Managing User Disk Quotas
- Securing User Data

Introduction

While installing the Windows 2000 operating system and preparing applications is important, we use these systems to create and store data. Without this ability, all of the previous work to install and create a desktop is worthless. This is the most critical component of any system. Creating and maintaining strategies for managing this data must be completed to ensure it is not lost.

Several techniques can be used to manage user data. First, you must understand and plan how to manage user data. It is much easier to implement a strategy prior to deploying Windows 2000 instead of completing it later. Next, managing user documents is done to verify that data is intact and recoverable. Disk quotas can be set up to enforce disk restrictions available for users and groups. This can be especially helpful if a computer is shared. Lastly, securing data from intrusion is critical in many cases. These are all helpful techniques that can be used to ensure the integrity of the data located on these systems.

Planning User Data Management

Since data is the lifeblood of any company or organization, it must be treated as such. Taking a lackadaisical attitude toward data will not only earn you a bad reputation within your organization, it could interfere with your job security as well! Imagine how you would feel if the payroll department lost your paycheck and didn't seem to care that much about finding it. Or worse yet, they tell you that it's not their responsibility that your check was lost.

Depending on your organizational structure, it is possible that data as important as payroll records, a presentation your president is making to shareholders, patient medical records, or your own favorable job review by your boss could be within your support structure. A well-planned data management process is key to keeping your company in business and profitable. Even if you don't understand what your users' data is, you must treat it like gold, and in doing so let them know that you understand its importance as well.

For Managers

Successful Data Management Requires Teamwork

A complete data management solution cannot be one-sided. In other words, the data management solution cannot rest solely on your shoulders, nor must it be entirely the responsibility of your user base. In order for a data management solution to be successful, both parties must share responsibilities.

One of the key elements for the success of this teamwork is communication. Even if you develop the best plan for your organization, it will be ineffective if your users have never heard about it. By the same token, you cannot develop a good plan if you don't know what your users' needs are. As you go through the process of developing your data management plan, involve key members of your user base. Select individuals from your user community who understand the data needs of their areas and are well respected within their group. They can help to effectively communicate the needs and requirements of their groups and take any issues back to their peers to explain them in an easily understood way. But do not rely solely on these team members to be your only line of communication with your user community. During the planning process, establish a routine of regular communications that provide a brief status update, without getting overly technical or going into great detail. You want to involve your users in the process, not beat them over the head with it!

Another critical aspect of the process is educating the user community in how to participate in the data management processes. It is not enough that you develop a plan with them and provide them tools to use; you must also show them how to use the tools. Not only will this help to strengthen your partnership with your user community, it will also lead to fewer calls for help.

Continued

Finally, make sure your user community understands what your limitations are, either financially or technologically. For instance, who would pay for a backup system that could handle completely backing up every workstation hard drive every night? If your users understand the limitations you are working within, they will be less likely to ask for the moon that you cannot afford to purchase, which could help avoid future conflicts or misunderstandings. Plus, in terms of monetary limitations, your user base might be willing to contribute some of their money to the project if doing so would help them achieve a level of service they might otherwise not have.

Through all of this, however, you may need to continue to assert your technical expertise, albeit gently and without malice. You and your team understand the technology that is being used, including all of its benefits and limitations. But by working in a team of people who have a solid understanding of their own skill area, you can develop a data management strategy that will survive past implementation and might help your company avoid a major data disaster.

Developing Data Management Strategies

In the ideal world, local computer resources would be used to store and execute applications, while application data would be stored on a remote server. This would make the data easy to back up and manage, as well as making it available to any user on the network at any time.

While we're dreaming, let's imagine a world where disk drives don't crash.

The simple truth is that more than bad media endangers computer data. Computer viruses, faulty network transmissions, and user interaction can all lead to the corruption or total loss of data. Any support professional can tell you his or her own favorite story of the horrible results of lost data and how it came to be. And while many of these stories tend to be humorous to the support community, their simple existence indicates that data loss is not an iso-lated problem.

But data security and integrity is only one aspect of data man-agement. Access to data is often as important, if not more so. A soft-ware developer who cannot access his or her code is just as unproductive as if the code had been damaged or destroyed. The Chapter 6 sidebar "For Managers—Where to Store User Data" takes a look at the evolution of data storage approaches, and addresses several issues related to server-based storage of user data. But a complete plan for managing user data must look at both local and remote storage of data. After all, we don't live in the ideal world.

If you are reading this book, you are probably in the planning or early implementation stages of a Windows 2000 rollout in your organization. Hopefully, you will be reading this far enough in advance of an implementation that you will be able to apply some of the knowledge and techniques in the book to your infrastructure, improving its stability and making the transition process smoother. Even if you don't fall into these categories, you can still use the ideas and techniques described in this chapter to help implement your data management solution, even if it comes after the full-scale upgrade. So let's take a look at some of the technologies Microsoft has given us in Windows 2000 and how to use them to implement an effective data management strategy.

Managing User Documents

As much as having users store their data on a file server would sim-plify a system administrator's life, that solution is not always the best. For instance, you may not be able to afford to give every user a 2GB allocation of disk space on a server (or set of servers!) for data storage. Also, system administrators may not want to give their users the permissions necessary to set up customized data shares from the network file system. And there are user files that users may not need or want on a network server, such as temporary files, Internet browser cache files, or other files deemed as expendable. In any case, users are going to keep some of their files on the local machine, even if a robust and reliable network storage solution is in place for them. Instead of going into combat with your users, trying to persuade them to use only the network solution, attempt to understand their data needs, and work with them to develop a solution that meets both of your goals.

Managing Personal Files

In this chapter, we will approach topics from a standpoint of your system environment is mixed. That is, you allow users to store data on their local machines and on network servers. However, the concepts detailed here can be applied if this approach does not match your environment. As it would be impossible to provide examples and explanations for every possible system configuration, the samples and exercises detailed here will be generalized to a certain degree. It should not, however, be difficult for you to adapt any concepts presented here to fit your specific environment.

Allocating Local Resources

As mentioned earlier, there are some types of application data that must reside on the local disk. It would make very little sense to store temporary Internet files on a network file server, as it would impact the performance of the Internet browser. By the same token, many applications create temporary work files in the process of editing or creating documents, and storing those files on the network would again negatively impact the performance of the application, network, and file server.

One example of an approach to allocating local disk resources is to designate one portion of disk storage into space to be used by the operating system and applications, and another into space for user data storage. In other words, drive C: for Windows 2000 and user programs, and drive D: for user data. In Chapter 6, we learned methods for redirecting folders such as the My Documents folder to alternate locations. For this example, the My Documents folder could be configured in Group Policy to point to drive D: by default. This approach has several benefits. In organizations where desktop backups are performed, the backup process could focus on drive D: where the data is stored, which would cut down on backup times and total backup capacity needed. In cases where a disk failure or other corruption occurred, preventing a normal system boot, the C: partition could be replaced with a standard installation image while leaving the data on the D: partition intact. User education is kept to a minimum in this approach as well. Users can be instructed to store all their data on drive D: if they choose to save data outside of the My Documents folder.

There are a myriad of ways that local disk space can be partitioned, and finding the right resource allocation is up to you. Some thought should be given to identifying drive C: as a location only for the operating system and a standard application suite, as doing so could have a positive impact on future support for your user base.

For IT Professionals

Partitioning Local Windows 2000 Disks

Computing technology often improves at a rate greater than we are capable of handling. One example of this that has been a constant factor for the last 10 years or so has been the ever-increasing capacity of disk drives. There have been many instances in that time where drive manufacturers would develop disk technologies that yielded capacities greater than the current operating systems could handle, forcing the OS developers to play catch-up with hardware developers. With Microsoft, we've moved from maximum disk sizes of 32MB to 2GB and beyond, each hurdle being addressed in an update to the operating system that might sometimes require a complete reformatting of the disk in order to work.

Continued

But the operating systems themselves have also led to the need for larger capacity disks. Early versions of Microsoft operating systems could fit on a 360K floppy, while Windows 2000 needs a 1GB partition just to install. At the writing of this book, it is not uncommon to find desktop and laptop computers shipping with 10GB (or larger) disk drives. In a year, we may look back and wonder how we survived in a world with disk drives that were so small. I remember the days when we could run an entire network with shared applications and user data on an 80MB disk drive.

Many computers in production today are running Windows 95 or Windows 98 using 16-bit file allocation tables (FAT-16) for partitioning. This system yields a maximum partition size of 2GB. The 32-bit file allocation table (FAT-32) structure, which allows for much larger partitions, is supported by Windows 98, but not many have adopted the use of this formatting system. Windows NT introduced the NTFS file system that is superior to FAT-16 and FAT-32 with its larger partition sizes and file system security options, but it can only be used on a local disk with the Windows NT operating system.

Windows 2000 is the first operating system that supports all three of these disk-partitioning schemes, and there are times when it may make sense to use more than one formatting scheme on a local disk. When moving users from an earlier operating system to Windows 2000, you should consider how to repartition the local disk, if at all. One thought is to immediately reformat the local disk with NTFS, making the disk one giant partition instead of several 2GB partitions, for disks that are larger than 2GB, of course. But consolidating the disk space into one partition may not make the most sense. By using multiple partitions under Windows 2000, you can provide a very clear separation of operating system and application storage space from user data space, for example. And even though NTFS is a more efficient file system than FAT-16 and FAT-32, there is still additional overhead associated with larger partitions that may prevent you from making the most efficient use of the disk space that is available.

Continued

Take some time to evaluate the pros and cons of several disk-partitioning approaches before deciding how to allocate local disk space for your Windows 2000 users. You may find that different schemes work better for some of your users than others, and you can help maximize the users' environment by tailoring disk allocation to best meet their needs.

No matter which approach you take, one factor you must consider is that your user base understands its data needs better than you do in many cases. If your user environment is a dynamic one, there may be times that your users need to share data amongst themselves outside of the normal communication or hierarchical channels of your organization. By giving your users an allocation of local disk space to use for themselves, you can empower them to set up their own shares and control access to those shares in ways they would not be able to do with server-based data storage. Additional information regarding the setup and maintenance of user shares can be found later in the chapter.

Finally, there are times when users may want a place to keep private data, a cubby hole where they can keep files away from prying eyes. Hopefully, your organization does not have the reputation of a group that peruses the contents of user data files regularly. Even so, most users acknowledge that system administrators have the tools to do these things, even if policy and procedures mandate otherwise. Allowing the user to have local disk space that is not monitored or backed up will allow the user to have a safe place where he or she can store sensitive, personal, or inconsequential data, knowing that only their eyes can see the contents. Methods and tools for helping the user to secure this kind of data are found later in this chapter.

Allocating Server Resources

While the actual hardware planning of a file server environment is beyond the scope of this chapter, the information here is presented with the assumption that ample disk space is available for every

user. That space may not be all in one location or used for one purpose, but we will assume that you have more than 1GB of shared
disk that several thousand users are going to access on a regular
basis.

Chapter 6 deals with redirecting certain folders in the Windows
2000 environment from local disk locations to network shares. But
while that chapter went through the mechanics of how to set up
redirection, it did not cover methods for determining where those
folders may be redirected. This section will provide a few brief
thoughts about planning for data redirection.

As mentioned in Chapter 6, the most commonly redirected folder
is the My Documents folder. Redirecting this folder to a network
location is almost invisible to the user, as most software applications written for the Windows 2000 environment use the My
Documents folder as the default location for storing data. Having
this folder, and by extension the user's data, on a file server can
ease maintenance of backups and make the data available to the
user from multiple workstations. In fact, each folder that can be
redirected through Group Policy has its own set of advantages and
disadvantages for being redirected to a server location.

The basic rule of thumb that applies here is not to keep all your
eggs in one basket. Setting up one server to provide storage for all
redirected data may make some sense from an administrative point
of view, but when that server is unavailable due to a system failure,
network outage, or disk crash, the entire user environment is put
on hold. Also, depending on the size of the user environment and
the amount of data involved, there could be serious performance
implications for storing the data in one location. Other factors
affecting performance include geographic location, network topology,
and group function. The server or servers you set up for redirected
data should not share hardware with key network services. In other
words, do not set up a large user data share on your primary Site,
Domain, or Organizational Unit server.

Since it is one of the most commonly used folders, let's examine
several factors that could impact the way you allocate resources for

the My Documents folder. If you have a few hundred users with minimal disk usage, you could probably maintain a single file server for storing all their data. On the other hand, if you have several thousand users who are working with massive amounts of data on a regular basis, a single server may not be able to provide a reasonable solution.

Other factors to consider when planning data storage include geography (keeping data servers physically or logically close to the user who will be accessing it), job function (multimedia developers may have different storage requirements than accountants), and department allocation (users within a department may need to share data amongst themselves or keep sensitive data away from other users). You could also set up additional storage locations based on more arbitrary means, such as username, account creation date, or seniority.

In any case, if you suspect that the data load you have planned for a server will affect the performance of the server, investigate bringing up additional servers, as necessary, to handle the data load. Transitioning users from one server to another can be handled seamlessly through Group Policy, if the redirection has been established in Group Policy initially.

Creating Shares

Once you have planned how to allocate disk resources to your user base and installed the resources on the network, you need to give your users access to the resources. This is done by creating network shares. Shares can be thought of as "virtual volumes" on the network. In practice, a share is a folder hierarchy on a disk drive that has been advertised to users on the network. Shares can also be shortcuts to disk locations to cut down on very long path names to data storage areas. And, if allowed by Group Policy, shares can be set up on local computers as well as servers.

Server Shares

One of the easiest and most common ways for creating shares on a server or workstation is through Windows Explorer. The Explorer window provides a graphical representation of shared folders, making them easy to spot by the system administrator. Figure 7.1 shows the Explorer window for the C: drive on a server. In the figure, three folders are shared folders—Home, Pictures, and Profiles—represented by a hand holding the folder. The other folders on the drive are not shared, with one exception. The WINNT folder is shared as a system share and is a hidden share. Information about special server shares will be presented later in the section.

Figure 7.1 Shared folders are indicated with a special folder icon.

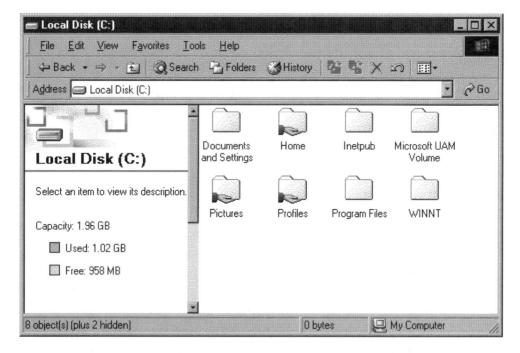

Network shares can be located by browsing to the server holding the shares. In Figure 7.2, we see the available shares for server Srv1, including the Home, Pictures, and Profiles shares. There are additional shares listed, some of which are system shares, like the

NETLOGON and SYSVOL shares, and others are arbitrary shares. In this figure we also see the Printers and Scheduled Tasks folders, which, as indicated by their icons, are not shares, but do provide user access to objects contained within them. The distinction indicated by the difference in the icons is that network drives can be mapped to the shares, but not to the Printers and Scheduled Tasks folders. Only accounts with administrative access to the computer will be able to access the Scheduled Tasks folder remotely. Normal user accounts will not see the Scheduled Tasks folder in the browser.

Figure 7.2 Server shares available on server Srv1.

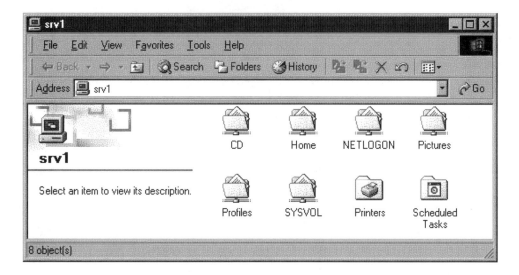

Setting Up a New Share

Let's suppose we need to create a new share on this server called Common. First, we create the folder on the server, then configure the sharing properties by right-clicking on the folder and selecting the Sharing... menu item, as demonstrated in Figure 7.3.

Figure 7.4 shows the Sharing tab of the Properties dialog for the Common folder. In this tab, you can specify the name the folder will be advertised as in the Share name: text box. Descriptive information about the share can be entered in the Comment: field, and this information will be displayed when a user views the properties of the

Figure 7.3 Selecting the Sharing... menu option for the Common folder.

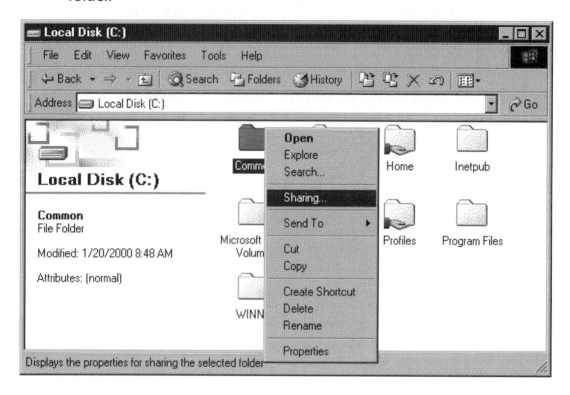

share or when the share is displayed in an Explorer window in Detail view. You can specify a maximum number of users who can access the share simultaneously in the User limit: selection. The Maximum allowed radio button is selected by default and allows the maximum number of connections permitted by the server to connect to the share. An alternate number can be specified in the Allow Users pick list. Share permissions can be modified by clicking PERMISSIONS, and if offline folders are configured in your network, settings for how this share is used with offline folders can be set by clicking CACHING.

Figure 7.5 shows the default permissions for the share. By default, every share that is created assigns Full Control permission to the Everyone group. Many inexperienced system administrators

Figure 7.4 The Sharing tab of the Common folder's Properties dialog.

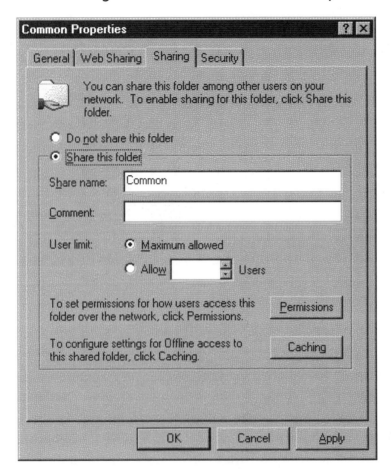

will forget this important fact and only get reminded when something happens relating to the share. Permissions can be modified in this dialog by clicking the Allow or Deny check boxes for the Full Control, Change, or Read permissions for the group/user selected in the Name list. Additional permissions for other user or group objects can be granted by clicking ADD..., and clicking REMOVE will remove the selected object from the Name list, removing the specific permissions assigned to that object.

A brief review of permissions is in order here. Share permissions are different from file system permissions (NTFS permissions), but both are needed to allow access to files and folders within a share.

.

Figure 7.5 Share permissions for this folder indicate full control by the group Everyone.

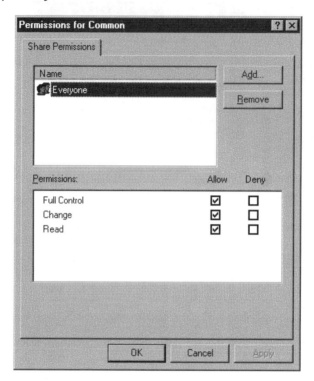

The permissions assigned in this dialog directly affect the share object only, and determine how the share object is accessed. In this case, if left alone, every authenticated user on the network could not only see the share advertised, but could modify the security permissions on the share. If the Full Control permission were removed, then authenticated users could see the share and access and modify the contents of the share, but they could not modify the security permissions. On the other hand, if only the Read permission were applied, then authenticated users could only see the share and the contents and not make changes to the contents. This is because share permissions filter file system permissions for the share. This means that if a user object has only Read permissions on the share, that user will only be able to read the contents of the files and folders in the share, no matter what the file system permissions may be. If the user has Read and Change permissions on the share, the user will be able to read and modify the files and folders in the

Table 7.1 Share Permissions

Permission Name	Permission Tasks
Read	■ View file and folder names ■ Traverse subfolders ■ Read data files and execute programs
Change	■ Same as Read ■ Add files and subfolders to shared folder ■ Modify data files ■ Remove files and subfolders
Full Control	■ Same as Change ■ Change NTFS permissions ■ Take ownership of NTFS objects

share, depending on the file system permissions. Table 7.1 details the capabilities of the share permissions.

These permissions can be set to Allow or Deny in the Permissions dialog. The Deny setting overrides other Allow permissions that have been set for the specific user or group directly or permissions that have been inherited from other groups. For instance, checking the Deny box for the Full Control permission will automatically set the Read and Change permissions to Deny as well. In addition, if the Full Control permission is set to Allow for one group but set to Deny for the Everyone group, then no users will be able to access the share, as the Deny permission for group Everyone overrides any Allow settings specified elsewhere.

In our example, we want the folder to be accessed, but not manipulated, by our entire user population. So, we would remove the check in the Allow box for Full Control in Figure 7.5. This configuration will allow all network users to open the share and work with the contents, assuming the file system permissions are set correctly.

NOTE

The share permissions only manage access to the files and folders in the share when accessed through the share. The share permissions have no effect if the user accesses the files and folders while logged on to the computer where the files are stored.

Before we continue with file system permissions on the folder, we will briefly examine the Caching settings for the share. Figure 7.6 shows the Caching Settings dialog for the folder. If offline folders are enabled by default on the server, then caching of the folder is enabled by default when sharing for the folder is activated. Folder caching can be disabled for individual shares by turning off the "Allow caching of files in this shared folder" check box.

Figure 7.6 Default settings for folder caching when offline folders are enabled.

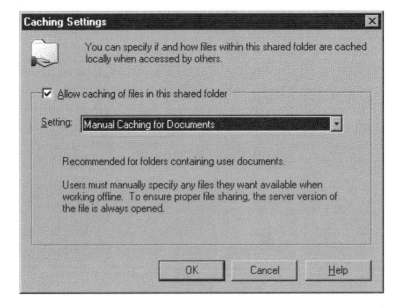

There are three settings possible for folder caching. The default setting is Manual Caching for Documents, as seen in Figure 7.6. This default setting is recommended when a folder share is being used to store user data. With this setting, users must specify which documents in this share are cached locally. This setting should be used when the share stores data accessed by multiple users. Another setting is Automatic Caching for Documents. This setting automatically caches every file a user opens from the share. It does not cache every file in the share, however. With this setting, users can still manually synchronize files into their local cache. The third setting is Automatic Caching for Applications. This setting is intended for shares that are read-only or contain data that is not to be changed. Unlike the other two options, cached files are opened from local cache first instead of opening off the server first. This reduces network traffic as the local copy of the file never changes since the share or its contents are read-only.

Figure 7.7 shows the Security tab of the folder Properties dialog. This tab contains the file system permissions for the folder. Again, by default the Everyone group has full control permissions for the contents of the folder. This will allow all users to make modifications to all contents within the share, including changing permissions on the files or subfolders themselves.

The file system permissions that can be configured in this tab include Full Control, Modify, Read & Execute, List Folder Contents, Read, and Write. Table 7.2 gives a breakdown of the file system tasks that are allowed by the different permissions.

When the "Allow inheritable permissions from parent to propagate to this object" check box is enabled, the default settings for the folder are matched to the settings for the parent folder. This box is enabled by default, and the Allow permission check boxes are grayed out. In order to specify an alternate set of permissions to be effective for this folder, you will first need to turn off that check box. When you do, you will be asked if you want to copy the permission settings from the parent folder, which will enable the specific permissions set in the parent folder, or remove all permission settings, which will create a blank list of permissions for the folder.

Figure 7.7 The default setting for file system security gives the Full Control permission to the Everyone group.

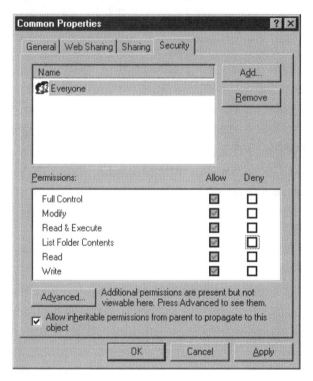

Table 7.2 File System Permissions

Permission Name	Permission Tasks	Additional Notes
Write	<ul><li>Create, write to, and append to files</li><li>Write attributes and extended attributes</li><li>Read permissions on files and folders</li><li>Synchronize files to this folder</li></ul>	The Write permission can be used by itself to create a "drop box," a place where files can be written, but not read. All other permissions must be removed for this effect.
Read	<ul><li>Read file/folder data</li><li>Read attributes and extended attributes</li><li>Read permissions on files and folders</li><li>Synchronize files from this folder</li></ul>	The Read permission can only open data files. With only this permission in effect, application programs within the folder cannot be run.

Continued

Permission Name	Permission Tasks	Additional Notes
List Folder Contents	▪ Same as Read ▪ Traverse folders	This activity only applies to and is inherited by folders.
Read & Execute	▪ Same as List Folder Contents ▪ Execute files	This activity applies to files and folders and is always present when viewing folder permissions.
Modify	▪ Same as Read & Execute ▪ All permissions for Write ▪ Delete files	This activity does not include removing subfolders, only files within the folder where the permission applies.
Full Control	▪ Same as Modify ▪ Delete subfolders and files ▪ Change permissions on files and folders ▪ Take ownership	Care should be given when granting this permission to a non-administrator user object.

WARNING

In file system and share permissions, the Deny setting overrides all other settings. For example, setting the Full Control permission for the Everyone group to Deny in an attempt to keep non-Administrators from modifying system settings will actually lock out all administrators as well as regular users. Since administrators are members of the Everyone group, the Deny setting would override any other settings, including an Allow for Full Control, the account may have. When modifying share and file system permissions, first try removing the Allow permission for settings you want to remove to see if you get the desired result. Once the Deny setting is applied in certain places, it cannot be undone, so use the setting wisely. For instance, if an administrator sets the Full Control permission on the C:\WINNT folder to Deny for group Everyone, then no user account, not even an administrator, will be able to access the folder, which will prevent anyone from being able to log on to the workstation or run any applications.

As with the share permissions discussed earlier, it is in your best interest to remove the Full Control permission for the Everyone group. Even though the Full Control permission will not be effective if the Full Control share permission is turned off for the Everyone group, that only impacts the Full Control NTFS permission when a member of the Everyone group accesses the files and folders through the share. If the user logs on to a computer and accesses the file directly from the file system, the share permissions no longer filter the NTFS permissions, and in this example the user would have Full Control over the contents of the folder. You may wish to modify other settings as needed for additional security.

For this example, we will give users the ability to read, write, create, and modify files in this folder, as well as the ability to traverse and create folders, by enabling all permissions except Full Control and Modify. First, we turn off the "Allow inheritable permissions from parent to propagate to this object" check box and copy the permissions from the parent folder. Then we remove the checks under Allow for Modify and Full Control to get the configuration shown in Figure 7.8. Clicking Apply will make these changes active. Now any user on the network can access the share we just created through \\Srv1\Common and read, write, and modify any file in the share and its subfolders. Since the Modify permission has not been set, no users will be able to change or remove any subfolders in this share.

Local Shares

Creating local shares on a Windows 2000 workstation follows exactly the same procedures as for creating server shares. In order for a user to be able to create a share, however, the user must belong to the local Power Users or Administrators groups. Therefore, it is possible that a user could create and manage shares on one workstation but not another. And regular users cannot create shares on the local workstation or any Windows 2000 server.

Figure 7.8 Final permissions configuration for shared folder Common.

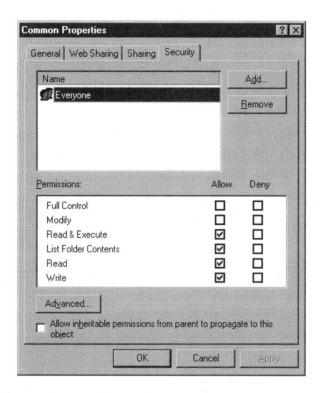

The most important thing to remember about supporting a local user base that maintains its own local shares is that when a new share is created, the Everyone group has Full Control permissions to the share and its contents, unless the creator of the share modifies the permissions. Communicating this information to the users who want to create local shares is important, as improperly configured shares are a security concern. For instance, if a user decides to share the C: drive on his Windows 2000 workstation and doesn't modify the share or security permissions, every user on the network will have full access to every folder on the drive, including the WINNT folder. And while Windows 2000 does have some internal security mechanisms that will prevent certain files from being modified or deleted, anyone taking advantage of this type of access can wreak havoc on the system, easily putting the computer into a state where it is no longer usable.

Managing Shares

In addition to creating shares and modifying permissions at the workstation and server, system administrators can also use the Shared Folders snap-in for Microsoft Management Console (MMC) to manage shares on servers and workstations. When adding this snap-in to an MMC console window, you will be asked to configure several settings, as shown in Figure 7.9.

Figure 7.9 Configuration options for the Shared Folders snap-in for MMC.

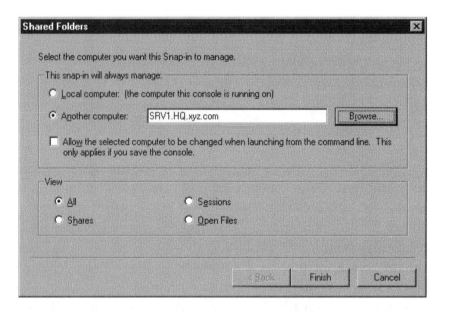

Once the snap-in has been added, the console displays information about the shares on the server SRV1.HQ.xyz.com as shown in Figure 7.10. The Console window shows the shares created earlier: CD, Common, Home, Pictures, and Profiles. The NETLOGON and SYSVOL shares we saw in Figure 7.2 are also shown here as Logon server shares. There are a few other shares shown that are worth mentioning, however.

Figure 7.10 Examining server shares with the Shared Folder snap-in for MMC.

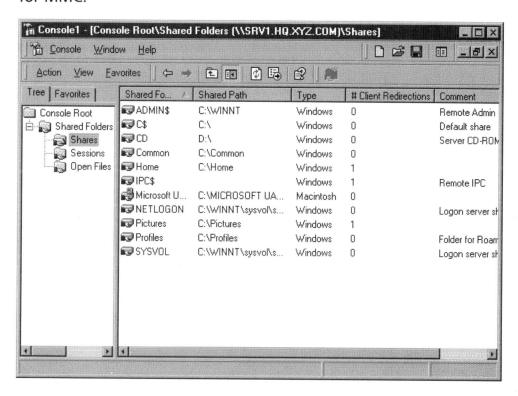

The ADMIN$, C$, and IPC$ shares are all hidden shares. The $ at the end of the share name indicates that the share is hidden. These three shares are system shares that allow for administrative access to some areas of the computer. While they are not advertised to users like the other shares seen in Figure 7.2, they can be accessed directly. For instance, if an administrator needed to access the root of the C: drive on server Srv1, he or she could browse directly to the share by entering \\Srv1\C$ in the Run... command in the Start menu.

One other share to point out is the Microsoft UAM Volume share. This share is made available when the server is also acting as an AppleShare server. The folder contains documents to be copied to the Macintosh in order to add the Microsoft User Authentication Method (UAM) to the security authentication methods available for Macintosh logons to the server.

Example: Adding a Cross-Platform Share through MMC

In this example you will see how to use the Shared Folders snap-in to MMC to create a cross-platform share on a server. This example uses a server that is acting as an AppleShare server to demonstrate the cross-platform functionality of the configuration wizard. You can ignore any portions of the following information that do not apply to your environment.

Creating a share through the Shared Folders snap-in is different from creating one directly from the computer file system. The process is handled by the Create Shared Folder wizard. To start the wizard, right-click on the Shares node in MMC and select New File Share, as shown in Figure 7.11.

Figure 7.11 Starting the Create Shared Folder wizard from MMC.

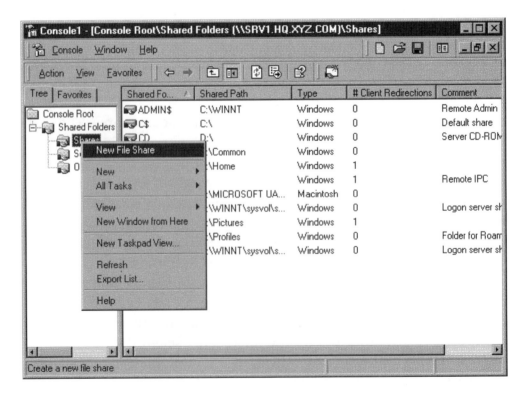

The first page of the Create Shared Folder wizard is shown in Figure 7.12. For this exercise, we will select C:\Data as the folder to share and call the share MacData. In order to make this folder visible to the Macintosh network, the Apple Macintosh check box in the "Accessible from the following clients:" frame must be checked. When that box is checked, the Macintosh share name: text box becomes active and copies the information in the Share name: field into its contents. Finally, we specify the Share description: as "Shared PC/Mac Data Folder." If AppleShare services are not installed on the Windows 2000 server, the Macintosh share name: and Apple Macintosh fields will be grayed out, as the Novell NetWare option is in Figure 7.12.

Figure 7.12 Entering information into the first page of the Create Shared Folder wizard.

The next page of the wizard is shown in Figure 7.13. In this page, you select the security permissions to apply to the share when it is created. The four options in this window are "All users have full control," where the Everyone group is given the Full Control permission; "Administrators have full control; others users have read-only access," where the Everyone group is given only the Read permission; "Adminstrators have full control; other users have no access," where all share permissions are removed (not denied) from the Everyone group; and "Customize share and folder permissions," where the administrator can specify a security profile different from the first three options. For this example, we select the Customize option and give the Everyone group Read and Change permissions on the share and remove the Full Control and Modify permissions on the file system. Once finished, click FINISH.

Figure 7.13 Specifying the type of permissions to set on the new share.

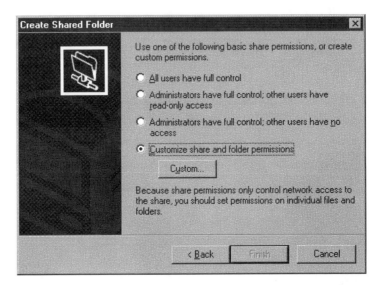

When the share is created, the MMC display updates to present the new configuration, as shown in Figure 7.14. The console shows two new shares: MacData, which is a Windows share out of the folder C:\Data, and MacData, which is a Macintosh share out of the folder C:\Data. The share icon in the console window indicates which shares are Windows shares and which type are Macintosh. Though we gave both shares the same name in this example, we could have called each interface to the share by a different name to help distinguish between them. Plus, we could have specified the share as a Macintosh-only share, as was done with the Microsoft UAM Volume.

Figure 7.14 Updated MMC display showing the new share configuration for server Srv1.

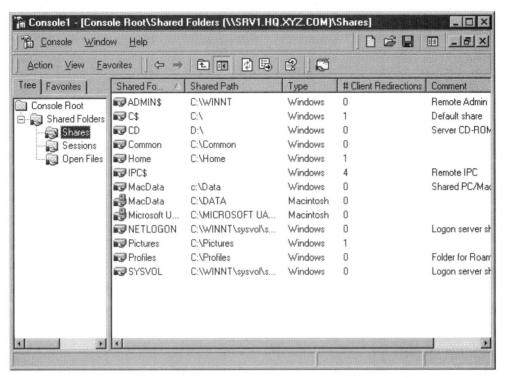

Managing User Disk Quotas

Disk quotas allow system administrators to track and control disk space usage on shared and local volumes. Through the use of quotas, administrators can prevent users from using more than a predetermined amount of disk storage, or log a system event when a user's disk usage exceeds a certain amount. This allows an administrator to run a tight, rigid, controlled system, or simply keep an eye on potential disk storage problems. Your approach to your environment will determine which way you choose to implement disk quotas, if at all.

Let me share with you a personal experience that illustrates why enforcing disk quota limits can be important. Several years ago, I was maintaining a user system that allowed each user to have a maximum of 10MB of storage on a 10GB shared volume. Even though there were close to a thousand users sharing the disk space, very few were using more than a megabyte of storage on the shared volume. So I was able to regularly maintain 2–3GB of unused storage on this volume.

One day I began receiving alerts that this particular shared volume was out of space. The day before, I had run a check and noticed that the space remaining on the volume had dropped just below 2GB. I was planning on performing some routine maintenance on the volume anyway, but I didn't expect to run out of space on the volume before I got started. I quickly checked and found that one user had used over 2GB of space on the shared volume. Looking at his account information, I realized that disk quota limitations on his account had not been enabled, so the account was able to use as much disk space as was available on the drive. And, sure enough, he had tried to use everything that was left.

I contacted the user to ask about the disk usage, and he informed me that he had realized several weeks ago that disk quotas had not been enabled for him. Instead of alerting me, however, he decided that he would use the server storage as a temporary backup for his local data so he could upgrade his local disk drive. As no other user could add any files to the shared drive at the time, I asked him to remove some of the data to free up space for other users of the drive. When I pointed out that I found he was also storing the installation tree from several operating systems on the shared drive, we were able to quickly recover a majority of the disk space he had been using, and full user access to the volume returned to normal.

After the crisis was over, I went back and found that I had neglected to enable disk quotas for all accounts I had created on the day this individual's account was made. I researched the disk usage of the other accounts and found that most of them were also using more than the 10MB limit I thought had been in force, but no other accounts were abusing the storage as this particular individual had been. When I contacted all the users who were over the quota limit and informed them that I was going to start enforcing the limit, most understood. Several responded with, "Yeah, I knew someone would figure it out eventually." Soon, all was restored to normal. I did add a regular maintenance check on user disk space usage to my monthly reporting activities to try and catch a slipup like this more quickly in the future.

But the moral of the story is that through one user's abuse of a hole in my disk quota security plan, all users of this server were unable to save files to the shared storage area for almost an hour. And while that may not seem like a long time to you and me, it did mean that several employees could not perform their jobs for an hour, and as a result, the organization lost several worker hours of productivity, something that can translate into real cost.

Quota Options

Quota settings for a disk drive are accessed through the Quota tab in the disk drive's Properties dialog box, shown in Figure 7.15. Quota settings apply to an entire disk drive, not just to a share on a disk. In the configuration that has been used for examples in this chapter, all shares reside on the same disk. Therefore, we cannot assign different quotas for the My Documents folder redirection and the Common share. To establish different quota settings for those two shares, they would have to exist on different disk drives on the server, or on disk drives on different servers. Also note that quota settings are only available on disk drives formatted with the Windows 2000 NTFS file system.

Quota settings are applied when the "Enable quota management" check box is checked. The remainder of the settings in the Quota tab provide configuration for monitoring disk usage or denying access for users on the disk. The "Deny disk space to users exceeding quota limit" check box will do exactly that when enabled. Any user whose disk usage exceeds the quota limit will be unable to write any additional data to the disk drive, directly or through a share, until existing data is removed and the usage drops below the

Figure 7.15 Quota settings in the disk drive Properties dialog.

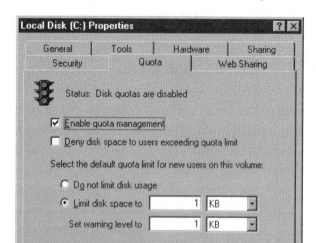

quota limit. This setting is used in conjunction with the "Select the default quota limit for new users on this volume" group, which is where you specify the default settings for quota limits on the disk. Selecting the "Do not limit disk usage" button will allow users to use as much disk space on the drive as is available. Selecting the "Limit disk space to" button will enable the two adjacent fields, which contain the specific disk space limit values. A numeric value goes in the first field, and the next field contains a pick list of the unit values: KB, MB, GB, TB, PB, and EB. The values available in the pick list will depend on the size of the disk drive. If a drive is less than 1MB, only the KB value will appear. If a drive is less than 1GB, only the KB and MB values will appear. If the drive is larger than 1GB, all values will be available. The "Set warning level to" fields are active even when the "Deny disk space to users exceeding quota limit" check box is turned off, so long as the "Limit disk space to" button is enabled. These values, which are set in the same manner as the "Limit disk space to" fields, indicate at which point a warning is generated regarding a user's disk space usage.

The last section of this dialog, "Select the quota logging options for this volume:," configures event logging for the quota system. When the "Log event when a user exceeds their quota limit" check box is enabled, an entry is written to the event log at the point when the user surpasses his or her disk quota limit and is no longer able to write data to the disk. When the "Log event when a user exceeds their warning level" check box is set, an entry is written to the log indicating the warning level has been surpassed. In either case, it is up to the administrator to act on the information in the log.

Quota Entries in this dialog allows the system administrator to create or modify individual user or group settings for quota management. Clicking this button will open the Quota Entries dialog, shown in Figure 7.16, where the administrator can specify quota settings on a user-by-user basis, if desired. The Quota Entries window displays the general quota settings for system groups and the disk space used by any user with data on the quota-enabled disk drive. In Figure 7.16, the HQ\Domain Admins and HQ\Administrator objects have no disk space used on this drive, but the BUILTIN\Administrators group and the user objects jsmith and templ1 are using space on the drive. The figure also shows that even though quota has been enabled, no values have been set for quota limit or warning level.

If you wanted to change the quota values on a particular user object, John Smith for instance, for the disk drive, you can do so in the Quota Entries window. Highlight the user object and open the Properties window for the object by right-clicking on the object and selecting Properties from the pull-down menu. This will open the Quota Settings window seen in Figure 7.17. In this window, you can see the amount of space already in use by the user object, and you can specify values for the quota limit or warning levels for this user. In this case, we have set the quota limit for John Smith at 100MB, and the warning level at 85MB. Once John has stored 85MB of data

Figure 7.16 The Quota Entries window displays the status of user disk space usage.

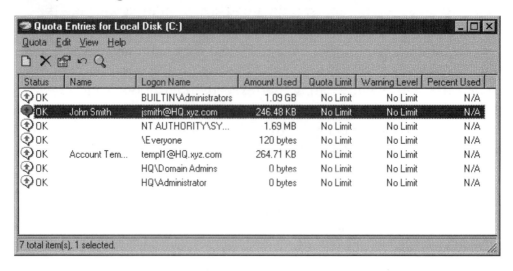

on the drive, he will get a warning message. When his storage gets up to 100MB, however, he will be denied access, and it will appear that the drive he is trying to write to is full. Once we apply the changes, the Quota Entries window will update and appear as in Figure 7.18.

Remote Management of Quota Settings

Quota settings management does not have to be performed at the system on which quotas are being set. Machine administrators can remotely connect to a Windows 2000 server or workstation disk drive and perform the same quota maintenance as if they were sitting at the computer's keyboard. And while you may choose to perform all your server quota maintenance at the server, remote administration of quotas on user computers makes more sense. Quota maintenance on a server can also be done remotely.

Figure 7.17 Individual quota settings for John Smith.

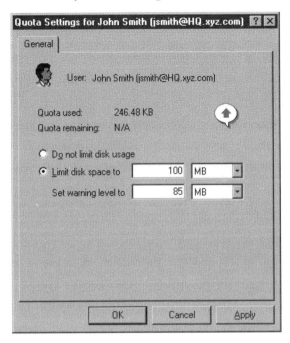

Figure 7.18 Quota Entries window showing specific quota settings for John Smith.

Status	Name	Logon Name	Amount Used	Quota Limit	Warning Level	Percent Used
OK		BUILTIN\Administrators	1.09 GB	No Limit	No Limit	N/A
OK	John Smith	jsmith@HQ.xyz.com	246.48 KB	100 MB	85 MB	0
OK		NT AUTHORITY\SY...	1.69 MB	No Limit	No Limit	N/A
OK		\Everyone	120 bytes	No Limit	No Limit	N/A
OK	Account Tem...	templ1@HQ.xyz.com	264.71 KB	No Limit	No Limit	N/A
OK		HQ\Domain Admins	0 bytes	No Limit	No Limit	N/A
OK		HQ\Administrator	0 bytes	No Limit	No Limit	N/A

Quota Entries for Local Disk (C:)

Quota Edit View Help

7 total item(s), 1 selected.

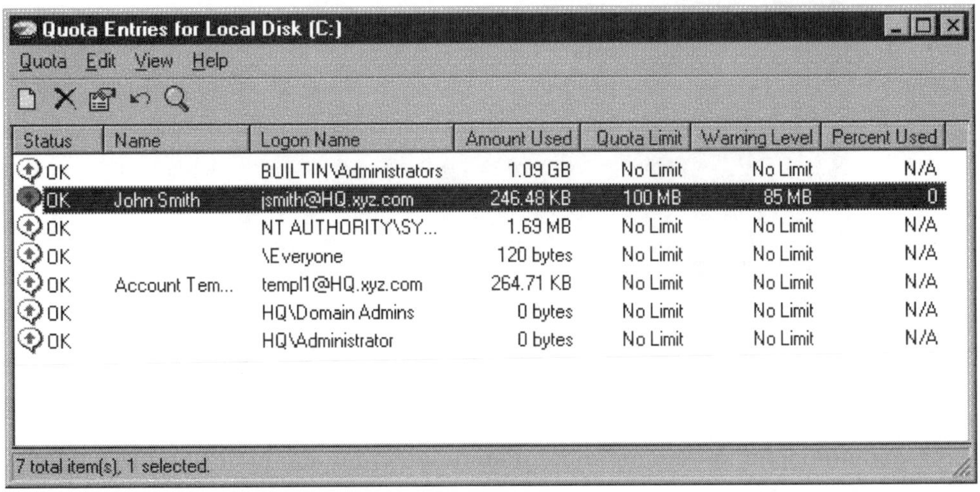

> **NOTE**
>
> Only administrators on a Windows 2000 workstation can add or modify quota settings for that workstation.

To remotely manage quota settings, you first need to map a drive to the remote server or workstation using the Map Network Drive Wizard, shown in Figure 7.19. This wizard can be launched by right-clicking on the My Computer or My Network Places icon and selecting Map Network Drive, or by selecting the Map Network Drive option under the Tools menu in any Explorer window. In order to manage the quotas for the disk, you must map to the disk drive and not just a share on the drive. In Figure 7.19, we map to the C: drive on Srv1 by using the hidden share \\Srv1\C$.

Figure 7.19 Mapping a network drive to a remote volume.

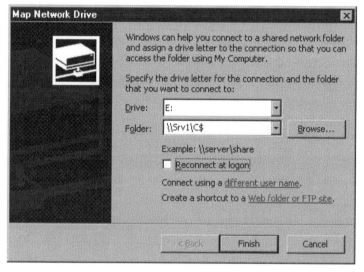

Once the drive is mapped, you can get to the quota settings for the drive by right-aclicking on the mapped drive in the My Computer window and selecting Properties, as shown in Figure

7.20. If you have the appropriate permissions and the drive you have mapped is a Windows 2000 NTFS volume, then the Properties window for the mapped drive will have a Quota tab as shown in Figure 7.21. You can work in the Quota tab for a remote drive exactly the same way you do for a local drive.

Figure 7.20 Selecting Properties for a network drive mapping.

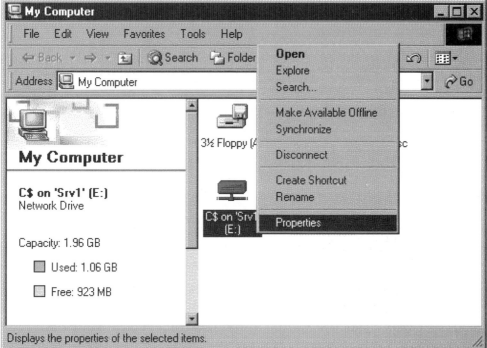

Securing User Data

After you have gone through the process of making sure your users have well-planned storage locations for their data, you might think that your job is complete. However, there is one other step involved in the process, and that step is ensuring the security of your users' and your organization's data. Data security is more than providing a reliable data backup solution or a stable and reliable location for data storage. You must also make sure that only the people who

Figure 7.21 Quota settings for a mapped network drive.

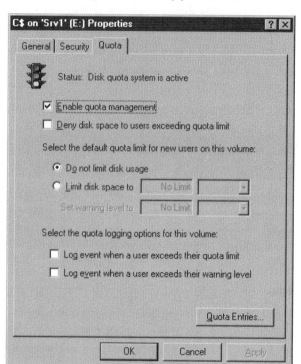

need access to the data have access to the data. How secure is your job if any guest logged on to your system can access your company's top-secret product development plans? Two tools provided by Microsoft with Windows 2000 can help to fully secure your data environment.

NTFS Permissions

We have already examined NTFS permissions earlier in the chapter in relation to data shares. However, share permissions are effective only when a data location is accessed from a network drive. If you have multiple users sharing a single workstation and you need to protect some of the data from some of the users, you will have to set up local disk permissions to ensure the data is protected.

Unlike share permissions, if multiple NTFS permissions apply to a user due to multiple group membership, the least restrictive permission is the one that applies. For example, the Accounting group is given Modify permissions on a disk folder, but the Finance group is only given Read permissions on the same folder. If user John Smith is a member of both groups, his effective permissions for the folder are Modify. For this reason, it is important to plan the folder structure and permissions map carefully when establishing NTFS permissions. You will need to make sure that the permissions you have enabled for a folder really provide the level of access you desire for the folder. For a review of the file system permissions, refer to Table 7.2.

With appropriate guidelines and training, some level of local security management can be left up to the owner of the workstation. Members of the local Administrators and Power Users groups have the ability to set permissions on files and folders on the local computer. While members of the Administrators group can set permissions on any file/folder on the system, members of the Power Users group are more limited in their capabilities. Members of the Power Users group can only add or modify security permissions on objects they have created or have been assigned ownership for. As such, Power Users cannot change the permissions on the C:\WINNT folder, for instance. In addition, Power Users cannot take ownership of files and folders unless they have been given Full Control permissions over the object through another security permission.

For Managers

When to Grant Local Administrator Privileges

The issue of giving users local administrator privileges on their computer is a tricky one at best. Unfortunately, Microsoft did not provide much flexibility in this area with the way local groups are set

Continued

up. In terms of local access, there are three levels of security that can be assigned to accounts in these three groups. The Users group contains objects that can log on to the machine, save files in directories where they have permissions, install some software packages, and modify personal environment settings such as changing system colors and desktop backgrounds, if Group Policy permits. All of the tasks that members of the Users group can perform affect only their account. Any colors they change appear only when they log on. Any software package installed is available only to the account that installed it. Some software packages cannot be installed, such as packages that add or update hardware device drivers or need to add tools into the operating system directories.

Members of the Power Users group can perform all the tasks that members of the Users group can. Membership in this group also allows users to create shares, modify NTFS permissions, install software that would be available to all users of the system, and create and share printer objects. Power Users members cannot modify file permissions of objects they do not own, and there are some kinds of software they still cannot install.

There are times when it is absolutely necessary to give a user administrative privileges on his or her machine. However, there are potential drawbacks in doing so. I have encountered this particular scenario more than once, and it provides a good explanation of the potential problems. A group of users were given new PCs with Windows NT, a book on how to use Windows NT, and administrative privileges on the computer. One of the exercises in the book was a description of working with file permissions and file ownership. In the process of working through the exercise, one user managed to take ownership of every file on the C: drive. Next, the user accidentally added a Deny permission on the Full Control permission for the Power Users group for the root of the C: drive. As a result, the user was unable to log on, and neither was anyone else. Another user in a different organization ended up with the same result but through a different route. In both cases, since no user object, administrator or not, could access the system locally or remotely, both systems had

Continued

to be rebuilt, and both users suffered some level of data loss as a result.

While it may not be possible to establish an organization policy that mandates that no users will have local administrator access to their computers, you should, at the very least, be aware of the issues that can arise as a result and plan for them, either in the delivery of user training to help prevent the problems or in the addition and training of support personnel to clean up when the problems arise. No matter how well-trained a user is in administrator issues, users are human and can make mistakes. Even administrators who have been supporting systems for years can accidentally lock themselves out of a system from time to time. I know this to be true, as it has happened to me more than once!

Encrypting File System

One significant addition to NTFS that Microsoft has provided with Windows 2000 is the Encrypting File System (EFS). When enabled, EFS stores user data in an encrypted format on the disk so that only the user who created the file can read the contents. The encryption process is invisible to the user who is working with the encrypted file or folder. In other words, users do not have to decrypt a file to open and modify it, and they do not have to encrypt it manually after saving the contents.

There are a couple of ways that files and folders can be encrypted. The first way is to set the encrypted attribute on the file or folder in the same way the read-only or hidden attribute is set. When this attribute is set on a file, the file will automatically encrypt. When set on a folder, the contents of the folder will be encrypted. Afterward, all new files created within the folder will be encrypted automatically.

To set the encrypted attribute on a folder, click ADVANCED... in the folder's Properties dialog, as shown in Figure 7.22. This will bring up the Advanced Attributes dialog shown in Figure 7.23. Click on the "Encrypt contents to secure data" check box and OK to enable encryption for the folder. The Confirm Attribute Changes dialog, shown in Figure 7.24, will appear, allowing you to select how you want the settings to apply. Select the appropriate radio button, and

Figure 7.22 Encryption settings can be accessed by clicking ADVANCED....

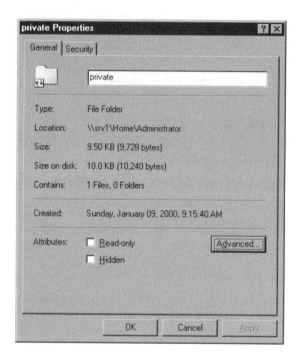

Figure 7.23 Advanced Attributes dialog showing encryption settings.

then click OK. Finally, click APPLY in the folder's Properties dialog, and the encryption settings will be applied as specified. This process can take some time, depending on the amount of data to be encrypted.

When the encryption attributes have been set on a folder, the Explorer information for the folder will show that the folder is encrypted, as depicted in Figure 7.25. This indicator does not specify if any or all of the folder's contents are encrypted, nor does it show if the entire subfolder tree is encrypted. However, each file or folder that is encrypted will have the same indicator in the Explorer window.

Figure 7.24 Applying changes to folder or folder and subfolder contents.

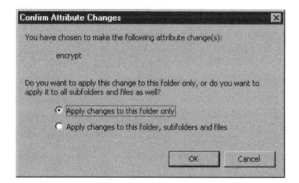

In addition to the primary data storage folders, there are a few other folders that should have encryption enabled when working with secure data. Any temporary folder used by an application that stores its data in an encrypted location should also be encrypted. For instance, if your Human Resource department generates their secure data with Microsoft Word, then the folders where Word stores its temporary, or scratch, data should be encrypted. If an employee is using a Web browser to access secure data, the cache folders for the Web browser should be encrypted.

Microsoft provides an additional tool with Windows 2000 to handle file encryption. This is the command-line utility cipher. Files and folders can be encrypted and decrypted quickly with this tool, which can also be used in system scripts. The cipher utility is controlled by a combination of command-line parameters, which are listed in Table 7.3.

Table 7.3 Cipher Command-Line Parameters

Command-line Parameter	Action
none	Cipher displays the encryption status of the current directory and any files it contains.
/a	Specifies the file on which to perform the selected action. If no filename is specified, this option is ignored.
/d	Decrypts the contents of the specified folder(s). The folder attribute will be changed so that new files added to the folder are not encrypted.
/e	Encrypts the contents of the specified folder(s). The folder attribute will be changed so that new files added to the folder will be encrypted.
/f	Forces the specified encryption or decryption action to take place. By default, files that have already been encrypted or decrypted are skipped.
/h	Displays hidden or system files. By default, these files will not be encrypted or decrypted.
/l	Cipher continues processing even if errors are encountered. By default, cipher will halt if an error occurs.
/q	Cipher will report only the most essential information.
/s:dir	Cipher performs the specified action on the folder and all its subfolders.

Figure 7.26 shows the cipher command executed with no command-line parameters to display the encryption status of the folder C:\secure. The "U" character at the beginning of the line for the Readme.txt file indicates that the file is unencrypted. To manually encrypt the file, the command cipher /e

Figure 7.26 Using the cipher tool to report the encryption status of a file and folder.

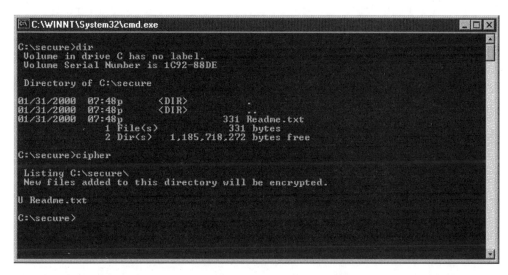

/a Readme.txt can be entered at the command prompt, as shown in Figure 7.27. Upon completion, the command reports the success or failure of the action.

Figure 7.27 Using the cipher tool to encrypt a file.

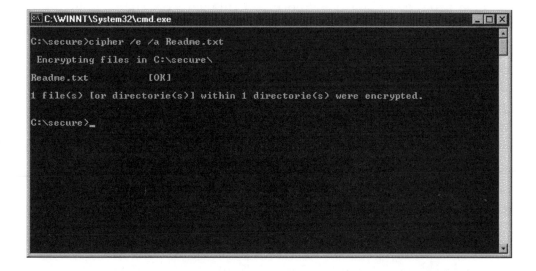

There are a few "gotchas" when dealing with encrypted files. First, only files and folders on NTFS volumes can be encrypted. Only the user who encrypts the file or folder has access to it afterward. Shared files cannot be encrypted and used by more than one user. Compressed files and folders cannot be encrypted. Files and folders that reside on a compressed volume must be uncompressed before they can be encrypted. Files can become decrypted when copied or moved to a non-NTFS volume. However, when these issues are kept in mind, keeping data secure with encryption can be effortless.

Summary

This chapter covered many issues relating to managing user data. Planning the user data environment is a key step in the process, and should be done well in advance of implementation. Understanding the needs of the user community starts with engaging the user community in a planning dialogue. Working with the user community to develop and implement a data storage solution can improve the support the user community receives and simplify the management and maintenance of the system. User data can be stored on local disk space or on network server space. Storing data on local disks gives the user more control over how the data is organized and accessed. Storing data on network servers provides a higher degree of security. Establishing a hybrid process of using both local and network storage space is straightforward and beneficial. Network shares can be configured as offline folders, where a local copy of the contents of the folder will be available when network access is down or the user is off-site. Even with no network access, users can access files in offline folders as though they were active on the network. When network access is restored, the local copy of the files are synchronized with the network copy, and the user resumes working with the network copy again.

Network disk storage is made available through shares. Network shares are created by setting up file and share permissions in the Properties tab on a data folder on a local or server hard drive.

Server shares can be used to store user data, user profiles, and system logon scripts. Shares can be restricted to access by individual users or user groups. There are three share permissions that affect how users gain access to the share: Read, Change, and Full Control. The Read permission allows users to see the share and its contents, but not make any changes. The Change permission allows users to see the share and its contents and modify the contents of the share. The Full Control permission allows users to see and modify the contents of a share, as well as change file permissions on the share. Share permissions are more restrictive than file permissions. If a user has Full Control permissions for the files in a folder, but only has the Read permission on the share through which the data is accessed, the user can only see the contents of the data through the share. Local shares can be established on Windows 2000 workstations by users who are members of the Administrator or Power Users groups. Normal user accounts cannot create shares or share printer objects.

Local access to data can be controlled thorough file system or NTFS permissions. The six NTFS permissions that can be configured are Read, Write, List Folder Contents, Read & Execute, Modify, and Full Control. The Write permission allows users to create, write to, and modify files. The Read permission allows users to read file and folder information. The List Folder Contents permission allows users to navigate the subfolder structure. The Read & Execute permission allows users to read and execute applications. The Modify permission allows users to delete files from the folder. The Full Control permission gives users complete access to the file system, including changing permissions and taking ownership of files. If a user or group is denied any of these permissions, the Deny permission overrides any permission granted or inherited for the file or folder.

Network and local shares can be managed using the Shared Folders snap-in with Microsoft Management Console (MMC). Only domain administrators can use this tool to manage shares on a server. Members of the Administrators group on a workstation can remotely manage shares on that workstation with this tool. The

Shared Folders snap-in displays all shares on a system, including the hidden system shares. Shares can be created for Macintosh volumes as well as PC volumes. New shares cn be created on a remote server or workstation with the Create Shared Folder wizard.

Disk quotas allow administrators to monitor and set limits on disk usage by user accounts. Quotas can only be set on Windows 2000 NTFS-formatted disks. In order for quotas to be monitored or enforced, quotas must first be enabled for the entire disk. Quotas cannot be set on a per-share basis. Quotas are enabled and configured through the Quotas tab of the disk's Properties dialog. Quotas can be set to prevent users from writing additional data to a disk once the quota has been reached, or an event can be logged when the quota threshold has been passed. Disk usage can also be monitored through this interface. When quotas are enabled for a drive, the breakdown of disk usage by user account and group is displayed in the Quota Entries window. Quota settings can also be managed remotely through the Properties dialog for the system disk drive share.

NTFS permissions and the Encrypting File System (EFS) can be used to secure user data. When overlapping sets of NTFS permissions are applied on a folder, the least restrictive setting takes effect. If a user has Read permissions through one group assignment and Full Control permissions through another, the user has Full Control access effectively. EFS allows user data to be stored on a Windows 2000 NTFS disk in an encrypted format. Only the user object that encrypted the file will be able to use the file afterward. File encryption should be used for very sensitive data. File and folder encryption settings should be applied to all folders where sensitive data will be stored, as well as temporary or work folders used by the applications that create and modify the data. Encryption settings are found in the Advanced Attributes dialog of the file or folder Properties dialog. When encryption is applied to an existing folder, the encryption process can take several minutes, depending on the amount of data to be encrypted. File encryption can also be managed with the command-line tool cipher.

FAQs

Q: My partner and I share a Windows 2000 workstation. When my partner logs on to the computer directly, he has full access to his My Documents folder, which is stored on C:. When I'm using the computer and he accesses his My Documents folder across the network, he cannot save any changes to any of his files. What's happening?

A: Check the permissions on the share your partner is using to access his My Documents folder. Chances are that the share permissions he has are Read and not Change. Even though he has permissions to modify the files locally, the share permissions are restricting his access to his files.

Q: I want to create a share on my workstation and restrict access to only certain network groups. When the share permissions are created, the Everyone group has all permissions allowed. I've added the groups I want to access the share and given them permissions, but no matter what permissions I assign to them, they cannot access the share on the network at all. What am I doing wrong?

A: If you left the Everyone group in the share permissions and checked the Deny box for the three permissions, no one will be able to access your share. The most restrictive permissions are the ones applied with shares. To keep Everyone from accessing your share, add the groups that you want to allow access to the permissions list and remove the Everyone group from the list.

Q: I want to set up a share so that several different groups have access to different folders within that share. I don't want all groups to have access to all the shares. I've set up the share so that all groups have Read permissions on the share, and then each group has been given additional permissions on the folders within the share. No one can do anything but read the files in their folders now. How can I fix this?

A: Since you have given only the Read permission to the share, everyone that connects to that share, no matter which subfolder they open, will only have read access to the files in the share. This is because the share permissions are inherited by all subfolders in the share. You will need to grant the appropriate permissions at the share, Read and Change, and then restrict the file permissions for the folders to get the kind of security you want. Or you can set up a separate share for each group and assign the correct permissions to each share point.

Q: I have started getting messages that I am about to reach my quota limit on a file server. I have set my large data files to be compressed on the server to save space, but I keep getting these messages. Why is this happening?

A: File compression has no impact on disk quota limits. Disk usage is always calculated for the uncompressed size of files when calculating quota limits. The only way to lessen your disk storage usage is to remove files and folders from the share that is nearing the quota limit.

Q: Members of our workgroup share a group of Windows 2000 PCs during the day. Some of us are able to create shares on some computers but not others. Others of us cannot create shares on any of the PCs. How can we get set up to create shares on all the PCs?

A: Only user accounts that belong to the local Power Users group can create shares on a Windows 2000 workstation. Those of you who can create shares on some machines are in the Power Users group on those machines. In order for all members of your workgroup to create and manage shares on the PCs, your administrator will need to add your accounts to the Power Users group on each machine.

Q: I work in an environment where I use a PC and a Macintosh, and I access my home directory on the server from both computers. I've started encrypting my data on the server from my PC, but now I cannot read those files from my Macintosh. I use the same account to access the server space. Why can't I see the files with my Macintosh?

A: The Windows 200 Encrypted File System (EFS) is only accessible from Windows 2000 computers. Your Macintosh will not be able to decrypt the files, even though you use the same account to access the files from each platform.

Chapter 8

Developing a Deployment Plan for Windows 2000

Solutions in this chapter:

- Defining the Project

- Assessing the Current Environment

- Building the Test Lab

- Training the Support Staff

- Conducting and Evaluating the Pilot Rollout

- The Production Rollout

Introduction

When deploying any application or change, a strategy and a plan are needed to ensure success. This is especially important when dealing with large-scale environments and with an operating system upgrade of this magnitude. Windows 2000 provides countless improvements and changes that provide a cleaner deployment than did previous versions of Windows operating systems. There are several steps for creating and executing a deployment strategy. First, you must define the scope and objectives of the project. Next, you must assess your current environment for the upgrade. Building the test lab and training the staff are two very important steps to validate and get ready for the deployment. A pilot project is then performed to validate the plan and prepare it for the final roll-out. The entire process flow is shown in Figure 8.1. Following these steps as part of a well-planned and executed deployment strategy is the key to a successful Windows 2000 deployment.

Defining the Project

The first step in your deployment strategy is to define what the project actually entails. This includes determining the scope of the project and its objectives.

Defining the Scope of the Rollout

The project scope determines the boundaries of the project and answers the question, "What is included in the project?" Scope defines the limits of the project and specifies a preliminary time line for project completion. Any tasks identified after planning and during the actual deployment need to be considered as to whether they are within the scope of the project. If they are outside the defined scope, the deployment team needs to decide whether or not the task is important enough to justify broadening the scope definition. Many projects suffer from "scope creep." Scope creep is the continuous

Figure 8.1 Deployment plan process flow.

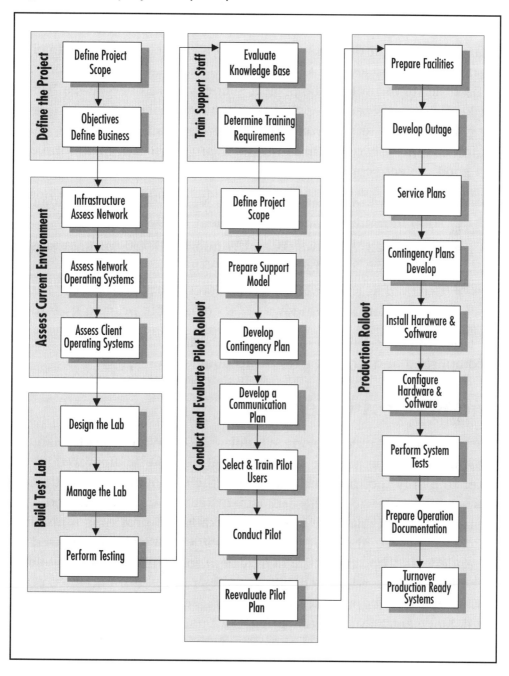

addition of tasks that are outside the defined project scope. These additional tasks usually affect the project team's ability to meet deadlines and provide quality assurance to the final output. Therefore, a thoroughly thought out and a strictly enforced project scope will help ensure that the project stays on track and that deadlines are met.

In order to formulate the project scope, you will need to gather the key business executives and functional managers who are driving your project. Get everyone in a room for a half-day meeting and try to flesh out a two- or three-sentence project scope. An example of a good project scope is:

- Upgrade all production Windows NT 4.0 servers to Windows 2000 in a mixed-mode environment by December 2000.
- Upgrade all Windows 9x and Windows NT 4.0 workstations to Windows 2000 by February 2001.
- Certify that all server-based and workstation-based applications are Windows 2000 compatible prior to upgrade.

This project scope is very succinct in stating what is to be accomplished and when it is to be accomplished.

Defining Business Objectives

Why is the company deploying Windows 2000? What does it wish to accomplish? These are the questions that need to be answered in order to justify the time and expense of the deployment project. To answer these questions, the deployment team must discuss and define a set of business objectives. In addition to providing a justification for the actual deployment, the business objectives are used as guideposts throughout the deployment to ensure that deployment activities are focused on achieving the desired result . So, when one of the departments proposes a change to the desktop configuration, the deployment team can use the set of business objectives as a metric to determine if the change falls within the scope of the project and to help decide whether it should be approved or not.

The business objectives do not all have to be focused on the technology being deployed. For the most part, the technology is business driven. Throughout this chapter the examples show the deployment plan being composed by XYZ Company. XYZ Company produces advertisement posters for the tops of taxi cabs. They have three offices situated in New York, Chicago, and Los Angeles, each a major metropolitan region with lots of taxis to carry their posters. Due to the graphically intense nature of their business, XYZ Company keeps current with technology and incorporates state-of-the-art equipment into their network.

In order to arrive at a set of business objectives for your company, the deployment team needs to conduct interviews with key business executives and functional managers. Here is a list of questions that may be helpful during these interview sessions:

- What does the company need to know to do business?
- What are the industry requirements and standards?
- Are there statutory or legal constraints that affect the data and information needs?
- What business processes does the network currently facilitate?
- Are these business processes expected to change with the implementation of a more functional operating system?
- What future business processes are anticipated, and what types of services will they require?
- What information needs to be accessed, and what groups need to access it?
- What are the end-user requirements?
- What are the priorities for providing a solution to each requirement?
- Are other projects currently in progress?

After conducting interviews with the key business executives and functional managers at XYZ Company, the deployment team documented the following business objectives:

- Support existing mission-critical applications
- Improve performance and reliability for end users
- Define a standard desktop configuration and application suite
- Reduce total cost of ownership by reducing support costs
- Improve overall security of corporate data

Assessing the Current Environment

After the project has been defined, the deployment team must determine what currently exists out on the network. This will involve an evaluation of the network infrastructure, the existing network operation system, and the existing client operating system architecture. The intent of gathering this data is to document what currently exists and to prepare what is needed to make both your hardware and software Windows 2000 ready.

Network Infrastructure

When performing the network infrastructure assessment, the objective is to obtain a clear understanding of how the network is divided, to determine the configured and available bandwidth on network links, to evaluate throughput and delay, and to evaluate whether the network will support the new applications and services that are being deployed. For example, if Dynamic Host Control Protocol (DHCP) is to be implemented, you will want to verify that the routers impacted support RFC 1542, which allows the forwarding of DHCP Discover packets across the routers. Another example is the ability of the existing WAN links to support the various replication and synchronization traffic that is generated when a new operating system or application is introduced onto the network.

Current network diagrams, if available, will provide valuable input into this process. Many times it is necessary to perform a high-level network infrastructure analysis in order to create or update network diagrams to a degree that they are usable for the deployment project.

Luckily, the network team at XYZ Company has kept their network documents accurate and up to date. Figure 8.2 shows the high-level network diagram for the company.

Figure 8.2 XYZ Company network diagram.

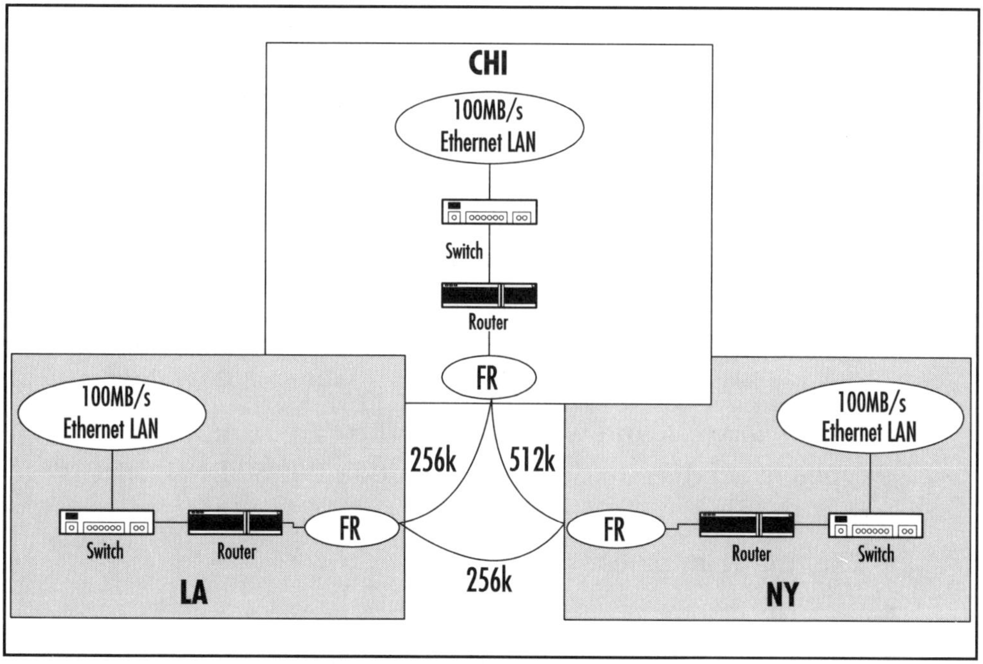

From this diagram we see that the three sites are all connected via a Frame Relay network. LA has 256k permanent virtual circuits (PVCs) to NY and CHI. NY is linked to LA via a 256k PVC and linked to CHI via a 512k PVC. CHI has a 256k PVC to LA and a 512k PVC to NY. At each physical site the WAN router is connected to an

Ethernet switch via a gigabit Ethernet uplink. Each LAN segment supports 100MB/s-switched Ethernet to the desktop.

Existing Network Operating System Environment

Assessing the existing network operating system environment helps in determining what changes may support the deployment of Windows 2000. If your company has not been diligent in keeping this type of data up to date, this task can be very time consuming in large environments. Depending on time constraints and budget availability, it might be wise to outsource both the network operating system and client operating system assessments.

When performing this assessment, some of the information that should be documented includes:

- Number, location, and configuration of servers.
- Current NT domain architecture, including the number of domains, existing trust relationships, location of the primary domain controllers (PDC) and the backup domain controllers (BDC) for each domain, and any existing profiles and policies in place.
- Service packs and hotfixes that have been applied to the servers.
- List of services and what servers they are running on. The types of services to document include WINS, DNS, DHCP, and RAS.
- Existing naming conventions.
- Security policy.
- Backup and disaster recovery applications and processes.
- Directory replication scheme.
- Any additional network operating systems that have been deployed, such asNetWare, Unix.
- Server-based applications.
- Management or administration tools.

There are tools available to help expedite this process and your company may already support one of them. Microsoft offers System Management Server, which provides both hardware and software inventory capabilities. The data collected is stored in an SQL database and can be used to generate reports for use during the deployment planning stages. Two third-party products (and there are many more) that perform hardware and software inventory include NETInventory from BindView and Inventory from Tivoli.

WARNING

If your company has not already implemented an application for hardware and software inventory, now is a good time to consider one. Keep in mind that implementing a product such as Systems Management Server is a large endeavor by itself and requires a significant amount of planning and testing. Developing a deployment plan for one of these applications in conjunction with the Windows 2000 deployment plan will require additional time and resources, but can prove very beneficial in the long run.

Existing Client Operating Systems Environment

The information obtained from a client operating system assessment provides guidance when determining what functionality is needed at the desktop level and documents the current desktop configuration. As with the assessment of your network operating system, assessing your current client operating system environment can be a very time-consuming and costly task. If the necessary people resources are not available to perform an adequate client operating system assessment, serious consideration should be given to outsourcing this task. Additionally, the tools mentioned previously in the network operating system assessment for hardware and software inventory are also applicable for collecting data from the client.

The types of data that should be collected include:

- Number, location, and configuration of desktop systems
- Applications
- Naming conventions
- Network configuration
- Security policy

For IT Professionals

Application Compatibility Testing

One of the most important outputs of the operating system assessment is the determination as to whether a particular application is Windows 2000 compatible or if it will require an upgrade or replacement. Microsoft provides a number of resources to assist you in application compatibility testing.

The Windows 2000 Setup allows you to check the applications installed on your system against a set of known applications that have compatibility problems prior to installing Windows 2000. The syntax for running Setup in this mode is WINNT32.EXE /CHECKUPGRADEONLY. This check is limited to applications currently on the system and will only check them against a small group of applications known to be incompatible with Windows 2000. You should still test applications that do not show up on the list.

Visit the Windows 2000 application list maintained on Microsoft's Web site, www.microsoft.com. This can assist you with the compatibility of many commercial applications, but will not

Continued

provide information for custom applications that your company developed.

Whatever your situation, you will want to develop a method for certifying your applications. Your testing process should, at a minimum, cover the installation and removal of the application, printing functionality, basic features functionality, and inter-operability with other applications.

Building the Test Lab

You have probably heard that in real estate the most important thing is location, location, location! In the technology industry we have a similar saying, which is test, test, test! Proper testing can save you hours of troubleshooting time and incalculable human and financial resources. To ensure that the tests you perform are of value, a proper testing environment must be designed and managed. A properly designed test lab also provides a training ground during the early stages of deployment for administrators and support personnel to become familiar with the new technologies being implemented. Two questions that need to be answered when building the test lab are, how will the lab be managed, and what will be the testing methodology? Even after the deployment, a test lab can be used for change management by testing new products, service packs, and hotfixes.

Designing the Lab

The test lab should reflect the current network and operating system environment as closely as possible. This does not mean you have to cram every piece of PC hardware and LAN/WAN hardware into your test lab and configure it to look like your real network. It does mean that you will have to prioritize what aspects of your current environment are the most important to simulate and how that can be done with the least amount of hardware. This will ensure that the tests performed in the lab, if successful, will have a high probability of succeeding in production. Using the information gathered during the assessments allows you to then design the lab.

After prioritizing which parts of the current environment will be simulated in the lab, you need to determine where the lab will physically reside. Your company might already have a test lab set up for the current infrastructure. The deployment team must decide whether it is possible to reuse the existing lab or if a new lab is required. The information gathered in the network and operating system assessment and the preliminary high-level design for the Windows 2000 deployment should aid in this decision. If new space is needed, the lab design team must ensure that there is adequate room, electrical power, cooling systems, and physical security to prevent unauthorized access to the testing resources. Once these requirements are documented, the appropriate executive personnel need to sign off on the new lab.

The lab must simulate the proposed server and client environment. This involves server and workstation configurations that will closely match the majority of systems that will be deployed. In the test lab, a single server can provide multiple services that normally would be distributed across more than one server. For example, one lab server can provide DNS, DHCP, and WINS services. The servers should be set up based on the preliminary high-level design. If a first-draft Active Directory architecture has been proposed, the lab should be configured to match that design. Figure 8.3 shows XYZ Company's proposed Active Directory namespace.

At the minimum, the test lab must contain one domain controller for each domain. Additional servers can be added to test down-level compatibility with legacy NT domains or interoperability with different operating systems, such as Unix or Macintosh. Also, if

Figure 8.3 Company's proposed Active Directory namespace.

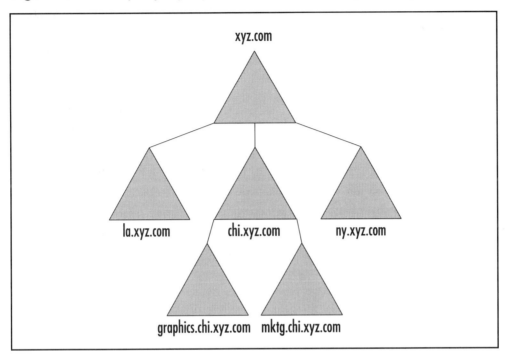

you need to test additional services, these servers can be configured to provide DNS, DHCP, WINS, RAS, or others. Figure 8.4 illustrates how XYZ Company's servers physically map to the proposed Active Directory namespace, and what services each server will offer in the test lab.

In addition to servers and workstations, the lab design team needs to provide a network infrastructure that emulates the existing LAN/WAN environment. In order to test how the architecture works over slow and fast network links, the necessary network equipment needs to be in place and configured. This step may require coordination with the network infrastructure department to provide support with equipment selection, procurement and configuration. As was discovered during our assessment, XYZ Company has standardized on 100MB/s Ethernet LAN switches with Gigabit Ethernet uplinks at each site. Each site connects to other sites across a Frame Relay

Figure 8.4 Example server roles in test lab.

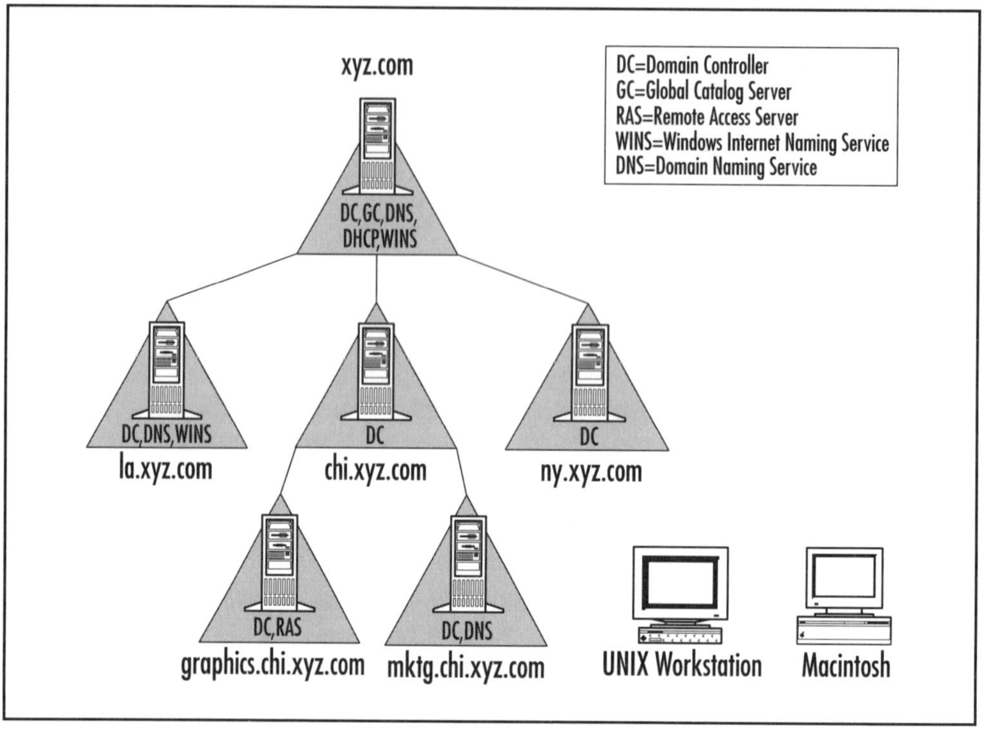

network via a router (see Figure 8.2). We have prioritized our testing needs to be able to test connectivity and performance across the different Frame Relay WAN links, since there are sites connected via 256k and 512k PVCs. The equipment we need are two routers with serial links to simulate the Frame Relay network and Gigabit Ethernet ports, and two 100MB/s Ethernet switches with Gigabit uplinks. The router operating systems, such as Cisco Internetworking Operating System (IOS), should be capable of providing clocking services to simulate the Frame Relay link via a serial cable between the two routers. The network infrastructure team can provide support in this area. The servers and clients can be placed on the separate networks, but the flexibility exists to be able to move them in order to test different configurations. Figure 8.5 shows one possible physical layout for XYZ Company's lab.

Figure 8.5 Physical layout for XYZ Company's test lab.

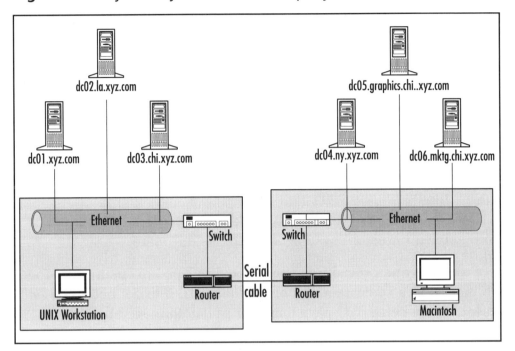

Now that the logical and physical design of the lab is complete, the deployment team should review the test lab design documents to ensure that the test lab will meet the deployment project's needs. Once sign-off is acquired, the equipment and software can be ordered, installed, and configured.

Managing the Lab

The lab has been set up and configured and you are ready to test. Most likely, many different deployment teams will want access to the lab for testing the technology for which they are responsible. Before you jump into testing head first (or mouse first), take the time to prepare some processes and procedures that can be used to manage the lab environment.

Depending on the size and complexity of the test environment, it may be necessary to dedicate a resource to manage the lab full time.

In most instances, the role of lab manager can be assigned to an existing employee as part of his or her duties. Managing the lab environment involves the following tasks:

- Ensuring that the lab documentation is kept up to date.
- Scheduling testing by different individuals/teams.
- Managing change control so that testing done by one group does not impact testing being performed by another group.
- Managing the hardware and software in the lab. This includes procuring new hardware and software and maintaining a consistent inventory.
- Managing the server and workstation images or backups used to restore systems to a consistent state.

Processes and procedures should be developed to ensure that the lab is used in a consistent and orderly fashion. It is not necessary or reasonable to pen a 100-page manuscript detailing step-by-step instructions on how to behave in the lab. However, guidelines need to be clearly written and enforced to help deployment team members make the best use of their time in the lab. These processes and procedures may include contact information, change control guidelines, and installation and configuration of servers and workstations.

For IT Professionals

Managing Server and Workstation Images in the Lab

Due to the number of configuration changes, application installations, and registry tweaks that occur during testing, there needs to be a way to manage a consistent installation of the operating system. This book has talked about a number of tools that can be used to ease the deployment of Windows 2000. The test lab provides an

Continued

excellent venue for testing these tools, while at the same time taking advantage of their functionality.

Using the tools discussed in previous chapters, the lab manager can create a base installation of the operating system and the applications being tested. Remote Install Services (RIS) can be installed on one of the lab computers and host all the available build images for the testing environment. Whenever a test group needs to test a feature or application against the default configuration, the machine can be rebuilt using RIS and the appropriate image file. By taking advantage of the enhanced deployment tools available in Windows 2000, an efficient and effective lab environment can be maintained.

Testing in the Lab

There are many different types of testing that take place in the lab. It may be helpful to categorize the types of testing into three phases, which will be called Phase One, Phase Two, and Phase Three testing.

Phase One testing is the time when functional testing takes place. The testing teams will determine whether the functionality that was advertised for the product actually works, and works the way it is supposed to. This phase can also be called "proof of technology" testing. This testing is also valuable in that it provides a training environment for deployment team members to become more familiar with the products.

Phase Two testing is more detailed and tests the functionality of components that are part of the proposed design to ensure that the design works as intended. This phase can be called "proof of concept" testing. During the end of this phase of testing, a small pilot group can start accessing the systems to test usability and productivity.

Phase Three testing is the final phase of testing with the intent of tweaking the environment prior to locking down a configuration prior to production deployment. A larger pilot group can be provided access to the systems and have access to more services.

All three phases require that detailed test plans be prepared. The objectives for the test plans will be slightly different for each phase, but the test plan framework should be the same. A test plan should include the following:

- **What aspect of the system will be tested**? For example, "Smart card logon will be tested from a Windows 2000 Professional workstation logging on to a Windows 2000 Server."

- **What are the expected results of the test**? For example, "The user should be authenticated using the smart card and an assigned PIN."

- **Any obstacles to performing the tests**. For example, "There may be difficulty in obtaining a smart card reader for the test environment."

- **Required hardware and software resources and any special configuration needed to perform the test**. For example, "Windows 2000 Server, Windows 2000 Professional, Certificate Services, Group Policy settings to allow Smart Card logon, Smart Card reader, and Smart Card."

- **How the test will be performed**. This section will be a detailed step-by-step description of how the test will be conducted, including what components are required and how the system is configured.

- **Test success measurement**. What criteria will be used to determine whether the test was successful or not.

Finally, a key component of testing is information sharing and knowledge transfer among deployment team members. Prior to testing, it is important to agree on a standard method for posting the test plans and results. This could be as simple as a shared folder on a network drive, or as complex as a customized Web site that serves as a front-end to a database to which all the testing information is stored. Whichever path you choose, ensure that the information is easily accessible and that new information is distinguishable from older material.

Training the Support Staff

As with any new product, it is imperative that the support staff is properly trained. These individuals provide two types of services. One is obvious; they provide the technical troubleshooting skills necessary to fix end-user and system problems. The second one is not so obvious: The success of all large-scale deployments is highly dependent on perspective. Is the CEO able to log on and access her important files? The Support Team helps in bolstering a positive image if they are well trained in the technology and are helpful and courteous. So, when the CEO calls to ask where her important presentation ended up after her desktop was upgraded to Windows 2000, the support person receiving the call is able to help her quickly become productive again.

Evaluating Existing Knowledge Base

Prior to developing a training plan, determine what level of expertise your support staff currently displays. In most cases, support staff will need to be trained on the new features and functionality being offered with Windows 2000. After this initial training, different levels of expertise will need to be obtained by different support personnel.

Help desk personnel who perform first-level support are usually familiar with basic administrative tasks and common end-user activities, such as file management, desktop applications, and logon issues. Server administrators who commonly perform second-level support often have a deeper understanding of the network operating system and how the operating system behaves on the network. System architects often act as third-level support and exhibit expertise in many areas related to operating systems and networking.

In order to evaluate the existing knowledge base, it is best to develop a skills self-assessment survey and distribute it to the support staff. This survey will list a number of technologies currently used by the company and those that will be implemented with Windows 2000. Ask each person to assess his or her skill level in each technology. For example, one technology might be *remote access services*. Next to this item is a list of check boxes labeled 1–10, with 1 being *no knowledge* and 10 being *industry expert*. The person would check a box that best reflects his or her level of knowledge in remote access services.

Once the surveys are handed back and the results tallied, you will have a better idea of where each person views his or her skill set and be better able to develop a training approach.

Determining Training Requirements

With the survey results in hand and an understanding of the challenges Windows 2000 brings to the table, you are now ready to determine training requirements for the support staff. As we discussed, the support staff can usually be broken down into three categories: first-level, second-level, and third-level support. Each level has different responsibilities and so, different training requirements.

It has already been identified that most of the staff will require an overview that discusses the new features and functionality of Windows 2000. Aside from this, each level of support will require different training. For example, the first-level help desk personnel will need to become familiar with how to use Active Directory Users and Computers so that they can reset passwords. They also need to be familiar with the upgrade process to help users experiencing difficulty during or after the upgrade. Second-level support requires more in-depth training. So, in addition to the training that first-level support receives, they will need to be familiar with upgrading, installing, and configuring Windows 2000. They will also require introductory and advanced training in server and workstation administration. Third-level support will most likely require the same training as first- and second-level support, but also be trained to understand how to design a Windows 2000 architecture, including Active Directory design, network services, and change and configuration management.

Depending on your requirements, it may be necessary for support staff to become certified at their respective levels. Microsoft offers a number of certifications, such as Microsoft Certified Professional (MCP), Microsoft Certified Systems Engineer (MCSE), and Microsoft Certified Solution Developer (MCSD).

Now that the *nature* of the training has been determined, you need to determine the *method*. There are a number of different training options available. The most common is instructor-led Microsoft Official Curriculum (MOC) courses offered at Microsoft Certified Technical Education Centers (CTEC). Most recently, a number of online, Web-based education sites have popped up, providing self-paced, MOC courses via their Web sites. Other self-paced training includes computer-based training and self-study books. To find a current list of Windows 2000-related MOC courses, visit Microsoft's Web site at www.microsoft.com/train_cert/.

Conducting and Evaluating the Pilot Rollout

Although your deployment pilot is considered part of the testing phase of the deployment, it needs to be treated as if it were a production rollout. The necessary steps for a pilot rollout are:

1. Define the scope of the pilot rollout; that is, set expectations.
2. Prepare a support model for pilot.
3. Develop a contingency plan.
4. Develop a communication plan.
5. Select and train the pilot users.
6. Conduct the pilot.
7. Reevaluate pilot plan.

Criteria for a Successful Pilot

There are several steps that must be taken to ensure that your pilot project is successful:

Define the Pilot Scope

Your first step is to define the scope of the pilot project. Remember, that scope describes what is to be included in the pilot. In large deployments, it is recommended that the pilot take place in a number of phases. The first phase is usually limited to a few individuals, mostly members of the deployment team. This correlates with Phase Two in the testing framework. The second pilot phase is larger and includes a wider range of end-user types. Additional phases continue to incorporate more pilot users and leads to production rollout. A single project scope can be defined for all phases as long as each phase is given consideration in the definition. A good scope also sets the appropriate expectation for all parties involved in the pilot.

Prepare a Support Model

Your second step is critical to the success of the pilot, and that is to prepare a support model for the pilot. End users who are participating in the pilot, especially in the early phases, can experience disruptions to their productivity, and a strong support model alleviates some of the hardships they will encounter. A good support model includes contact lists, problem tracking systems, populated knowledge bases, and trained staff.

Develop a Contingency Plan

In addition to major and minor disruptions to the end–user's workday, some users may experience catastrophic problems. In these cases, it is essential to have a well thought-out contingency plan to allow you to back out of a deployment. This includes recent backups and a tested disaster recovery plan to put the user's previous configuration and data back on his desktop.

Develop a Communication Plan

Documentation and communication are vital to a successful pilot. A communication plan outlines how parties will communicate during the pilot, when communications take place, and what information is exchanged during these communications. Several methods can be used to communicate between pilot participants, such as pilot group meetings held in person or via video/teleconference, e-mail discussion lists, chat rooms, bulletin boards, Web pages, and frequently asked questions. These tasks all provide valuable feedback that needs to be processed and documented. The deployment team must then make the necessary changes to the system to correct any identified problems. This is an iterative process that will recur at each phase of the pilot rollout.

TIP

The pilot relies heavily on end-user feedback. Common perceptions of end users need to be set aside at this point. Perceptions that users resist change, ask for features, but want something different in the end, and are only concerned about non-essentials such as screen colors and icons, must be replaced by an open-minded attitude. An environment where open and honest communication takes place needs to be established in order for problems to be discovered and eventually resolved.

Select and Train Pilot Users

Concurrent to the planning steps discussed earlier, you can start the process of selecting pilot users. If you are taking a phased approach to the pilot rollout, the criteria for pilot-user selection is different for each phase, but there are general guidelines for selecting all pilot users. The following list outlines characteristics of good pilot users:

- Strong proponent of change
- Technically savvy
- Exhibits propensity to champion new technology
- Willing to participate in pilot-group communications
- Able to tolerate computer downtime associated with the pilot
- Prior pilot group experience
- Ability to free up time to participate in trainings and discussions

Pilot users for the first phase of pilot testing are usually limited to the deployment staff themselves. The next phase of pilot testing encompasses a larger group. During this phase, a single department or a limited number of users from multiple departments can participate. Subsequent phases should consistently incorporate a more diverse user population that is representative of different user groups within the company.

Conduct the Pilot and Reevaluate Plan

You have a pilot plan and you have pilot users. You are now ready to conduct the pilot. Be true to your plan and ensure that you are providing exceptional support to you pilot group. At the same time, collect as much information as possible during each of the pilot phases. After each phase, review the information that was collected and make any necessary changes to the pilot so that you experience that much more success for the next pilot phase. The pilot rollout is an iterative process and is complete when the deployment team is satisfied it has worked through any issues that could cause problems during the production rollout.

The Production Rollout

It's show time! The pilot phases have been completed and the deployment is ready to go prime time. The production rollout includes the deployment details, outage service plans, site preparation requirements, and contingency plans. Be sure to consider your company's culture while developing the production rollout plan. It must not be counter to the culture. There is more than one way to look at deployments. First, incremental change. One step, followed by the next step, until the target solution is in place. Another approach is to consider revolutionary change: by directly implementing the target solution. This approach is often effective in reaching a goal fairly quickly. However, it must be designed and approved, with sufficient senior management support, for a successful deployment.

Many of the tasks associated with the production rollout are similar to those we covered in the pilot rollout. Only new topics are discussed in this section.

Prepare Facilities

Although most of your efforts have been concentrated around preparing a stable operating system configuration, the facilities that will support the rollout cannot be neglected. If additional hardware is being deployed, adequate electrical and data jacks must be available. The facilities preparation also ensures that a staging area is available for setting up equipment. These tasks usually need to be coordinated with the facilities personnel at each site.

Develop Outage Service Plans

One tool that can be used to prepare for the production rollout is a "Risk Assessment Table of Functionality," shown in Table 8.1. This table can be developed with representatives from the departments that will be affected by any outages associated with the deployment.

The table includes information about the functionality, critical components affected, and the acceptable outage duration for the function.

Table 8.1 Risk Assessment Table of Functionality

Functionality	Critical Components	Acceptable Outage Duration
Messaging	Mail server, SMTP gateway, transport system, desktop	3 hours
Printing	Print server, printers, transport system, desktop	5 hours
Internet Access	Internet gateway, external messaging, transport system, desktop	2 hours

Turn Over Production-Ready Systems

Once the production rollout is completed, you are ready to turn over the systems to the operation teams to administer and manage. This process can involve a short transition period where the deployment team works side by side with the operation teams to provide support and knowledge transfer.

Diligent planning and hard work contribute to a successful production rollout. Clear and accurate documentation, along with a well-executed communication plan and trained support staff, help ensure that end users are satisfied and quickly back to being productive.

Summary

Your Windows 2000 deployment plan begins by defining what will be included in the project, and what the project will accomplish. These considerations are addressed in the project scope and business objectives, respectively. Next, you must assess your current network and client/server infrastructures. This involves an inventory of existing equipment and network links to ensure that they support the new technologies. You then embark on testing.

The testing phases include designing the test lab to ensure that it provides the necessary resources to support the deployment team's testing needs. Second, a method for lab management must be established to handle change control and scheduling. Third, testing can begin following a standardized framework that helps with the evaluation of all the test results.

In order to provide deployment support for Windows 2000, your staff must be properly trained. To ensure effective training, evaluate your staff's knowledge base. After you discover what they know, you can evaluate the number of different training mechanisms available in the marketplace.

Next, you select a group of end users to test your deployment processes. This is the pilot phase and usually occurs as an iterative process, with reevaluations taking place after each pilot group is deployed.

Finally, you are ready to roll out Windows 2000 to the remainder of your production users. This assumes that the facilities and your team are ready in the event that a recovery effort needs to take place. Once the product is successfully deployed, the production environment can be turned over to the operations group for day-to-day management.

FAQs

Q: Is it always necessary to run a pilot rollout, even if you have tested everything?

A: Depending on the size and diversity of your end-user population, it is recommended that at least one pilot is conducted. A pilot rollout allows the deployment team to test deployment scenarios within a controlled group of participants who have agreed to tolerate the interruptions to productivity associated with pilots. If your user population is large and diverse, multiple pilots addressing as many different groups as possible is recommended.

Q: We don't have a thorough inventory of our network and client/server systems. Is it worth it to take a step back and deploy an application to inventory our environment?

A: This is a tough question without a simple answer. There is no question that an up-to-date and accurate inventory of your environment can save you time and money during this deployment, as well as provide valuable data for future projects. If your company is willing to invest the additional resources to deploy an inventory application, while at the same time postponing the Windows 2000 deployment, I would suggest that you take the extra step. Otherwise, prioritize which systems need to be inventoried and start there.

Q: We have a number of applications that run just fine under Windows NT 4.0. Do we need to still test them to see if they will run under Windows 2000?

A: Yes. In most cases, the application that ran fine under Windows NT 4.0 will run just as well under Windows 2000, but it may not take advantage of Windows 2000's new features. The reason for testing is to make sure that this is the case. Even though many of your applications will make the move to Windows 2000 gracefully, it is a good practice to test them first prior to deploying Windows 2000 in order to avoid any surprises that may rear their ugly heads after your rollout.

Chapter 9

The Windows 2000 Fast Track

Solutions in this chapter:

- Windows 2000 Platform Models

- Important New Features in Windows 2000

- Advantages and Disadvantages of Windows 2000

Introduction

This chapter provides an overview of Windows 2000 deployment for IT professionals or managers who need information "on the fly." Pre-planning is a critical first step in the deployment of any new operating system, so much of this chapter focuses on helping you determine whether or not Windows 2000 is right for your organization.

First, the history and development of Windows 2000 is discussed. You'll also learn about some of the main improvements and new features of Windows 2000, as well as the hardware requirements of the OS. This chapter also explores the types of users likely to benefit from Windows 2000 and provides you with some common advantages and problems associated with it.

Before installing Windows 2000, you should be familiar with the steps associated with successful deployment. This chapter wraps up with a handy Frequently Asked Question (FAQ) section to help you quickly look up important deployment information.

What Is Windows 2000, and Why You Need to Know about It

Windows 2000 is Microsoft's newest operating system, released on February 17, 2000. Windows 2000 was designed to combine the networking abilities and stability of Windows NT with the ease of use of Windows 98. This section focuses on the history and evolution of Windows 2000, and introduces you to the four versions in the Windows 2000 family.

A Brief History

Windows 2000 is a network operating system, and is an evolution of the Microsoft Windows NT (New Technology) platform. The history of the NT platform actually began in the late 1980s when Microsoft and IBM paired up to create two different operating systems: a network operating system called OS/2, and a stand-alone operating system called Windows.

Although OS/2 enjoyed great success, Windows remained largely unpopular until its release as Windows 3.0 in 1990. At that time, the partnership between Microsoft and IBM broke up, and Microsoft went on to release its own network operating system, called Windows NT 3.1. Windows NT combined the network technology of OS/2 with the interface of Windows 3.0, and was released in 1993.

Microsoft Windows NT 3.1 was a 32-bit operating system and was not restricted to the same memory boundaries and hardware access as Windows 3.0 and DOS. It was also designed to run 16-bit programs in a special environment that would not disrupt 32-bit operations (these features were later incorporated in Windows 95 and Windows 98).

Microsoft has since released version 4.0 of Windows NT, in Workstation, Server, and Enterprise versions. Windows 2000 (originally called Windows NT version 5.0) shares much of the same core architecture with NT 4.0, but also incorporates many of the user-friendly features found in the 9x lineup. These include Plug and Play, support for USB, and Active Desktop (these features are described in more detail later in the chapter).

The Windows 2000 Family

Like Windows NT 4.0, Windows 2000 comes in several versions to meet the needs of both administrators and end users. This section looks at the four versions, their uses, and hardware requirements.

Windows 2000 Professional

Windows 2000 Professional is the workstation model, and allows users to access server-provided features and resources. Professional is the 2000 equivalent of Windows NT Workstation 4.0. This operating system can join a Windows 9x, NT 4.0, or Windows

2000 network, or it can be installed in a stand-alone configuration. As part of the effort to make the OS user friendly, Professional includes easy-to-use help and wizards and provides an Active Desktop, designed to conform to the way the user accesses desktop features.

Windows 2000 Professional can support up to two CPUs (two-way SMP), and can address up to 4GB of memory. The minimum system requirements to run Windows 2000 Professional are 133 MHz or higher Pentium-compatible CPU, 64MB of RAM, and 1GB free disk space. Refer to Table 9.1 for information about required versus recommended hardware.

Windows 2000 Server

Also called Windows 2000 Server, Standard Edition, this operating system is the 2000 version of Windows NT Server 4.0, and as such, it is designed to provide security and resources to small- to medium–sized networks. This OS includes all of the features found in Windows 2000 Professional, and is also able to provide the network with file, print, application, and Web services.

Windows 2000 Server is designed to reduce the number of reboots and crashes, and includes enhanced storage space management and repair features. This operating system supports four-way SMP (Symmetric Multi-Processing) and can address up to 4GB of memory. Windows 2000 Server requires a 133 MHz Pentium-compatible CPU, 128MB RAM, and 1GB of disk space.

Windows 2000 Advanced Server

This operating system is built on the technology of Windows NT Server 4.0, Enterprise Edition. It is designed for use in medium- to large-sized networks, and provides higher availability and scalability than Windows 2000 Server. Windows 2000 Advanced Server includes all of the features found in Windows 2000 Server, but also allows for server clustering, which involves combining the functions of multiple servers that act as a unified unit on a network. When servers are clustered, they can provide load balancing, in which network requests are divided equally among the network's servers. Clustering also provides fault tolerance. If a network server goes down, the network's remaining servers will take over its functions until it is up and running again.

Windows 2000 Advanced Server can support four-way SMP for those performing a clean install. Those performing an upgrade from Windows NT Server 4.0, Enterprise Edition, will retain that operating system's support for eight-way SMP. Advanced Server can address 8GB of memory. The full version comes with 25 client-access licenses. Like Windows 2000 Server, Advanced Server requires 133MHz Pentium CPU, 128MB RAM, and 1GB free disk space.

Windows 2000 Datacenter Server

This is the high-end operating system in the Windows 2000 family. It is designed for very large networks, and can support 10,000 users at once. Datacenter Server is ideal for hosting large databases or ISPs. This operating system has no predecessor in the Windows NT 4.0 lineup.

Windows 2000 Datacenter Server supports all of the features found in Advanced Server, and can support 32-way SMP and address up to 64GB of memory. Datacenter Server is set to be released approximately three months after the release of Advanced Server, and pricing and system requirement information is to be announced by Microsoft.

Important New Features in Windows 2000

Windows 2000 is more than just an upgrade from Windows NT 4.0. Although the two platforms share some of the same core technologies, Windows 2000 includes many new features and improvements over Windows NT 4.0. It also includes many of the features that made Windows 9*x* popular, but were not previously available in the NT lineup. This section focuses on these new features, and how they can affect performance on a stand-alone or networked computer.

Plug and Play

All versions of Windows 2000 support Plug and Play (PnP), which had been previously seen only in the Windows 9*x* lineup. When a PnP-compatible device is installed, Windows 2000 will automatically detect it, load the appropriate device driver, and assign the proper IRQ and I/O address. This means less manual configuration on the user's part, and it reduces the possibility of resource conflicts within the system.

To determine whether a device is PnP compatible, you can refer to Microsoft's Hardware Compatibility List (HCL) at www.microsoft.com/hcl. Generally, devices that are PnP compatible with Windows 9*x* will also be PnP compatible with Windows 2000.

Power Management

Windows 2000 offers BIOS-independent power management. This means the operating system is in complete control of power-saving features such as blanking the screen and powering down the hard drive after a specified period of inactivity. Windows 2000 also supports a "wake on LAN" feature that allows you to remotely set a workstation to wake or sleep via the network.

Windows 2000 also includes a hibernate feature, in which the entire contents of RAM are copied onto the hard disk before powering down. When the computer is restarted, the desktop is restored to its previous state, including all open applications and files.

Dynamic Partitions

Windows 2000 includes a new file system technology called NTFS v5.0. This file system allows you to create or change partition sizes on the fly, without losing existing information on the disk, or rebooting the computer. Windows 2000 will also support older NTFS 4.0, FAT 16, and FAT 32 file systems.

Hardware Support

Previously seen only in the Windows 9*x* platform, Windows 2000 supports AGP, FireWire, USB, DVD, and multiple monitors. Windows 2000 also includes DirectX 7.0 video support.

Active Directory

One of the most talked about new features of the Windows 2000 platform is the new multidomain directory service, called Active Directory. Active Directory is a server-provided technology that uses *multimaster replication*, which means that each domain maintains information only about resources on the network to which it has access. This greatly reduces the amount of information that must be maintained by each domain host.

Furthermore, when resources on the network are updated, all domains that reference that resource are automatically updated. This is a far cry from earlier directory services that required a manual update of each domain host when a new resource was added to the network. Because less manual configuration is required to add new resources to a network, Active Directory allows for high scalability (growth).

Finally, Active Directory provides users with a more logical view of resources on a network. Rather than viewing resources in terms of their domains, users can view resources in *containers*. Active Directory containers can be organized so that resources belonging to a single department appear together on the network, regardless of which domain they belong to. This makes it easier for users to find resources without having to remember exact locations or long path names.

IntelliMirror

Another new Windows 2000 improvement is server-provided IntelliMirror. IntelliMirror provides roaming access and availability to Windows 2000 networks. When a user creates or edits a file, it is saved locally to the hard disk, and a mirrored copy is saved on the server. Because the server contains a copy of the files, the user can access them from any machine on the network. This is called roaming access. Also, since a copy is kept on the user's own machine, the files can be accessed even in the event of a server crash. When this is the case, the user's files will be automatically updated on the server as soon as it rejoins the network.

Kerberos Security

One of the more advanced features of Windows 2000 Server is the use of Kerberos security. In this new security model, users can quickly access resources across domains without authenticating themselves over and over.

When a user first logs on to his or her domain, the domain controller (server) issues that user a Ticket Granting Ticket (TGT). The TGT contains information about which resources the user is allowed to access. When the user tries to access a resource in another domain, the TGT is presented to that domain's controller. The user is then granted a Service Ticket, which entitles him or her to access a specific resource (for example, a printer). The user remains authenticated for the remainder of the session, making interdomain access much faster.

Industries and Companies Affected by Windows 2000

With all of its new features and improvements, Windows 2000 seems very powerful. However, keep in mind that it is essentially a network operating system and is not designed for every user. This section describes the target market for Windows 2000 and explains why this new operating system may or may not be appropriate for certain types of users.

Organizations with Small- to Medium-Sized Networks

Organizations that have small- or medium-sized networks should definitely consider using Windows 2000 Professional along with Windows 2000 Server. It offers a greater range of hardware support than Windows NT 4.0, and is designed to offer high stability. Recall that Windows 2000 supports PnP and allows you to add most devices without rebooting the system. Windows 2000 is also designed to crash less often than other operating systems. It will block unrecognized or corrupt drivers, and does not allow new applications to overwrite existing shared .DLL files. Furthermore, when you end a process using CTRL-ALT-DEL, Windows 2000 will also end all related processes, freeing up memory and processor resources.

Windows 2000 Server also offers easier and higher scalability than many other operating systems, because the Active Directory automatically updates the network's domain controllers when a resource is changed or added to the network. Finally, Windows 2000's use of IntelliMirror and Active Desktop can help decrease network traffic. When users move from one machine to another, their desktop settings follow them, but server-provided applications are not loaded into the workstation until the users try to access them. This reduces unnecessary network traffic and leads to faster access on the network as a whole.

Organizations with Large Networks

Large networks may experience great benefits from using Windows 2000 Professional in conjunction with Windows 2000 Advanced Server. Advanced Server includes all of the features of Windows 2000 Server, but also offers enhanced server-clustering services. The clustering services can provide fault tolerance and load balancing to large networks, which translates into greater availability of network resources and faster network access. Kerberos inter-domain security will provide faster access to network resources than

Windows NT 4.0, and Active Directory will make it easier for users on a large network to find the resources they need. Depending on resource use, very large networks, such as ISPs or networks with up to 10,000 users per server, may benefit from using Windows 2000 Datacenter Server. It provides all of the functions of Advanced Server, but can support many more users, and has enhanced database management and computer simulation capabilities.

Gamers

Those who use their computers to run games have a more difficult decision when considering an upgrade to Windows 2000 Professional. An advantage of the OS is that it is more stable than Windows 9*x*, so it will experience fewer crashes. Another advantage is Windows 2000's support of DirectX 7.0. Users who play games that run in Windows 9*x* will definitely benefit from Windows 2000's new features.

However, as you have already seen, Windows 2000 Professional has some pretty hefty hardware requirements. Users with the minimum requirements will probably experience a decrease in performance over Windows 9*x*. Another disadvantage of Windows 2000 for gamers actually stems from the stability of the OS itself. Like Windows NT, Windows 2000 was designed to prevent applications from directly accessing the computer's hardware. Therefore, applications that try to access the hardware directly (including most DOS games) may not run properly, or at all, in Windows 2000.

Home Users

Home users include casual users who want to do word processing, access the Internet, play a game or two, or create desktop publications. Some advantages of Windows 2000 Professional for this group are its intuitive interface, easy-to-use features, and advanced help and wizards.

However, recall the steep hardware requirements. Most casual users have computers that do not, or just barely, meet the minimum hardware requirements. In these cases, Windows 2000 will take up more resources than Windows 9*x*, and cause a degradation of performance. Because Windows 2000 is designed for network use, stand-alone users will not be able to take advantage of the real benefits of the operating system. Therefore, home users will probably get little or no benefit from using Windows 2000 Professional, and are better off using an operating system from the 9*x* lineup (Windows 95 or Windows 98).

Advantages and Disadvantages

Before deploying any new operating system, administrators must perform thorough research of the product. Because Windows 2000 is so different from previous operating systems, administrators need to be fully aware of its advantages and disadvantages. Only by weighing the pros and cons and being prepared for possible problems can administrators make an educated decision about making the switch to Windows 2000. However, keep in mind that all networks are different, and the benefits or disadvantages listed here may not apply to your configuration.

Advantages of Windows 2000

Many of Windows 2000's advantages have already been discussed throughout this chapter. To recap, Windows 2000 is a more stable and secure operating system than Windows 9*x* and provides more hardware access and user-friendly features than Windows NT.

The first advantage that most users will notice is the interface itself. Windows 2000 uses Active Desktop, in which frequently accessed features and applications appear more prominently than rarely used features. Windows 2000 also includes balloon help, which offers more detailed information than traditional Tool Tips. Finally, Windows 2000 offers help and wizards that are easier to use, and provides error messages that attempt to guide the user through the proper troubleshooting procedures.

Network access across domains is also improved in Windows 2000. Kerberos security means less authentication and faster network access than seen in Windows NT 4.0. Also, Active Directory makes it easier for users to find resources on the network because objects are organized in a more logical manner.

Windows 2000 also provides greater scalability than other operating systems. When a resource is changed or added to the network, the Active Directory is responsible for automatically updating all domain hosts that reference that resource. This means less manual configuration for network administrators.

Another advantage of Windows 2000 is its improved availability and support of roaming access. Windows 2000 uses a new technology called IntelliMirror, in which users' data is stored both locally and on the domain server. Because data is stored on the user's workstation, it is available even in the event of a server failure. Because data is stored on the server, users can access their data from any machine on the network.

Another advantage of Windows 2000 over other operating systems is its stability. Windows 2000 employs System File Protection, which prevents applications from overwriting .DLL files that are shared by other applications. The OS also includes better repair features that will block or warn about the installation of corrupt drivers. Windows 2000 is also designed to repair damaged features to avoid a complete reinstallation of the OS. Finally, Windows 2000 includes a feature called *kill process tree*. In older operating systems, users could end a task or process using the Windows Task Manager. Windows 2000 also has this ability, but goes one step further by also ending all processes related to the offending process. This prevents stray processes from taking up the computer's resources, and can help avoid computer crashes.

Windows 2000 has better hardware support than Windows NT 4.0, including its use of Plug and Play and its support of USB, multiple monitors, DVD, and FireWire. Windows 2000 also includes enhanced Power Management and hibernation features.

Disadvantages and Problems with Windows 2000

Because Windows 2000 is a network operating system, it is not for everyone. This section focuses on possible disadvantages of the program, as well as problems one may encounter when implementing Windows 2000 in a network.

Plug and Play

A common complaint about Windows 2000 is that it provides incomplete or no support for certain hardware devices, particularly sophisticated sound and video cards. In many cases, users found that Windows 2000 Plug and Play would locate and load a device, but would not allow access to the device's more advanced features. In some cases, Windows 2000 would not recognize the device at all. In these cases, a manufacturer-provided driver is necessary to configure the device and make use of all of its features.

The reason for this is that Windows 2000 is primarily a business-oriented operating system. Windows 2000 PnP is geared toward business-oriented hardware, such as scanners, networking hardware, and smart cards. You can check your hardware's compatibility with Windows 2000 PnP at www.microsoft.com/hcl.

Device Driver Compatibility

This point is related to the Plug and Play issue described above. When Windows 2000 (or any other OS) cannot provide a device driver for a piece of hardware, you must supply a manufacturer-provided driver. Although Windows 2000 can use many of the same drivers that work in Windows NT 4.0 or Windows 9x, it cannot take advantage of the accompanying .inf files.

Many users have found that they can "fool" Windows 2000 into using older drivers by combining a Windows 9x driver with a Windows NT .inf file, or vice versa. However, this solution does not always work, or may allow you to install a device without access to

its more advanced features. The best solution is to obtain or wait for
a manufacturer-provided Windows 2000 compatible driver. Again, to
check your hardware's compatibility with Windows 2000, visit the
Microsoft Hardware Compatibility List Web site.

Application Compatibility

Most applications and Windows-based games will run in Windows
2000. However, you may run into problems when using system
applications, such as defragmenters, anti-virus programs, and disk
management tools. These types of applications may not run at all,
or may try to alter the Windows 2000 operating system in ways that
will render it nonfunctional. Fortunately, Windows 2000 includes
disk defragmenter and disk management programs. However, before
using third-party management tools or anti-virus programs, make
sure they are Windows 2000 compatible.

You are also likely to run into problems running DOS-based
games, or other applications that try to access the hardware directly. Many manufacturers have released patches or code changes
that can navigate around these problems. However, keep in mind
that Windows 2000 is not designed to run these types of games, and
"tricking" it into doing so can lead to configuration problems or corrupt OS files.

Hardware Requirements

The hardware requirements of Windows 2000, which were explained
in detail earlier in the chapter, are pretty steep for most home and
some business users. Upgrading to Windows 2000 on a machine
with the minimum requirements will probably result in slower performance. Before deciding to upgrade or install Windows 2000, you
should make sure your computers have the *recommended* hardware
requirements, listed in Table 9.1.

For Managers

Important Upgrading Information

There are many pros and cons to performing an upgrade rather than a clean install of Windows 2000. The upgrade versions cost less, do not require you to reformat your hard drive and reinstall all applications, and can be much faster than performing a full install. However, you should be aware that Microsoft recommends performing a full installation, to avoid migration problems.

If you do decide to use a Windows 2000 upgrade, determining what will upgrade what can be a confusing issue. Because Windows 2000 is a network operating system, Windows NT 4.0 provides the easiest upgrade path. Each Windows NT 4.0 model has a corresponding model in the Windows 2000 platform: NT Workstation ~ 2000 Professional; NT Server ~ 2000 Server; NT Server, Enterprise Edition ~ 2000 Advanced Server. Beyond that, however, things get more complex. For example, you can only upgrade from Windows 95 or Windows 98 to Windows 2000 Professional, and you cannot upgrade from Windows 3.x to Windows 2000 at all. The following table summarizes which Windows operating systems you can upgrade to and from.

I'm Using:	Can I Upgrade to Windows 2000:			
	Professional	Server	Advanced Server	Datacenter Server
Windows 3.x	No	No	No	No
Windows 95	Yes	No	No	No
Windows 98	Yes	No	No	No
Windows NT 3.51 Workstation	Yes	No	No	No
Windows NT 4.0 Workstation	Yes	No	No	No
Windows NT 3.51 Server	No	Yes	No	No
Windows NT 4.0 Server	No	Yes	No	No
Windows NT 4.0 Server, Enterprise Edition	No	No	Yes	Yes
Windows NT 3.50 Server with Citrix	No	No	No	No
Windows CE	No	No	No	No

Upgrading Problems

Windows 2000 is available in upgrade versions for systems using Windows 9*x* or Windows NT. However, before choosing an upgrade version, you should be aware that performing a Windows 2000 upgrade could lead to system file migration problems that would not occur during a clean installation.

In some cases, the Windows 2000 upgrade may overwrite a working device driver with one of its own generic drivers, or you may find that some applications won't run after the upgrade. Windows 2000 may even completely refuse to upgrade your system. In most cases, performing a clean installation will not result in these types of problems. Fortunately, the Windows 2000 upgrade packages include a report mode, in which the setup program will report potential problems before making any changes to your system.

Before choosing the upgrade version over the full version, check your computer's hardware on Microsoft's Windows 2000 Hardware Compatibility List. It is also important to note that Windows 2000 does not include an uninstall feature that will undo the upgrade and revert to the previous OS. See the *For Managers* sidebar for more information about upgrading to Windows 2000.

Windows 2000 Summary Points

The decision to implement Windows 2000 in your network can be a difficult one, and should not be taken lightly. This chapter has provided you with much of the information you need to make informed decisions about whether or not and how you can implement Windows 2000 in your organization.

The first objective of this chapter was to familiarize you with the models in the Windows 2000 platform. Because Windows 2000 is an evolution of the Windows NT platform, it shares much of the same core architecture as Windows NT 4.0, and is designed to perform the same type of roles in a network. Windows 2000 Professional is the workstation model. It supports 2-way SMP and 4GB of memory, and provides an easy upgrade from Windows NT 4.0 Workstation. Windows 2000 Server is the 2000 version of Windows NT 4.0 Server, and supports 4-way SMP and 4GB of memory. Windows 2000 Advanced Server is built on the same technology as Windows NT 4.0 Server Enterprise Edition. It supports 8-way SMP and 8GB of memory. Finally, Datacenter Server is breaking the mold with 32-way SMP and support for 64GB memory access.

By presenting you with information about Windows 2000's new features, this chapter also attempted to help you determine how you might benefit from implementing Windows 2000 in your network. Windows 2000 supports more advanced Plug and Play capabilities than Windows NT, and includes better Power Management and hibernation features. Due to its use of Active Directory and IntelliMirror, Windows 2000 is able to provide networks with higher availability and scalability than other operating systems, and can reduce your organization's total cost of ownership.

Some disadvantages of Windows 2000 include its Plug and Play support for mainly business-oriented hardware and its inability to run many DOS-based applications. The hardware requirements of Windows 2000 may also prove to be a disadvantage, as they exceed the hardware configurations of many home computers.

Another objective of this chapter was to provide you with important upgrading information, in an attempt to help you weigh the benefits of upgrading versus performing a clean installation of Windows 2000. The Windows 2000 upgrade packages cost less than the full versions, and do not require you to format your hard drive and reinstall all applications and devices. However, some migration problems can occur when using an upgrade package, which can result in device and/or application problems within the computer system.

Finally, the following FAQ section will help get you started with a deployment strategy, and tell you where to find additional information.

FAQs

Q: Who should use Windows 2000?

A: Anyone can use Windows 2000, as long as their computer meets the minimum hardware requirements. However, Windows 2000 is not beneficial for all users. The target market for Windows 2000 Professional includes workstation users on small to large networks. Windows 2000 Server was designed to provide network resources on small- to medium-sized networks. Windows 2000 Advanced Server should be used on medium to large networks, and Windows 2000 Datacenter Server should be used on networks that will host large ISPs or very large databases.

Q: I've decided to use Windows 2000. Where do I start?

A: By now, you should have decided whether to perform an upgrade or full installation, and your machines should be Windows 2000 compliant. Your next step should be to define the objectives of the deployment, including the application, security and connectivity needs of your organization. This will help you determine which Windows 2000 features you will need to use.

Next, gather information about the current status of your organization, including naming conventions, user types, and application use. Before deploying Windows 2000, you should set up a pilot lab in which to practice the deployment before actually making changes to your network's workstations. The network's support staff must be informed of all changes and be trained in the new operating system. When you are confident in the soundness of the deployment strategy and the support staff's abilities, you are ready to perform the Windows 2000 deployment.

Q: Our organization is planning to deploy Windows 2000. What deployment options do we have?

A: This depends on the current configuration of your workstations and the type of installation you want to perform. If you want to perform an unattended scripted installation, use the Windows 2000 Setup Manager. In this technique, an "answer" file is created, which will automatically answer any questions asked by the Windows 2000 Setup program. This is a good method to use when your network's workstations have dissimilar hardware configurations. See Chapter 2 for more information about deploying Windows 2000 using the Setup Manager.

Another technique you can use is called imaging. Windows 2000 comes with a utility called Sysprep, which allows you to "copy" exact replicas of one hard drive to other workstations on the network. This method is very fast, but can only be used if your workstations have the exact same hardware configuration. Chapter 3 describes Windows 2000 imaging in more detail.

Finally, you may decide to deploy Windows 2000 using a Remote Installation Server (RIS). This is similar to the imaging technique, in that parts of the operating system are copied onto the user's workstation. However, hardware configuration, and anything else that is unique to that workstation (username, computer name, etc.) must be manually configured. Chapter 4 provides information on deploying Windows 2000 using the RIS technique.

Q: What does Microsoft mean by "Lower Total Cost of Ownership?"

A: Total Cost of Ownership (TCO) indicates how much it costs an organization to configure and maintain a computer. This figure includes the price of the hardware and software, maintenance and administration of the computer, and user training. Microsoft has designed Windows 2000 to be deployed and maintained by a single, centrally located server. This means that administrators do not need to visit every workstation to change or install the Windows 2000 configuration. This decreased administration and maintenance time leads to a lower TCO.

Q: I'm a Windows 9x user and I've decided not to use Windows 2000. What other upgrade options do I have?

A: When Microsoft first began development of Windows 2000, they intended to put an end to the Windows 9x lineup. However, because Windows 2000 is a network operating system and has fairly hefty hardware requirements, it is not suitable for many home users, or others using stand-alone computers. Microsoft is therefore planning to continue the Windows 9x lineup in a new version, code named Windows Millennium. Windows Millennium will not offer the same security as Windows 2000, but will target home users, and as such, will support more sophisticated home-use and gaming hardware and applications.

Q: Will Windows 2000 run on laptops?

A: Yes. However, because laptops are proprietary in nature, with few standards in place, the ability to run Windows 2000 will depend largely on the laptop itself. Furthermore, the power management and hibernation features of Windows 2000 are quite different from that of Windows 9x, so many features that previously worked on your laptop may fail to do so following a Windows 2000 upgrade or install. Finally, many laptops fall short of the Windows 2000 minimum hardware requirements, so make sure you check Microsoft's Hardware Compatibility List before making the switch.

Q: What is a Windows 2000 CAL?

A: A CAL is a Client Access License, which gives you the right to use Windows 2000. For example, if you purchase Windows 2000 Server with 5 CALs, five users can access the server. Microsoft offers two types of CALs for Windows 2000. A per-seat mode CAL indicates the number of clients on the network, regardless of the number of servers they can access. A per-server mode CAL indicates the number of users that can access a particular server at any one time.

Q: Where can I get more information on Windows 2000 Professional deployment strategies?

A: If you have read the relevant information in this book and still have questions, you should go straight to the source. Microsoft's Web site offers reviews, technical information, and white papers about deploying Windows 2000. A good place to start is www.microsoft.com/windows2000/library/planning/default.asp.

Q: I'm still undecided about Windows 2000. Where can I get more information?

A: There are lots of places to learn more about Windows 2000 and get opinions about the product. Talk to colleagues or other people who have used Windows 2000. Because Windows 2000 is currently a hot topic, you'll probably find lots of reviews and recommendations in computer magazines. Finally, use the Internet. Here, you'll find opinions about Windows 2000, as well as deployment information, including tips and tricks and pitfalls to watch out for. Two excellent sources, for example, are www.zdnet.com and www.winmag.com.

Windows 2000 Professional Deployment Secrets

Solutions in this chapter:

- For Experts Only
- Under-Documented Features and Functions
- Additional Resources

For Experts Only

Included with Windows 2000 are additional tools or features that should only be administered by IT professionals very experienced with Windows 2000 who fully understand the impact of making changes. As you have probably heard repeatedly about the registry, changing options such as the following can render the system inoperable.

Driver Signing

Windows 2000 provides a unique new feature that is a long-awaited dream for desktop administrators. Hardware drivers that are written must now be signed by Microsoft to be compatible with Windows 2000. You can administer the system to disallow the installation of any driver that has not met this requirement. This can help to ensure that certified devices found only on the Hardware Compatibility Listing (HCL) are installed. The options include ignoring all drivers, signed or not, displaying a message for unsigned drivers, and blocking all unsigned drivers.

To set driver signing options, open the Control Panel and select System properties. Choose the Hardware tab, and select Driver Signing. The default configuration is shown in Figure A.1.

Figure A.1 Default driver signing options in Windows 2000 Professional.

Security Configuration Tool Set

Security is a major part of the new Windows 2000 operating system and the number of new enhancements proves that Microsoft takes security seriously. With Windows 2000 comes a new tool set that allows an administrator to create and deploy a security template to multiple computers very easily. This utility is called the Security Configuration Tool Set.

The security configuration tool set can set security permissions and configure various tools such as:

- Account Policies
- Event Logs
- File Systems
- Group Policy Settings
- Group Membership Policies
- Registry
- Services

Setting and configuring these options can be accomplished through various tools within the suite of security products available. Each tool provides an integral piece to this tool set and is used to configure security settings for the tasks listed above.

The *Security Configuration and Analysis MMC snapiin* is used to apply and configure a security template to a Windows 2000 computer. Security templates are files that have configurations saved to apply to multiple computers. This tool can also be used to analyze a Windows 2000 system to create a security template to use for future installations.

The *Security Template MMC snap-in* can be used to create a new security template or manage existing templates. Several default templates are provided in a basic Windows 2000 installation including a high-security template and a basic-user template. Templates are stored in files with an *.inf* extension such as *BASICDC.INF*. Figure A.2 displays an example of the Security Templates snap-in within the Microsoft Management Console.

Figure A.2 Default Security Templates provided with Windows 2000.

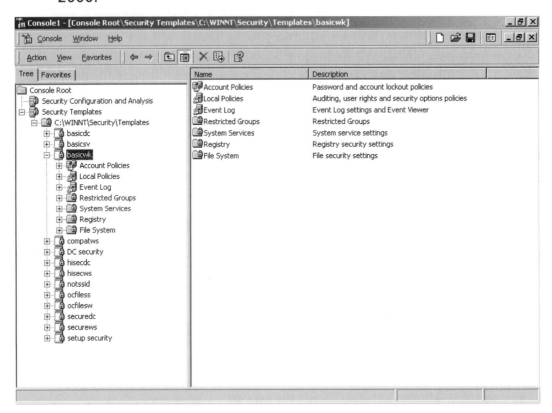

In addition to these graphical tools, a command line version of these utilities is available called *SECEDIT.EXE*. Because secedit is a command line version of this utility, it works well in automating the analysis, creation, and deployment of security templates throughout the enterprise.

Finally, *Security Setting extensions* are also added to the Group Policy editor for security policies for global and local resources. These can be set up on domains, organizational units, or sites. As part of the overall security framework, these extensions allow an administrator greater functionality in managing the client desktop environment.

Under-Documented Features and Functions

Because Windows 2000 provides so many new features and updates, many items do not get the attention they may deserve. This section is provided to discuss some of the under-documented features and functions that are provided and how they may assist you in deploying Windows 2000 Professional.

Windows 2000 Professional Resource Kit

As with many other versions of Microsoft's operating systems, a resource kit has been developed to provide additional tools and information to further customize Windows 2000 to the needs of an organization or user. This resource kit includes utilities ranging from troubleshooting Microsoft browsers to automating mass user creations, to installing applications as a service. Some of these tools were included with older resource kits and have been updated, while there are a few new utilities and scripts. The list below provides only a sample of the available tools provided on the Windows 2000 Professional media located in the Support directory:

- **BROWSTAT.EXE** A utility used to troubleshoot computer browsers such as forcing elections

- **CLONEPR.VBS** A VB-Script utility for migrating users from one domain to another. Can be used for Windows 2000 migrations.

- **DEPENDS.EXE** Lists dependencies for an individual application. Useful in troubleshooting application related problems.

- **DEPLOY.CHM** Contains the Windows 2000 Deployment Planning Guide (DPG), which provides methodologies and techniques for deploying Windows 2000.

- **KILL.EXE** Used for killing process. Good for stopping a malfunctioning application from the command line.

- **PVIEWER.EXE** Monitors the processes running on a server and allows you to kill them remotely.
- **SIDWALK.EXE** Used to change the Security Identifier (SID) for a given computer. This utility is especially helpful when using disk-imaging tools with prior versions of Windows NT.
- **W2000MSGS.CHM** Error and event messages including detailed explanations of all Windows 2000 events.

ADMINPAK

With Windows 2000 comes a set of administrative tools that can be used for various remote and local support. In deploying Windows 2000 Professional, you may require a workstation to have the associated administrative tools to provide support to the user community. For example, Windows 2000 does not include some of the older NT 4.0 tools such as User Manager and Server Manager. Although a new improved version is provided that is Windows 2000 aware, in some cases these older tools are required to administer legacy systems. Newer utilities are also included within the ADMINPAK, such as Terminal Services Manager, WINS Manager, and Active Directory administration tools.

The following steps take you through installing the ADMINPAK to a local Windows 2000 Professional computer.

1. Place the Windows 2000 Server or Advanced Server media into your CDROM
2. Open Windows Explorer and navigate to the \I386 directory of the root of the CD.
3. Run the **ADMINPAK.MSI** program to begin the installation.
4. Follow the prompts to complete the installation (Figure A.3).

Figure A.3 Installing ADMINPAK for Windows 2000 Professional.

WINNT32.EXE Switches

Similar to its predecessor, Windows 2000 uses WINNT32.EXE to start the setup installation program. With this utility come many options that can be used to further automate or customize the installation procedure. Although many of these options are very well documented and well known, there are a few that are new or are not discussed in many resources.

/DEBUG [level]:[filename]

This option can be used to further debug your Windows 2000 installation. It allows administrators to not only log the installation details, but to specify the level of detail they wish to have. In addition, the log file and location can be specified. By default, the logging detail level is set to 2 and is logged to %WINDIR%\WINNT32.LOG. The various detail levels are specified below and each includes the information from the numbered levels below it.

- 0: Severe Errors
- 1: Errors
- 2: Warnings
- 3: Information
- 4: Detailed

/CMDCONS

This option is used to add the Recovery Console to the operating system selection screen. The recovery console is used to debug problematic installations of Windows 2000. This option can only be used after installation has been completed.

/COPYDIR VS. /COPYSOURCE

The /COPYDIR and /COPYSOURCE switches are used in Windows 2000 to provide a method for automatically copying customized files and directories during installation. Although both perform a similar function, there is one major difference. The files copied with the copydir switch remain after the installation while the files copied with copysource are deleted after setup is completed. Both can be very useful under the correct circumstances.

For example: you may use the copydir switch when copying application source files over to be used after setup is completed. An example of using copysource is for hardware driver installation. Once the hardware driver is installed, you may want the source files to be deleted.

/CHECKUPGRADEONLY

This option was added to Windows 2000 to help ensure application compatibility and a smooth upgrade path. Although discussed within this book, it warrants another brief discussion. This utility will help to check existing hardware and software to verify that it is compatible with Windows 2000 prior to upgrading. It creates a report of the issues that are found and stores it in ungrade.txt for Win 9x and winnt32.log for WINNT installations. Figure A.4 shows an example of a report.

Figure A.4 An example of the /CHECKUPGRADEONLY command line switch.

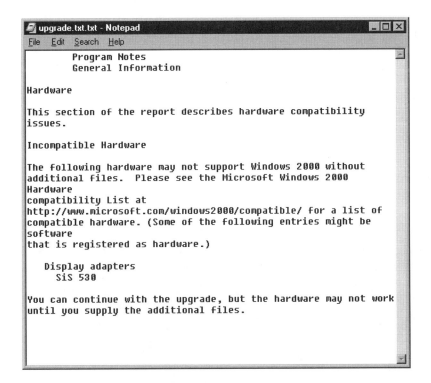

/MAKELOCALSOURCE

Another new switch provided is the /MAKELOCALSOURCE command-line switch. This instructs the setup utility to copy all of the Windows 2000 source code locally before the first reboot. This is an excellent tool to minimize the need for the source installation media. For example, if using the Windows 2000 CD to install client desktops, you may use this switch to prevent the need to continually leave the CD in one machine until it is completed.

MAKEBOOT.EXE & MAKEBT32.EXE

Although the successor of Windows NT, many changes have occurred to better the Windows 2000 operating system as a whole. In its former version, three setup boot floppies could be created using the WINNT32.EXE and WINNT.EXE command line utilities. These boot floppies were used for running the Windows NT setup program used for new installations or for recovering from system failures. With Windows 2000, this utility has been separated from the WINNT32.EXE and WINNT.EXE into its own tool. Located in the BOOTDISK directory on the Windows 2000 CD ROM, this utility is composed of six files: four image files, a 16-bit creation utility (MAKEBOOT.EXE), and a 32-bit creation utility (MAKEBT32.EXE).

An example of the MAKE32.EXE utility is shown in Figure A.5.

Figure A.5 Using MAKEBT32.EXE to create the four floppy diskettes used for the setup utility.

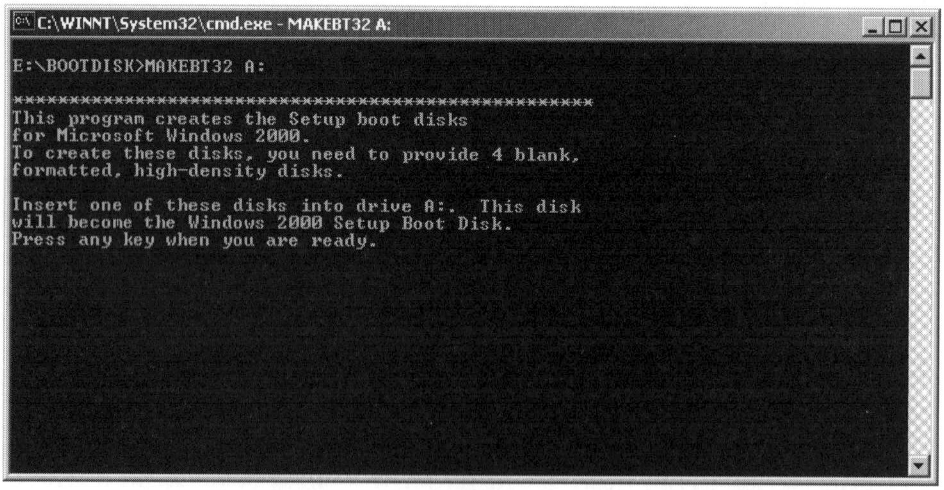

Although using these floppy diskettes is very similar to running the setup utility from the CD, there are differences which may help you decide how you perform installations.

- You cannot use the floppy diskette installation for an upgrade. This method only works with clean installations.

In addition, Windows 2000 has some slight differences in how it handles boot floppies compared to Windows NT 4.0. These are listed below:

- The Windows NT floppy creation utility always created them in reverse. First disk 3 was created, than disk 2, and finally the boot diskette. The Windows 2000 utility creates them in numeric order: disk 1, disk 2, disk 3, and finally, disk 4.
- Windows NT used three boot floppies, while Windows 2000 uses four. This is required to handle the additional installation information.

High Encryption Pack

Windows 2000 was built on the idea that strong security is one of the top five major design objectives, based on the fact that security is a growing concern within the IT industry. Microsoft provides an upgrade that is available free to allow the Windows 2000 operating system to use a 128-bit encryption algorithm when required. This update, shown in Figure A.6, is also inclusive of any future patches, such as a service pack. In other words, if you installed an update, you would not have to reapply the encryption pack again. Also, once the update has been applied, it cannot be removed. Because of laws governing the export of 128-bit software, be sure to check before applying this update.

Figure A.6 Installing the Windows 2000 high-encryption pack.

Windows Update

A new utility has been included in Windows 2000 that is quickly growing in popularity. Microsoft has created a Web site that customizes itself to your Windows 2000 computer to provide you with a listing of all the updates available. It scans the computer locally to ensure speed and security, and offers a listing of updates that have not been applied in various categories, such as critical updates, minor updates, or device drivers. To use it, browse through the updates that are listed, select the updates to download, and continue to install these updates to your computer. Once the updates have completed installing, the catalog listing removes these items from the available updates that are provided the next time you access this Web site. The Windows update is available at http://windowsupdate.microsoft.com.

Although this may work well for home users, some corporate administrators may prefer to keep their users from updating computers with patches that have not been tested. Microsoft has provided a mechanism to remove the Windows Update feature if need be. The following procedure explains how to remove Windows Update from a Windows 2000 Professional computer.

1. Open REGEDT32.EXE
2. Navigate to the following key:
   HKEY_LOCAL_MACHINE\Software\Microsoft\Windows\CurrentVersion\Policies\Explorer
3. Add the following entry: NOWINDOWSUPDATE=1. (Setting of 0 enables Windows Update)

4. To remove the icon from the Start menu, type the following at a command prompt:

WUPDMGR.EXE -SHORTCUT

Additional Resources

As with any software release, additional resources can provide a great deal of information pertaining to the subject to which it is dedicated. With Windows 2000, Microsoft provides several great resources to help an administrator in learning about, deploying, and supporting Windows 2000. Listed below are a few of the major resources made available.

Deployment Planning Guide (DPG)

The Windows 2000 Deployment Planning Guide was created to help administrators plan and deploy Windows 2000 throughout an enterprise environment. It provides tips and techniques on deployment technologies and managing Windows 2000.

Included within the guide are chapters covering a wide array of topics, including:

- Deployment Planning
- Building a Test Lab
- Conducting a Pilot Deployment
- Network Infrastructure Preparations
- Designing Active Directory and DNS
- Application Compatibility
- Client Connectivity Strategies
- Client Administration Techniques
- Automated Client Installation Techniques
- Planning Worksheets
- Sample Deployment Plans

TechNet

One of the most infamous and heavily used by any Microsoft professional, TechNet is a monthly subscription that provides recent knowledge-base articles, white papers, and service packs. TechNet is an indispensable tool in the network administrator's arsenal when implementing and supporting Microsoft products, and Windows 2000 is no exception. Beyond the normal resources provided within this CD set, additional utilities, code, and information has been provided to help you make a Windows 2000 deployment as painless as possible.

Microsoft Web Site

Another good resource is the Microsoft Web site located at: http://www.microsoft.com.

It provides up-to-date information, such as release schedules for service packs, support information, and news about the various products. Many of the first deployment tools appeared here on the Web site for downloading, to help administrators further customize large-scale deployments. For example, the *Deployment Planning Guide* was published on the Web site for anyone to download before the product was even released. Because it is continually updated, it can be an invaluable tool when trying to deploy and maintain Windows 2000.

The Global Knowledge Advantage

Global Knowledge has a global delivery system for its products and services. The company has 28 subsidiaries, and offers its programs through a total of 60+ locations. No other vendor can provide consistent services across a geographic area this large. Global Knowledge is the largest independent information technology education provider, offering programs on a variety of platforms. This enables our multi-platform and multi-national customers to obtain all of their programs from a single vendor. The company has developed the unique CompetusTM Framework software tool and methodology which can quickly reconfigure courseware to the proficiency level of a student on an interactive basis. Combined with self-paced and on-line programs, this technology can reduce the time required for training by prescribing content in only the deficient skills areas. The company has fully automated every aspect of the education process, from registration and follow-up, to "just-in-time" production of courseware. Global Knowledge through its Enterprise Services Consultancy, can customize programs and products to suit the needs of an individual customer.

Global Knowledge Classroom Education Programs

The backbone of our delivery options is classroom-based education. Our modern, well-equipped facilities staffed with the finest instructors offer programs in a wide variety of information technology topics, many of which lead to professional certifications.

Custom Learning Solutions

This delivery option has been created for companies and governments that value customized learning solutions. For them, our consultancy-based approach of developing targeted education solutions is most effective at helping them meet specific objectives.

Self-Paced and Multimedia Products

This delivery option offers self-paced program titles in interactive CD-ROM, videotape and audio tape programs. In addition, we offer custom development of interactive multimedia courseware to customers and partners. Call us at 1-888-427-4228.

Electronic Delivery of Training

Our network-based training service delivers efficient competency-based, interactive training via the World Wide Web and organizational intranets. This leading-edge delivery option provides a custom learning path and "just-in-time" training for maximum convenience to students.

Global Knowledge Courses Available

Microsoft
- Windows 2000 Deployment Strategies
- Introduction to Directory Services
- Windows 2000 Client Administration
- Windows 2000 Server
- Windows 2000 Update
- MCSE Bootcamp
- Microsoft Networking Essentials
- Windows NT 4.0 Workstation
- Windows NT 4.0 Server
- Windows NT Troubleshooting
- Windows NT 4.0 Security
- Windows 2000 Security
- Introduction to Microsoft Web Tools

Management Skills
- Project Management for IT Professionals
- Microsoft Project Workshop
- Management Skills for IT Professionals

Network Fundamentals
- Understanding Computer Networks
- Telecommunications Fundamentals I
- Telecommunications Fundamentals II
- Understanding Networking Fundamentals
- Upgrading and Repairing PCs
- DOS/Windows A+ Preparation
- Network Cabling Systems

WAN Networking and Telephony
- Building Broadband Networks
- Frame Relay Internetworking
- Converging Voice and Data Networks
- Introduction to Voice Over IP
- Understanding Digital Subscriber Line (xDSL)

Internetworking
- ATM Essentials
- ATM Internetworking
- ATM Troubleshooting
- Understanding Networking Protocols
- Internetworking Routers and Switches
- Network Troubleshooting
- Internetworking with TCP/IP
- Troubleshooting TCP/IP Networks
- Network Management
- Network Security Administration
- Virtual Private Networks
- Storage Area Networks
- Cisco OSPF Design and Configuration
- Cisco Border Gateway Protocol (BGP) Configuration

Web Site Management and Development
- Advanced Web Site Design
- Introduction to XML
- Building a Web Site
- Introduction to JavaScript
- Web Development Fundamentals
- Introduction to Web Databases

PERL, UNIX, and Linux
- PERL Scripting
- PERL with CGI for the Web
- UNIX Level I
- UNIX Level II
- Introduction to Linux for New Users
- Linux Installation, Configuration, and Maintenance

Authorized Vendor Training
Red Hat
- Introduction to Red Hat Linux
- Red Hat Linux Systems Administration
- Red Hat Linux Network and Security Administration
- RHCE Rapid Track Certification

Cisco Systems
- Interconnecting Cisco Network Devices
- Advanced Cisco Router Configuration
- Installation and Maintenance of Cisco Routers
- Cisco Internetwork Troubleshooting
- Designing Cisco Networks
- Cisco Internetwork Design
- Configuring Cisco Catalyst Switches
- Cisco Campus ATM Solutions
- Cisco Voice Over Frame Relay, ATM, and IP
- Configuring for Selsius IP Phones
- Building Cisco Remote Access Networks
- Managing Cisco Network Security
- Cisco Enterprise Management Solutions

Nortel Networks
- Nortel Networks Accelerated Router Configuration
- Nortel Networks Advanced IP Routing
- Nortel Networks WAN Protocols
- Nortel Networks Frame Switching
- Nortel Networks Accelar 1000
- Comprehensive Configuration
- Nortel Networks Centillion Switching
- Network Management with Optivity for Windows

Oracle Training
- Introduction to Oracle8 and PL/SQL
- Oracle8 Database Administration

Custom Corporate Network Training

Train on Cutting Edge Technology

We can bring the best in skill-based training to your facility to create a real-world hands-on training experience. Global Knowledge has invested millions of dollars in network hardware and software to train our students on the same equipment they will work with on the job. Our relationships with vendors allow us to incorporate the latest equipment and platforms into your on-site labs.

Maximize Your Training Budget

Global Knowledge provides experienced instructors, comprehensive course materials, and all the networking equipment needed to deliver high quality training. You provide the students; we provide the knowledge.

Avoid Travel Expenses

On-site courses allow you to schedule technical training at your convenience, saving time, expense, and the opportunity cost of travel away from the workplace.

Discuss Confidential Topics

Private on-site training permits the open discussion of sensitive issues such as security, access, and network design. We can work with your existing network's proprietary files while demonstrating the latest technologies.

Customize Course Content

Global Knowledge can tailor your courses to include the technologies and the topics which have the greatest impact on your business. We can complement your internal training efforts or provide a total solution to your training needs.

Corporate Pass

The Corporate Pass Discount Program rewards our best network training customers with preferred pricing on public courses, discounts on multimedia training packages, and an array of career planning services.

Global Knowledge Training Lifecycle

Supporting the Dynamic and Specialized Training Requirements of Information Technology Professionals

- Define Profile
- Assess Skills
- Design Training
- Deliver Training
- Test Knowledge
- Update Profile
- Use New Skills

Global Knowledge

Global Knowledge programs are developed and presented by industry professionals with "real-world" experience. Designed to help professionals meet today's interconnectivity and interoperability challenges, most of our programs feature hands-on labs that incorporate state-of-the-art communication components and equipment.

ON-SITE TEAM TRAINING

Bring Global Knowledge's powerful training programs to your company. At Global Knowledge, we will custom design courses to meet your specific network requirements. Call (919)-461-8686 for more information.

YOUR GUARANTEE

Global Knowledge believes its courses offer the best possible training in this field. If during the first day you are not satisfied and wish to withdraw from the course, simply notify the instructor, return all course materials and receive a 100% refund.

REGISTRATION INFORMATION

In the US:
call: (888) 762–4442
fax: (919) 469–7070
visit our website:
www.globalknowledge.com